Screening Violence

Screening Violence
Edited by Stephen Prince

This volume provides an even-handed examination of the history and effects of graphic violence on film. It is an area very much disputed and theories abound. Following the release in 1967 of *Bonnie and Clyde* and *The Dirty Dozen,* leading on to *The Wild Bunch* and *The Terminator,* violence has been seen as a defining feature of modern film. Is it art or exploitation? Danger or liberation?

These are questions considered by the contributors to this volume, including active reviewers, scholars of film, sociologists and psychologists.

Stephen Prince is Associate Professor of Communication Studies at Virginia Tech. His publications include *Savage Cinema: Sam Peckinpah and the Rise of the Ultraviolent Movie* (Athlone, 1998).

Edited and with an introduction by
Stephen Prince

Screening
Violence

THE
ATHLONE
PRESS
LONDON

First published in Great Britain 2000 by
THE ATHLONE PRESS
1 Park Drive, London NW11 7SG

This collection copyright © 2000 by Rutgers, The State University.
For copyrights to individual pieces, please see first page of each essay.

British Library Cataloguing in Publication Data
A catalogue record for this book is available from the British Library
ISBN 0 485 30095 8

Manufactured in the United States of America

For My Parents and Tami

Contents

Screening Violence

Stephen Prince

Graphic Violence in the Cinema: Origins, Aesthetic Design, and Social Effects

Graphic violence is an inescapable and ubiquitous characteristic of contemporary cinema. Severed heads and spurting arteries are plentiful on today's screens, and filmmakers of all stripes, from auteurs to hacks, have become proficient at staging sanguinary spectacles. Martin Scorsese has shown characters with their faces shot apart (*Taxi Driver* [1976]) and beaten into bloody but still living pulp (*Casino* [1995]). Paul Verhoeven's giant bugs in *Starship Troopers* (1998) rip their victims into ragged, bloody pieces. Exploding bodies (*The Fury* [1978], *Videodrome* [1983]), decapitation (*The Omen* [1976], *Wild at Heart* [1990]), dismemberment (*Re-Animator* [1985], *Henry: Portrait of a Serial Killer* [1990]), and homicide committed with unconventional weapons ranging from ice pick (*Basic Instinct* [1992]) to power drill (*Body Double* [1984])—such bloody spectacles now crowd the screen. Indeed, their popularity demonstrates the widespread embrace of violence by contemporary moviegoers and the film industry, despite ongoing social controversies about the unhealthy effects of viewing ultraviolence.

This introduction examines the origins of ultraviolent movies, the long-standing controversies over the effects of viewing film violence, the evidence furnished by social science about these effects, and the inherent characteristics of screen violence that subvert its progressive, legitimate uses (the reasons why, in other words, filmmakers cannot control the reactions of viewers to the graphic violence they put on screen). Screen violence provokes an inherently volatile set of viewer responses. These do *not* include catharsis, and they should make us pessimistic about the psychological health promoted in viewers by much contemporary visual culture.

Violence in the movies is not of recent origin. Screen violence is deeply embedded in the history and functioning of cinema. It is as old as the medium and has arguably been of central importance for the popular appeal of film. Edwin Porter's *The Great Train Robbery* (1903) shows a beating victim (albeit transmuted into a none-too-convincing dummy) thrown from a moving train and climaxes with a massacre of the train robbers. D. W. Griffith's *Intolerance* (1916) shows decapitation and other gruesome sights and climaxes, as did many of his pictures, with thrilling scenes of physical action. The appeal of violence in cinema—for filmmakers and viewers—is tied to the medium's inherently visceral properties. These make the cinema especially suited to the depiction of violence. Brian De Palma, a well-known contemporary exponent of movie violence, has noted this fundamental connection between the plastic components of the medium and the emotional pleasures it offers. "Motion pictures are a kinetic art form; you're dealing with motion and sometimes that can be violent motion. There are very few art forms that let you deal with things in motion and that's why Westerns and chases and shoot-outs crop up in film. They require one of the elements intrinsic to film: motion."[1]

Although movie violence has a long history, in contrast with today's films, screen violence in earlier periods was more genteel and indirect. From 1930, when it was formulated, until the 1960s, Hollywood's Production Code regulated all aspects of screen content, with an elaborate list of rules outlining what was permissible to show and what was not. These regulations placed great constraints on filmmakers and helped to prevent the emergence of ultraviolence in American film during these earlier periods. (With its decapitation [and its nudity], *Intolerance* was a pre-Code film.) In filmic depictions of crime, for example, the Code stipulated that brutal killings must not be shown in detail, murder must not be glamorized so as to inspire imitation, and the use of firearms should be sparing. This censure against excessive depictions of firearms stands in sharp contrast with the fetish for high-tech firepower in today's action films, which devote long, lingering close-ups to weapons, as cradled in the arms of Sylvester Stallone, Arnold Schwarzennegger, and other superheroes.

From 1930 on, filmmakers had to shoot and cut their material with the Code's provisions in mind because the major studios would not distribute films that lacked a Code seal of approval. Thus, explicit footage showing King Kong trampling his victims or Frankenstein's

Figure 1. In earlier decades, gunshot victims gracefully expired with minimal fuss. In Casablanca, *Major Strasser (Conrad Veidt) takes a bullet in the chest at close range and drops out of the frame without losing his grip on a telephone.*

monster tossing a little girl into a lake (she drowns) was deleted from the final cuts of those pictures. And in countless Westerns and urban crime dramas, shooting victims frowned and sank gracefully out of frame, with their white shirts immaculate.

With its roots in Catholic Church doctrine, the Production Code aimed to enforce a strict morality and healthy-mindedness in the movies. This policy was the industry's response to a prolonged period in the 1910s and 1920s of social agitation over movie content,[2] during which time many citizens' groups and state and local agencies tried to censor the movies. To protect itself, the industry passed the Production Code and created in 1934 an enforcement agency, the Production Code Administration (PCA). For decades, the Code and the PCA held violence on screen to a minimum.

Inevitably, though, some films and filmmakers pushed the boundaries of what was deemed acceptable. The gangster film cycle of the early 1930s, in particular, inflamed national controversy about the unwholesome effects of the movies. *Little Caesar* (1930), *The Public*

Figure 2. Tony Montana (Al Pacino) expires in an ultrabloody showdown at the end of Scarface. *The ferocity of his death scene could not have been shown in earlier decades of American cinema.*

Enemy (1931), and especially *Scarface* (1932) showed cold-blooded murder by tommy-gun, and these pictures boasted an extraordinary body count. The violence of this cycle, and the viciousness personified in the gangster heroes portrayed by James Cagney, Edward G. Robinson, and Paul Muni, helped instigate the PCA, as well as the Payne Fund Studies, the first systematic effort to use social science methodologies to study the effects of motion pictures on their audiences. Conducted in the early 1930s in response to controversies over allegedly indecent film content, the studies comprised eight volumes of research on the effects of movies on children and youth, with particular emphasis on issues of delinquency and sexuality. I will have more to say about the Payne Fund Studies later in this introduction.

For now, the salient point to grasp is that Hollywood's Production Code restricted the possibilities for graphic depictions of screen violence, although, as the inception of the Payne Fund Studies shows, it did not end controversy over the social effects of motion pictures. For the most part, screen violence remained relatively discreet, and the camera turned away from its uglier manifestations. Consider the representational differences at work in similar material in the gangster genre filmed during Code and post-Code eras. At the end of *White Heat*

Figure 3. In the 1930s, Hollywood gangster films aroused public outcry over their violence and romantic depiction of criminals. In The Public Enemy *(1931), Tom Powers (James Cagney) prepares to coldly execute a boyhood pal.*

(1949), a government sniper repeatedly shoots Cody Jarrett (the film's gangster hero portrayed by James Cagney), but Jarrett refuses to fall. He takes the high-powered shots without succumbing in an episode of sustained and brutal violence. The visual treatment, though, makes the violence implicit and surprisingly indirect. The action shows Jarrett at a distance, in longshots that make it difficult to see that he is, in fact, being shot repeatedly. Furthermore, in keeping with the period's filmic norms, none of the bullet strikes on Jarrett are visualized. The pictorial treatment glosses the scene's exceptional brutality by hiding its details. A viewer has to look through the style to grasp the content that it has buried. By contrast, at the conclusion of Brian De Palma's remake of *Scarface* (1984), the gangster hero (Al Pacino) is gunned down by a rival gang using automatic weapons. Blasted by a hail of gunfire, he is shot many times over. The gore is detailed and inescapable. The bullet hits peppering the character are shown in a graphic spray of blood and torn clothing and flesh. Instead of hiding it, the style flamboyantly emphasizes the physical carnage. The contrast between these scenes in *White*

Heat and *Scarface,* the difference between concealing and displaying hyperviolence, shows the disparity between the Code and post-Code eras and is the result of complex changes in the film industry, and in society, that helped produce the turn toward explicit violence.

The Genesis of Ultraviolence

The beginning of the shift, that point when the graphic representation of physical violence first became a distinct stylistic possibility in the American cinema, is easy to date. Ultraviolence emerged in the late 1960s, and movies have never been the same since. The factors that helped produce this new violence were instigated by two watershed events in Hollywood history: the revision in September 1966 of Hollywood's thirty-six-year-old Production Code and the creation two years later of the Code and Rating Administration with its G-M-R-X classification scheme. These changes were responses to the more liberal and tolerant culture of the period, particularly the revolution in social mores tied to the youth movement. Shackled by the Production Code, movies were thirty years behind the times. Accordingly and led by the Motion Picture Association of America (MPAA), the Hollywood industry mounted an aggressive campaign to make films relevant again for a society whose attitudes and practices no longer coincided with the morality institutionalized in the Production Code.

Thus, the 1966 revision scrapped the Code's injunctions about specific content areas and substituted in their place a few broadly phrased guiding principles that, as MPAA head Jack Valenti pointed out, significantly expanded the creative license of filmmakers. Where the old Code told filmmakers precisely how they were to approach and show scenes of violence, the revised Code merely recommended that filmmakers exercise discretion in showing the taking of human life. "Discretion" is an elastic and relative concept, and as the intensifying violence in American cinema in the late 1960s shows, it was mostly an ineffective principle. But the scrapping of specific content injunctions was not the most significant revision. In a development that was far more important and influential for subsequent filmmaking, the MPAA created a new Suggested for Mature Audiences (SMA) designation for films that had harder, more adult content. This new designation enabled filmmakers for the first time to target an adult audience and on that basis take sex and violence much further than in the past when the audience mix included young viewers.

An additional revision a few years later accelerated these developments. In 1968, the MPAA unveiled a four-way classification system—G-M-R-X—that differentiated films by audience segment. G-rated films were suitable for the entire family, while underage viewers were prohibited from seeing X-rated films and could only view R-films if accompanied by a parent or adult guardian. The G-M-R-X scheme made even greater freedoms available to filmmakers because films could now be niche-marketed to adult audiences, bypassing the content restrictions that the presence of young viewers had hitherto necessitated. These modifications of the Production Code helped produce a wave of tougher, harder-edged, and controversial films whose graphic violence, profanity, and sexuality exemplified the new artistic freedoms that the MPAA had been seeking and promoting. Films like *Bonnie and Clyde* (1967), *The Fox* (1968), *The Detective* (1968), *In Cold Blood* (1967), *Point Blank* (1967), and *Barbarella* (1968) would have been unthinkable a mere five years previously, and they collectively demonstrate the emergence of the new, adult-themed cinema that the MPAA helped inaugurate.

Indeed, the MPAA's advocacy of new filmmaking freedoms was a remarkable feature of this revolution in American cinema. The MPAA pushed aggressively for these freedoms despite vocal protest from groups opposed to these changes. Testifying before the National Commission on the Causes and Prevention of Violence on December 19, 1968, Jack Valenti proudly announced, "There is a new breed of filmmaker. And mark you well this new filmmaker, because he's an extraordinary fellow. . . . He's reaching out for new dimensions of expression. And he is not bound—not bound—by the conventions of a conformist past. I happen to think that's good."[3] In another context, Valenti stressed the importance of bringing "old movie standards out of the archaic and arcane and into current trends."[4] Criticizing viewers who protested the rising levels of violence, sexuality, and profanity in the movies, an MPAA community relations associate cited the "new revolutions" in taste and morality in society. She recommended that viewers reorient themselves to these social changes and the new cinema they were helping to produce. "They [the public] fail to realize that films have changed to reflect our changing culture."[5]

The MPAA's responsiveness to late 1960s culture, in this respect, was strikingly different from the posture and policy it assumed in the early 1980s, when a more conservative national climate produced vehement criticism of movie violence by government officials and social watchdog groups. Brian De Palma's lurid and bloody thriller *Dressed to Kill* (1980) aroused tremendous criticism because of its violence against women. Anticipating problems, the MPAA threatened during post-production to slap an X-rating on the picture unless De Palma trimmed its violence. De Palma protested the cuts but nevertheless made them so that the picture could be released with an R-rating. Explaining the tough line taken by the MPAA with regard to *Dressed to Kill,* Jack Valenti pointed to the political realignments of the Reagan era and implicitly announced that the agency's late 1960s liberalism was over. He said, "The political climate in this country is shifting to the right, and that means more conservative attitudes toward sex and violence. But a lot of creative people are still living in the world of revolution."[6]

During the 1960s, however, in its period of high liberalism, the MPAA aimed to bring films into closer accord with the youth audience and its general questioning of Establishment values. This was a vital demographic and one that the agency was determined to court; a 1968 MPAA audience survey showed that 16- to 24-year-olds were responsible for 48 percent of national ticket sales.[7] To capture this young audience, the MPAA believed that films would have to become more attuned to contemporary mores, which adherence to a thirty-six-year-old Production Code prevented. In addition to the youth audience, however, a multitude of other factors influenced and helped shape the new direction of American cinema. The period's general social turmoil, its climate of political violence, and, most especially, the war in Vietnam convinced many filmmakers and the MPAA that movie violence paled next to the real-life bloodshed in the nation's cities and the jungles of Southeast Asia. The savage bloodshed of the Vietnam War established a context whereby filmmakers felt justified in reaching for new levels of screen violence. Moreover, the war and the political assassinations of the 1960s fed a general cultural fascination with violence to which the movies responded.[8]

Jack Valenti remarked on the interconnections between the era's social and media violence and did so in a manner that claimed film's prerogative in responding to real-world violence. In 1968, he remarked, "For the first time in the history of this country, people are exposed to instant coverage [on television] of a war in progress. When so many movie critics complain about violence on film, I don't think they realize the impact of 30 minutes on the Huntley–Brinkley newscast—and that's real violence."[9] *Bonnie and Clyde* was the most explicitly violent film that had yet been made, and its director, Arthur Penn, claimed that he didn't consider it especially violent when taken in context of the Vietnam era. "Not given the times in which we were living, because every night on the news we saw kids in Vietnam being airlifted out in body bags, with blood all over the place. Why, suddenly, the cinema had to be immaculate, I'll never know."[10]

Resulting from the industry's efforts to connect with a young, contemporary audience and the period in which that audience lived, motion picture violence began its remarkable escalation in 1967. United Artists released Sergio Leone's *Dollars* trilogy of Westerns—*A Fistful of Dollars*, *For a Few Dollars More*, and *The Good, the Bad, and the Ugly*—on staggered dates throughout that year to accentuate the series nature of the films. Their release triggered a storm of protest over Leone's more cold-blooded and brutal depiction of the West. A reviewer for *Variety*, the film industry's trade journal, called *Fistful* a "bloodbath," with "sadism from start to finish, unmitigated brutality, a piling up of bodies."[11] The paper's subsequent review of *The Good, the Bad, and the Ugly* objected, "One sequence in particular, a five-minute torture session that climaxes in an attempted eye-gouging, may well serve as the battle cry for opponents of screen violence."[12]

The Leone films, which had been made in Italy, aroused considerable protest from groups opposed to the new screen violence, but it was two American films that year—*The Dirty Dozen* and *Bonnie and Clyde*—that ignited the loudest cries. *The Dirty Dozen* was an uncommonly cynical World War II action picture about hardened criminals recruited for a suicide mission into Nazi Germany. In the climax of the picture, the Americans incinerate their Nazi enemies by locking them in closed quarters, dousing them with petrol, and setting them afire. The sadism of the sequence appalled many commentators. Among the most vocal of these was Bosley Crowther, the prominent *New York Times* critic. He condemned the film, and the new movie violence of which it was part, for its "glorification of killing" and for blatantly appealing to an audience's aggressive and sadistic appetites.[13] *Bonnie and Clyde* went even farther by explicitly portraying the details and physicality of violent death, concluding with an extended slaughter sequence that shows the outlaws raked with automatic weapons' fire, their bodies riddled by bullet strikes. Both *Time* and *Newsweek* condemned the film as bloodthirsty trash in initial reviews, only to issue retractions in an unprecedented second round of reviews that praised the picture as trendsetting.

Indeed, Penn was the first American filmmaker to utilize the cinematic techniques that quickly became the normative means of filming violent gun battles. Taking his cue from Japanese director Akira Kurosawa, who had used these techniques in *Seven Samurai* (1954) and other films, Penn employed multicamera filming (i.e., filming with more than one camera running simultaneously), slow motion, and montage editing (i.e., building a sequence out of many, very short, brief shots). To these techniques which rendered gun violence with greater intensity than ever before, Penn added squibs. Probably more than any other effects tool, squibs changed the way screen violence looked.

Squibs were condoms filled with fake blood, concealed within an actor's clothing, and wired to detonate so as to simulate bullet strikes and blood sprays. Squibs enabled filmmakers to graphically visualize the impact of bullets on the human body, a detailing that is ab-

Figure 4. Squibs registering bullet strikes are an essential component of contemporary movie violence. His face obscured with blood spray, Mr. Blonde (Michael Madsen) is gunned down by Mr. Orange (Tim Roth) in Reservoir Dogs. *The character's white shirt provides maximum contrast for the squibs.*

Figure 5. In The Wild Bunch, *Peckinpah innovated in the use of squibs by employing them to represent exit wounds. When a bounty hunter shoots an army soldier, viewers see the exit wound but not the bullet strike on the victim's chest.*

sent in film prior to 1967 and which helped give violence in these earlier periods an unreal and sanitized appearance. To be sure, certain pictures in these earlier periods anticipated the modern staging of gun violence. In *Shane* (1953), for example, a gunfire victim is hurled backward by the force of a bullet's impact, and in Penn's own *The Left-Handed Gun* (1958), a hapless deputy is literally blown out of his boot by a gun blast. But despite such striking details, these scenes lacked squib-work and the palpable physicality that it lent gun violence. During and after 1967, by contrast, the savage impact of gunfire on human flesh became an enduring feature of screen killing. Films released in the same year as *Bonnie and Clyde* and which lacked squib-work—*The Professionals, El Dorado*—seemed bloodless, irrevocably part of a now-archaic era in screen violence and not at all contemporary with Penn's film. In the film's climactic sequence, Bonnie (Faye Dunaway) and Clyde (Warren Beatty) are ambushed by the Texas Rangers, who are armed with machine guns. The actors were rigged with multiple squibs. When detonated in sequence and augmented by the writhing of the actors, these provided a horrifying visualization of the outlaws' bodies being punctured by scores of bullets.

Penn filmed this action with four cameras running at different speeds. Most operated at very high speeds to provide slow-motion footage for the construction of a complexly edited sequence. Penn and his editor Dede Allen assembled a brief but sophisticated montage of the ambush. The editing juxtaposes differential rates of slow motion to extend the outlaws' death agonies and to capture, as Penn put it, the balletic and the spastic qualities of their violent deaths. Penn said,

"What I did do, which I think had not been done, was to vary the speeds of the slow motion so that I could get both the spastic and the balletic qualities at the same time."[14] These are qualities in tension with one another, yet Penn and Allen's masterful editing conjoin movements that are equally dancelike and convulsive. The scene's alternately beautiful and horrifying qualities are the result of its choreography and specifically of Penn's determination to yoke dance and convulsion together in a novel combination. The results were truly seminal. The montage of slow-motion, squib-fired death agony powerfully influenced subsequent filmmakers, especially Sam Peckinpah, who took the design to new extremes the following year in *The Wild Bunch*.

The Dirty Dozen and *Bonnie and Clyde* sent the industry a clear signal that would not be ignored. These controversial pictures were extraordinarily popular. *The Dirty Dozen* was the biggest money-maker of 1967, and so extraordinary was repeat business for *Bonnie and Clyde* that *Variety*, tracking its box-office performance, placed it in an "impossible to project" category.[15] The picture's popularity placed it on *Variety*'s weekly list of the top dozen box-office earners twenty-two times, a record topped at the time only by *Mary Poppins* (thirty-two times on the list in late 1964–early 1965). *Time* magazine noted the industry's response to this success and its implications for the future: "There is an almost euphoric sense in Hollywood that more such movies can and will be made."[16]

The outstanding commercial success of Leone's *Dollars* trilogy, *The Dirty Dozen*, and *Bonnie and Clyde* showed that the public had hitherto unappeased appetites for screen carnage and that the industry could make a lot of money from filming hyperviolence. Thus, in short order, the threshold that *Bonnie and Clyde* had crossed in 1967, with its images of slow-motion bloodletting, was surpassed. Director Sam Peckinpah's *The Wild Bunch* (1969) offered two extended slaughter sequences, opening and closing the film, that were far more gruesome, graphic, and protracted than the gun battle in Penn's picture had been. Nothing in the American cinema had been as remotely violent as what Peckinpah now put on screen in *The Wild Bunch*.

Its gun battles had ferocity and an intensity that *Bonnie and Clyde* only approximated. Peckinpah and his producer Phil Feldman knew exactly what they were doing in crafting blood-soaked images that were the most audacious yet conceived. While Peckinpah was in pre-production on *The Wild Bunch*, Feldman wrote to congratulate him for offending the MPAA with the savagery of the picture's proposed bloodshed and urged him to view the Leone films before deciding how far to go. "I think it might be good for you to have a comparative basis before you finally decide just how far other people have gone in the field of blood and gore and what the public is comparing us to."[17] Furthermore, on March 19, 1968, Warner Bros. sent a letter to Peckinpah's production manager confirming that a print of *Bonnie and Clyde* would be shipped to Parras, Mexico, where Peckinpah was on location for *The Wild Bunch*.[18] The film would arrive for screening the weekend of March 23–24. This was just prior to the start of principal photography on March 25. Peckinpah evidently wished to take another look at Penn's achievement, to reinforce his understanding of that achievement and his desire to surpass it.

Many viewers were appalled by the film's gore. An early test screening of the film elicited such negative responses as "The movie is nothing but mass murder" and "Nauseating, unending, offensive bloody violence."[19] But the film also had its passionate defenders, and these included ordinary viewers as well as prominent film critics. Penn and Peckinpah were enormously talented filmmakers, and they had crafted the two most vivid, audacious, and ambitious films that Hollywood had seen in many years. Thus, these pictures gained a significant measure of respect and critical stature that helped legitimize the in-your-face bloodletting that otherwise made them so notorious. Penn and Peckinpah were both radical social critics, disturbed by the corruption of America in its Vietnam years, and they proved that filmmakers in the late 1960s could use graphic violence for serious purposes. Peckinpah, for example, repeatedly remarked that he wished to deglamorize movie violence in order to show how ugly and awful real violence was.[20]

Unfortunately, and perhaps inevitably, the stylistics of graphic violence proved to hold tremendous fascination for subsequent generations of filmmakers who did not share Penn and Peckinpah's radical social objectives. The explicitness of this violence quickly escalated. Made only a few years after *The Wild Bunch*, for example, *Taxi Driver* (1976) was far bloodier and much more graphic, with images of dismemberment and a gunshot victim's brains splattered on a wall. Penn and Peckinpah helped establish the stylistic features of ultraviolence, while subsequent filmmakers have replicated and exaggerated them. Squib-work, multicamera filming, and montage editing utilizing differential rates of slow motion—this combination of elements became one of the two dominant aesthetic forms of ultraviolence. It is today

Figures 6 & 7. One of the most horrific moments of violence in recent cinema occurred in Alien, *when a baby monster bursts from the chest of its human host. Graphic imagery of physical mutilation would become a staple of horror films.*

very difficult to find gun battles in movies that have not been stylized in this fashion. (The elaborate gun battles in *L.A. Confidential* [1997] are notably deviant because they lack slow motion.) Moreover, the form has been internationalized. Hong Kong director John Woo (*The Killer* [1989], *Hard Boiled* [1992]) is the best-known contemporary exponent of the furiously bloody gun battles in the style elaborated by Penn and Peckinpah. Despite the fact that Woo's work is situated in another culture and country (at least until his current Hollywood period), the formal design of violence in his films follows the now-familiar and conventional parameters of the Penn–Peckinpah stylistic.

Contemporary ultraviolence exhibits a second predominant aesthetic form. In addition to the Penn–Peckinpah stylistic, ultraviolence includes graphic imagery of bodily mutilation. This type of imagery was not part of the Penn–Peckinpah stylistic, beyond the use of squib-work, because that style stressed the kinetic effects of montage, making violence balletic, a dance of death. But graphic mutilation—eye gouging, impalement, and dismemberment—surfaced in the horror film in the late 1970s and the 1980s, as that genre abandoned the atmospherics of earlier decades and offered instead stomach-churning and gut-wrenching experiences. As Carol Clover notes,

> The perfection of special effects has made it possible to show maiming and dismemberment in extraordinarily credible detail. The horror genres are the natural repositories of such effects; what can be done is done, and slashers, at the bottom of the category, do it most and worst. Thus we see heads squashed and eyes popped out, faces flayed, limbs dismembered, eyes penetrated by needles in close-up, and so on.[21]

The genre's remarkable resurgence in the 1980s was tied to this investment in ultraviolence. The decade opened with a huge spike in horror film production, which rose from 35 pictures produced in 1979 to 70 in 1980 and 93 in 1981.[22] Films in this spike included *Dressed to Kill, Friday the 13th, Prom Night,* and *Maniac,* all notoriously violent pictures. The genre spiked again in 1986–87, hitting a peak of 105 pictures in 1987. By mid-decade, the video market was thriving, and many of these pictures, especially the most violent and disreputable, were low-budget, throw-away entries aimed at this ancillary market.

Developments in two areas of makeup special effects, practiced by a new generation of makeup artists, stimulated the genre's turn to ultraviolence. The artists included Tom Savini (*Dawn of the Dead, Maniac, Friday the 13th, Eyes of a Stranger*), Rick Baker (*It's Alive, Squirm, The Funhouse*), and Rob Bottin (*The Howling, Piranha, The Thing*). These artists employed prosthetic limbs and latex (as a convincing stand-in for human skin) to simulate exquisitely detailed body mutilations. Limbs could be hacked off with a convincing show of bone and gristle, and skin (latex) could be ripped, scored, punctured, and peeled away, much to the roaring delight of audiences who patronized these films and enjoyed the new sadism.

The most controversial of the new horror pictures were the slasher films about serial killers slaughtering promiscuous teenagers. These slaughterfests seemed to demonstrate rampant sadism in popular culture, and they disturbed many observers inside and outside the film industry. Horror film bloodfests were present in high numbers at the international film markets in 1980, the first year of the genre's big production boom. Distributors and studio sales reps expressed revulsion at these products. "All they want is blood pouring off the screen. I question the mental balance of the people making and buying this stuff," noted a Carolco executive.[23] The imagery of victims dismembered by spikes, axes, chain saws, or power drills, or run through meat grinders evoked a swift and stern backlash from critics, especially feminist scholars, who pointed out that a basic slasher film premise was a male killer stalking and slaughtering female victims.

Moreover, the extended subjective camerawork in these films, showing the killer's point of view as he stalks his victims, seemed to invite viewers to accompany the killers and to participate in their stalking rituals. Prominent film critics Gene Siskel and Roger Ebert used their newspaper columns and television show to attack the slasher films. Calling them "gruesome and despicable," they argued that the pictures expressed a hatred for women. Ebert noted his personal discomfort watching the pictures with an audience. "Audiences are cheering the killers on. It's a scary experience."[24] The *Chicago Tribune* noted, "The public would not tolerate this kind of eye-ball gouging sadism if it were directed against animals instead of women. But in these new films, the fact that the horror is inflicted on women appears to be the very point."[25]

Not all viewers or scholars felt that the slasher films were objectionable or were without nuance. In her book *Men, Women, and Chain Saws*, for example, Carol Clover offered an interpretation of these films that emphasized the presence of a recurring character type—a heroic woman who eludes the killer, survives his rampage, and eventually defeats him. Clover thus argued (see the essay included in this volume) that a heroic female archetype repeatedly emerged from these narratives. She also presents a persuasive case that viewers identify with the characters in these films, killer and victims, in a fluid and dynamic manner and particularly that male viewers identify with the pain and anguish of the female victims. "Just as attacker and attacked are expressions of the same self in nightmares, so they are expressions of the same viewer in horror film."[26] In contrast to most observers, Clover emphasizes the complexity of slasher film discourse, the way it plays on ambivalent gender messages. But, as she acknowledges, this discourse contains sadistic elements. Whatever their manner of sublimating and displacing viewer anxiety, the films appealed in part, at least, to a prurient sadism, vividly visualized, and this is what motivated much of the critical outcry. The controversies, though, did not

Figure 8. In the prelude to a highly detailed killing scene, a knife-wielding and masked assailant grabs his victim (Drew Barrymore) in the opening sequence of Scream. *Because she does not die easily or quickly, the sadism goes on at length.*

stop the productions, although by the late 1990s the slasher cycle was nearly played out, as evidenced in part by the degree of self-consciousness it attained in Wes Craven's *Scream* films. But ultraviolent horror films remain very popular, as the huge collections of gory movies in video stores demonstrate and as the Web pages devoted in cyberspace to Jason, Freddy Kreuger, and the other killer heroes indicate.

Ultraviolent films since 1967 have utilized these two aesthetic formats—montage-slow motion and graphic mutilation—to provide very powerful and intense experiences for spectators. The medium's power to agitate, horrify, and excite movie audiences has generated persistent concern about the psychological and social effects of violent films. These concerns have appeared throughout film (and television) history. The 1930 Production Code, for example, was premised upon characteristics of the medium and the audience, which in combination were deemed socially undesirable. These characteristics were formally written into the Code as its reasons for being. They included cinema's intense appeal to mature as well as immature viewers, the spread of cinema to all sectors and regions of society and consequent erosion of local community standards, the suggestibility of a mass audience, and the vividness and emotional appeal of the medium. "In general, the mobility, popularity, accessibility, emotional appeal, vividness, [and] straightforward presentation of fact in the film make for more intimate contact with a larger audience and for greater emotional appeal. Hence the larger moral responsibilities of the motion pictures."[27]

An empirical examination of the effects of movies on young

viewers, the Payne Fund Studies (1933), closely followed passage of the Production Code. The studies were not concerned with violence per se but with juvenile delinquency more broadly conceived in terms of young lives given over to petty crime and sexual promiscuity, possibly resulting from Hollywood's influence. The studies are an early manifestation of a persistent fear that visual media may have harmful effects on viewers due to the media's vivid presentation and modeling of undesirable behaviors. In *Movies and Conduct,* a volume in the series, the sociologist Herbert Blumer developed the concept of "emotional possession" to explain the impact of film on viewers and the potential of the medium to exert strong effects.[28] For Blumer, emotional possession had three components. Viewers identify strongly with characters and situations on screen (e.g., romantic lovers in a kissing scene), and this leads to the arousal of normally repressed feelings. Heightened arousal produces a loss of ordinary self-control as the unleashed feelings gain or threaten to gain expression. Blumer speculated that, for some viewers over time, the emotions and behavioral repertoires associated with emotional possession may become entrenched and lead to a long-term alteration of character.

Blumer's terminology—emotional possession—tends to sound a bit lurid, and it certainly overstates the affective components of cinema viewing at the expense of their cognitive correlates and the viewer's cognitive framing of the experience. Most viewers, for example, doubtless realize they are watching a movie and understand that there are boundaries between movie experience and real-life experience. But Blumer was right to consider the special vividness and emotive power of the medium as key variables affecting viewer responses. By varying camera positions, editing rhythms, and using music and special effects, filmmakers stylize violence and heighten its emotional and visceral impact. The history of cinema is, in part, a history of increasingly vivid presentational techniques. Public fears that the medium's intense appeals might bypass traditional avenues of socialization and reconfigure social mores were acute in the 1930s, as the Payne Fund Studies demonstrate, but these anxieties did not receive definitive answers in the period's research. The evidence furnished by the Payne Fund Studies was ambiguous, and it pointed toward limited media effects. Moreover, graphic violence was not a feature of American movies in that period. After 1967, though, when the censorship barriers came down and explicit sex and violence filled the screen, the old fears about the medium's impact were again relevant. The rise of ultraviolence compelled a reconsideration of the medium's vividness and emotive power, those factors that Blumer had identified as constituents of the medium's ability to influence viewers. Generations of film and television viewers were being socialized to accept graphic violence as a screen norm, and this development created a vital need for continuing research on the effects of screen violence. Scholars in cinema studies, though, neglected questions of social effects because the field as a whole was hostile to empirical methodologies; scholars from the fields of psychology and communication took up the questions.

The Empirical Evidence on the Effects of Viewing Violence

Empirical investigations of media violence have confronted and discredited a deeply entrenched popular notion about the nature of probable effects. This is the idea of catharsis, the notion that screen violence provides a viewer with the opportunity to purge hostile feelings in the safe realm of art. The idea of catharsis has acquired tremendous force in contemporary culture and has become a foundational concept for explicating the relationship between visual media content and viewers. Critics routinely refer to the cathartic effects of violent films—and defend them on this basis—as in Mark Crispin Miller's description of the concluding gun battle in *The Wild Bunch* as a "cathartic holocaust."[29] Defending the new violence of late 1960s pictures, Jack Valenti cited their probable cathartic effects. He told the National Commission on the Causes and Prevention of Violence, "I am personally convinced that there is genuine validity in the belief that disturbing emotions may be purged through the vicarious experience of aggressive acts on screen."[30]

The concept of catharsis derives from Aristotle's well-known discussion in the *Poetics* wherein he asserted that tragedy uses language and acting to evoke pity (*eleos*) and fear (*phobos*) in a manner that purges such feelings from the spectator. Aristotle's discussion is brief, and, rather than constituting a theory, it provides only the hint of an idea. He does not work out the body or the implications of his idea in any detail. As the critic and philosopher of classical tragedy, Walter Kaufmann, points out, "The celebrated doctrines of the *Poetics* are for the most part peremptory dicta of a few lines, and not theories that Aristotle tries to establish with care."[31] Significantly, Aristotle does *not* mention aggression, and, furthermore, he identified *language* and *acting* as the vehicles effecting the cathartic purge. He described a medium—classical tragedy—which conveyed its effects through language and in which horrific violence occurred offstage.

Thus, his remarks about catharsis do not necessarily generalize to a medium like cinema, whose design is so different than classical tragedy. Cinema images are far more sensual and powerful. As I noted previously, filmmakers use editing, camerawork, and sound to heighten the sensory qualities of violent episodes, and these are *shown* in film rather than described verbally, as in classical tragedy. Thus, as Singer and Singer point out, "When you see a violent image on the screen in all its graphic gore, that image intrudes with greater shock as a literal picture, relatively uncontrolled by one's own imagination [or] values."[32] As a result of these differences, film and television images of violence have a greater ability to excite and arouse their viewers, and these medium-specific differences point away from the cathartic ideal.

The empirical evidence on media effects has discredited the idea of catharsis, and it points toward a link between viewing film or television violence and subsequent aggressive behavior. As Leonard Berkowitz, a prominent researcher in this area, writes, "the majority of researchers are agreed that the depiction of violence in the media increases the chances that people in the audience will act aggressively themselves."[33] A meta-analysis of 217 studies on television violence conducted between 1957 and 1990 found a consistent and significant correlation between viewing violent television and aggressive or antisocial behavior.[34] In Felson's recent review of the literature (included in this volume), he concedes that the empirical inquiries have demonstrated media effects on aggressive behaviors, although he adds the qualifier that, in his assessment, these effects are likely to be weak, to affect only a small percentage of viewers, and are unlikely to be a significant factor in the high crime rate in this country. Berkowitz, however, points out that a small percentage of affected viewers, in a country with a large population, may produce a not insignificant number of violent acts.

Studies on the viewing of media violence show aggression-inducing effects, rather than cathartic ones, and they have pointed in this direction for some time.[35] In 1972, for example, after examining the relation between television viewing and social behavior, the Surgeon General's Committee concluded that there was little evidence supporting the catharsis hypothesis (that viewing film or television violence would *lessen* an individual's propensity to behave aggressively).[36] From an empirical standpoint, the catharsis hypothesis is primarily associated with the work of Seymour Feshback, who has reported some evidence offering conditional support for the cathartic effects of viewing fantasy aggression.[37] Feshback's findings, though, do not represent the consensus of most researchers in this field, and even Feshback reported evidence pointing away from the catharsis hypothesis.[38]

Based on the empirical evidence, it is now possible to specify the program characteristics that are most implicated in the findings of aggression inducement. These involve violence that is relatively free of pain and suffering victims who deserve what they get, stories that postulate scenarios of righteous, justifiable aggression, and a match between the cue properties of situations and characters on screen and the viewer's real-world situation. When the salient characteristics of film victims, for example, match the characteristics of available targets in everyday life, aggressive responses toward those real-life targets may become more likely. Many of the most notorious and widely reported cases of apparent media-inspired violence fall into this category. The incineration of a Manhattan subway-token clerk following the release of the film *Money Train* (1995), which depicted a similar incident, seems to exemplify this principle, but it has also been demonstrated experimentally.[39]

A huge proportion of our film and television programming presents stories in which the hero or protagonist must behave aggressively in order to defeat the villain, avenge some crime, or realize goals. In this context, the depiction of the antecedents and consequences of aggression has been shown to influence viewers' tendencies to aggress. When aggression is rewarded in a film or television show, it tends to elicit more imitative aggression from viewers. Albert Bandura, who has argued persuasively in favor of a social learning theory of aggression,[40] points out that the persuasive example of successful villainy in a show or film "may outweigh the viewers' value systems."[41] Summarizing his experimental work in which he found young viewers imitating the aggressive behavior of a film character whose behavior was rewarded, Bandura noted that children watching television "have opportunities to observe many episodes in which anti-socially aggressive behavior has paid off abundantly."[42] In light of this, the villain's routine punishment at the end of an episode "may have a relatively weak inhibitory effect on the viewer."[43]

Bandura has also demonstrated the modeling functions of aggressive media content—that is, the tendency for observed filmic aggression to shape the form of a viewer's subsequent antisocial behavior. Children's play activities and choice of toys tended to assume forms imitative of the aggressive activities they had seen on film. Seeing film aggression not only seemed to heighten subsequent aggressive reactions; it offered a model for imitative learning.[44] When aggression was rewarded in a show, the salience of this modeling increased. Similarly, when a show or film presents aggression as a justifiable response by the hero or protagonist, it may have a disinhibiting effect on viewers.[45] When Rocky patriotically pummels the robotic Soviet boxer Drago in *Rocky IV* (1985), or the rebel forces battle the Empire in the *Star Wars* sagas, the film narratives present scenarios of justifiable aggression that provide a moral orientation for the explicit violence that ensues. Summarizing the association between filmic aggression, presented as justified, and antisocial responses by viewers, which they demonstrated experimentally, Berkowitz and Rawlings conclude that "Seeing the fantasy villain 'get what he deserved' may make the angered individual more inclined to hurt the villain in his life, the person who had angered him."[46] Zillmann has framed this process of enjoying the villain's fate as one of 'counterempathy.' "As we have morally condemned a villain for raping and maiming, for instance, we are free to hate such a person, can joyously anticipate his execution, and openly applaud it when we finally witness it. In fiction, we can enjoy his being bullet riddled; and outside fiction, we can rejoice at the drop of the guillotine."[47]

Zillmann has suggested that viewers form affinities for screen characters based on how such people would be viewed were their behavior occurring in the real world (i.e., the one outside the fiction). "Fictional characters toward whom an audience holds particular dispositions will draw emotional involvement and responses similar to nonfictional persons toward whom the same dispositions are held."[48] Depictions of suffering may complicate these affinities, that is, the viewer's disposition to feel for or against the perpetrators of screen violence. The presence or absence of a victim's pain, and, when present, its degree of severity, tends to affect a viewer's disposition to aggress. Visible or audible signs of a victim's suffering, for example, tend to depress, or inhibit, aggressive responses[49] and may also diminish a viewer's enjoyment of the film violence, depending on the amplitude of the expressions of pain.[50] One of the striking facts about much screen violence is its relatively pain-free quality. In the action epics of Arnold Schwarzenegger or Sylvester Stallone, the heroes massacre hordes of bad guys with little evident feeling and with no evident agonies on the part of those righteously dispatched. Of importance in this regard, viewers may perceive scenes that lack expressions of suffering by victims as being less violent than those in which the victim's pain is apparent. Blanchard, Graczyk, and Blanchard note that viewers tended to rate the violence level as much higher in *The Deer Hunter* (1978) than in either *The Bugs Bunny Movie* (1979) or the James Bond film *For Your Eyes Only* (1981), because the latter two films show relatively pain-free violence, unlike *The Deer Hunter*, which presents scenes of physical and emotional suffering.

> This suggests that suffering of victims is a major constituent of perceptions of violence. This interpretation is supported by the reliably lower ratings on violence of the Bond film, which contained relatively little emphasis on suffering of victims although several dozen characters appeared to be injured or killed as the result of a nonstop action episode. It is also congruent with the very low suffering ratings for the cartoon, which was rated much lower in violence than any of the live-actor sequences despite portrayals of exaggerated physical violence, including physical consequences such as heads being shot off."[51]

In assessing these consequences of screen violence for the viewing audience, I wish to emphasize two points. First, the viewing audience is not monolithic but is stratified by personality variables. These latter may interact strongly with program content and genres to produce undesirable effects. Zillmann and Weaver, for example, have shown that male viewers, whose personality characteristics show hostile dispositions and lack of empathy, preferred violent means of conflict resolution after watching the "superviolence" in contemporary action films and that these effects are relatively nontransient.[52] My second point is that the reactions of viewers are not mechanistic but, instead, have strong cognitive components, and these cognitive components may operate to reinforce undesirable effects. Berkowitz provides (in the essay included in this volume) a detailed explanation of the role that cognitive factors (thoughts and ideas) play in viewer reactions to media violence. Specifically, he examines the role of thought (induced by media programming) in activating bodily reactions. He terms this a priming process that involves the "spreading activation" of thoughts related to media images and content and which, under the right conditions, can dampen a viewer's inhibitions against acting aggressively. "The aggressive ideas suggested by a violent movie can prime other semantically related thoughts, heightening the chances that viewers will have other aggressive ideas in this period."[53] Berkowitz maintains that a high level of aggression-related thoughts can activate aggressive inclinations. This perspective is consistent with the phenomenon of desensitization, that is, the tendency for viewers accustomed to media violence to show a lowered physiological response to the material.[54] Berkowitz points out that these lower levels of physiological arousal should be understood as signs of lowered anxiety levels and that they can coexist with a higher disposition to aggress. "It is important to note that the lower arousal is presumably an indicant of a reduced concern about aggression and not a sign of a decreased inclination to aggression."[55] Berkowitz's view that people derive ideas from aggressive material in the media and that these ideas can, for a time afterward, foster antisocial behavior has a great deal of empirical support, which he cites in his discussion. His view suggests that the aggression-inducing characteristics of media violence have cognitive consequences for viewers, in addition to emotional and physiological ones. (Of these latter, several studies have shown that the arousal of excitement, in itself and independently of specific program content, is associated with inclinations to aggress.)[56]

The interplay of these physiological and ideational responses is complex and can be, at the nonstatistical level of an individual viewer, difficult to assess. This complexity may account for some apparent contradictions in the empirical literature and in efforts to predict the likely effects of violence in a given film or sequence. In the Blanchard et al. study, for example, respondents rated the Russian roulette scene from *The Deer Hunter* as being the least enjoyable and most violent scene of all the material under study, yet that scene was associated with thirty-one violent incidents involving use of a handgun in rituals of Russian roulette between 1978 and 1982.[57] Some viewers reacted aversely to the sequence, while others were apparently stimulated to reenact it. In another context, anecdotal evidence about the effects of *Bonnie and Clyde* ran counter to speculations that the carnage in that film was so graphic as to inhibit aggressive responses. In 1969, for example, Leonard Berkowitz spoke to the National Commission on the Causes and Prevention of Violence and speculated that the graphic violence in *Bonnie and Clyde* might inhibit a viewer's aggressive responses because of the manner in which that film showed the horrific consequences of violence. The film, he said, may have "a good effect of dampening the likelihood of the audience member acting aggressively himself, if he says to himself, yes, it can have this effect."[58] Congressman Boggs followed up on this point during a subsequent interview before the Commission with MPAA president Jack Valenti. "I was interested in the responses about *Bonnie and Clyde*," Boggs said. "I might tell him that we had a murder in my town committed by an 18-year-old boy who had come out of *Bonnie and Clyde* one hour before. He killed a young man who was running a drive-in grocery store. And it was just a senseless murder. Now, whether or not what he saw in *Bonnie and Clyde* had any impact on the murder, I don't know. But I know that what I say to you is a fact—that he saw this movie which glorifies violence."[59]

Aestheticized Violence and Volatile Responses

As these examples indicate, viewers respond to graphic violence in often divergent ways, and this may be one reason why the observable effects in the empirical literature occur in a small percentage of viewers, albeit a statistically significant one. The reactions of viewers to screen violence tend to be inherently volatile, a phenomenon encouraged by some of the essential features of cinema and one that has significant social import. In light of the empirical findings, I now examine these issues. Prior to releasing *The Wild Bunch* in June 1969, Warner Bros. tested the film before preview audiences and sampled their reactions. Viewers were invited to fill out preview cards describing their responses, and the film's producer, Phil Feldman, and studio marketing personnel studied these responses for clues about the demographics of the film's likely audience. The studio's analysis of 768 preview cards, derived from screenings in Fresno and Kansas City, showed a preponderantly negative response to the film.[60]

Sixty percent of those viewers who turned in cards rated the film unfavorably. Only 20 percent rated the film as excellent or outstanding, and these tended to be viewers in the 17–25 age group, the audience segment that Warners subsequently targeted in its release. The written responses on the cards run a gamut of extreme reactions:[61] "Truly a product of our sick society." "Nauseating, unending, offensive, bloody violence." "The kind of picture [mass murderer] Charles Whitman would have enjoyed." "It's difficult to believe someone could make such a movie—Let's all kill more!" "When a film like yours (and *Bonnie and Clyde*) makes me cheer for the bad guys—it is not a good picture." "Stark realism at its best." "It is the most honest and accurate film of human nature I have ever seen." "Most realistic motion picture yet conceived." "I hope the viciousness of the fights stays in the film so people can really know how bad killing is." "The violence obviously was handled at a point near brilliance. The really shocking horror of this mass killing definitely makes one think."

As these responses indicate, disturbing or outré images of violence may stimulate some viewers to reflect upon the filmmaker's moral point of view and probable intentions in crafting the images, although such viewers may arrive at very different conclusions about these issues. At the same time, other viewers of *The Wild Bunch* clearly exhibited less reflective and more excitatory reactions. Contemporary reviewers commented upon the laughter that greeted the film's violent episodes: "At all this the audience laughed (and so did I), not with merriment, exactly, but in tribute to such virtuosity of gore."[62] Screenwriter Charles Higson recalled his first reaction to the film as a teenager, one marked by a rush of excitement: "Once the film was over,

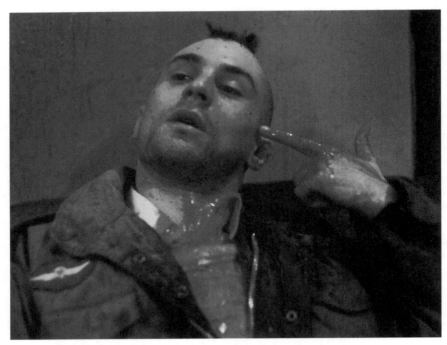

Figure 9. Covered in blood after a frenzy of shooting and stabbing that claims multiple victims, Travis Bickle (Robert De Niro) taunts the police by mimicking suicide. Taxi Driver *escalated the threshold of permissible violence well past what Sam Peckinpah had shown in* The Wild Bunch.

I was exhausted and in a state of high nervous excitement. I wanted to go out in a blaze of glory. I wanted a Gatling gun. I wanted to be pierced by a hundred bullets."[63]

Bonnie and Clyde and *The Wild Bunch* were not made as exploitation pictures. Nevertheless, the gore in these films, and others, elicited reactions from viewers that troubled the filmmakers who created the images. Hearing that a group of Nigerian soldiers screened *The Wild Bunch* to get psyched-up before going into battle, Peckinpah remarked, "I heard that story and I vomited, to think that I had made that film."[64] Similarly, the climactic shoot-out in *Taxi Driver* aroused vigilante reactions in excited viewers, and Scorsese remarked that he found these reactions disturbing. While wishing to distance himself from these reactions, however, he nevertheless admitted that he derived tremendous pleasure as a filmmaker in staging and filming this material. The audience, he said,

> was reacting very strongly to the shoot-out sequence in *Taxi Driver*. And I was disturbed by that. It wasn't done with that intent. You can't stop people from taking it that way. What can you do? And you can't stop people from getting an exhilaration from violence, because that's human, very much the same way as you get an exhilaration from the violence in *The Wild Bunch*. But the exhilaration of the violence at the end of *The Wild Bunch* and the violence that's in *Taxi Driver*—because it's shot a certain way, and I know how it's shot, because I shot it and I designed it—is also in the creation of that scene in the editing, in the camera moves, in the use of music, and the use of sound effects, and in the movement within the frame of the characters. . . . And that's where the exhilaration comes in.[65]

Viewers who whoop with approval at ultraviolence are often intuiting the filmmaker's own aesthetic pleasure in creating such scenes. It is not simply that the design elicits the response. Rather, the viewer grasps the filmmaker's own relationship to the materials, the sensuous pleasures that a Penn, Peckinpah, Scorsese, or Tarantino has derived from the audiovisual design of graphic violence and is manifesting through those designs.

To a large extent, the cinema cannot present violence in other than a pleasure-inducing capacity, and as the foregoing review of the empirical literature suggests, serious social consequences follow from this. The medium inevitably *aestheticizes* violence. The arousal and expression in cinema of 'negative' emotions— fear, anxiety, pain—typically occur as part of a pleasure-inducing aesthetic experience. Admittedly, there is much about this phenomenon—why viewers seek emotional experiences in art that they would avoid in a nonfictional context—which is little understood.[66] But it seems likely that representations of violence on screen that are unrelentingly horrifying, nauseating, or disgusting will fail to attract viewers, in comparison with films that provide aesthetic pleasures, even when the work in question, like Peckinpah's, aims to be shocking and upsetting. McCauley, for example, reported showing a sample of university undergraduates three documentary-style films depicting extreme violence.[67] One film showed head surgery on a young girl, during which the surgeons pulled her face inside out, away from her skull. Another film showed cattle stunned and butchered in a slaughterhouse, and the third showed a group of diners butchering a live monkey and eating it. The students watching the films were given the option of turning them off whenever they chose to do so. On average, they turned the films off halfway through, and only 10 percent of the sample watched the films until the end. Unlike Hollywood films, the screen violence here was a record of real events, and it lacked the normative aesthetic frame of commercial features, that is, attributes such as music and special effects. The students found these films unattractive and did not wish to watch them. McCauley suggests that "these three films were disgusting rather than enjoyable because they were loaded with cues for reality and were lacking the frame of dramatic fiction."[68]

The evident contrast with commercial cinema is quite clear, even in categories of film, like horror, that present extremely graphic images of violence. Changing camera positions, controlled lighting, montage editing, music, and special effects create significant aesthetic pleasure and emotional distance for viewers, who can use these cues as a means of insulating themselves from the depicted violence.[69] The episodes can be enjoyed because they are perceived as being 'not real' by virtue of their elaborate design and special effects. A recent study by the United Kingdom's Broadcasting Standards Commission examined male viewers' responses to a variety of violent film and television programming. With regard to the elaborate violence in contemporary Hollywood films, viewers reported using the special effects to distance themselves from the otherwise shocking violence: "I think when it goes that far it's not really disturbing." "You see the guy getting pierced all over the place and blood spurting out, it doesn't really bother me, but having to watch a documentary or something like that, and there was an operation getting carried out, you just saw a simple incision and stuff like that, you'd be cringing, turning away from the telly."[70] Zill-mann has discussed a similar concentration on special effects by male viewers of horror films.[71]

Even a film whose violence is as harrowing as that in *Saving Private Ryan* employs an elaborately artificial audiovisual design. Spielberg and cinematographer Janusz Kaminski used a number of un-usual techniques to get the striking, vivid, and unexpected visual qual-ities of that film's battle scenes. For some shots, they employed a shutter set at 45 and 90 degrees, instead of the more usual 180-degree configuration, in order to pixelate the action. They stripped the coating off the lenses to flatten contrast and get a foggy but sharp look. They shot with the camera shutter out of sync to produce a streaking effect from the top to bottom of the image. They used a Clairmont Camera Image Shaker to produce horizontal and vertical shaking of the camera, and they flashed the film to desaturate the color and used ENR to add contrast. (Named after Technicolor technician Ernesto N. Rico, ENR is a bleach-bypass process that leaves silver in the print during develop-ing. This gives the film image richer, deeper shadows and desaturated pastels.) These effects made the battlefield carnage more vivid, but they also supplied the visual effects that viewers could use to create some emotional and cognitive distance from the depicted violence. These techniques gave the violence an elaborate and explicit aesthetic frame, which was intensified by the picture's narrative of heroism and moral redemption. The violence was not raw, that is, it was not 'real.' It was staged for the cameras and filtered through the various effects and tech-niques employed by the filmmakers. By contrast, when screen violence lacks this aesthetic dimension, its evocation of negative emotions can be markedly unpleasant for viewers, as in the McCauley study.

These considerations suggest some uncomfortable and unpleas-ant facts about the medium of cinema. Filmmakers who wish to use graphic violence to offer a counterviolence message—that is, to use vi-olence in a way that undercuts its potential for arousing excitatory re-sponses in viewers—may be working in the wrong medium. The medium subverts the goal. In significant ways, the aesthetic contract that the filmmaker must honor with viewers entails that screen vio-lence be made to offer sensory pleasures. These pleasures are implicated in the aggression responses studied in the empirical literature. The prob-lem is especially serious due to the phenomenon of divergent audience responses. The difficulty here can be stated very simply: filmmakers cannot control the reactions of their viewers. Neither Peckinpah nor

Scorsese, both consummate filmmakers, wished to arouse aggressive, vigilante reactions among their viewers, but the scenes that they crafted did so. To a large extent, the formal design of the scenes is implicated in these reactions. Each plays up the aestheticizing organization of the violence. In addition to the squib effects common to both scenes, Peckinpah's montage editing enhances the artifice and spectacle of the violence, and in *Taxi Driver* Scorsese ends the shoot-out with an elaborate series of tracking shots to emphasize the artfully arranged bodies and Jackson Pollack-like collage of blood spatters. In these ways the scenes play to responses the filmmakers wished to disavow.

But even when a filmmaker goes to great lengths to avoid playing violence to spectacle, strikingly divergent viewer reactions may ensue. In *Schindler's List,* Spielberg films a number of killing scenes—Nazis executing prisoners—with an excruciating intensity. In one particularly disturbing scene, a Nazi officer executes a Jewish woman employed as an engineer helping construct a new building in the death camp. In this scene, Spielberg lets victim and executioner interact in an extended, lengthy take. Spielberg avoids montage here in order to enhance the emotional horror of the killing, in other words, to minimize the viewer's ability to take refuge in the spectacle and visual effects that montage offers. In addition, by playing the action in an extended take, he captures the humanity of the victim by letting the action unfold in the real time of the shot, as opposed to edited time. The filmic design is carefully considered, and it demonstrates serious moral purpose. A life is being taken, and the filmmaker tries to show in honest terms what that means and to show horror in the lack of existential reciprocity between victim and executioner, in the disparity of their emotional reactions (i.e., the earnest intensity of the victim in contrast to the cool indifference of the killer).

It is safe to say that Spielberg did not intend for any of the violence in *Schindler's List* to be funny or to provoke laughter, yet that is what this execution scene did for a group of Oakland, California high school students.[72] Promised an outing on Martin Luther King Day when the school was closed, the students were taken to a screening of the film with little preparation or context for the picture. Their laughter prompted complaints from other patrons in the theater, a request from the theater manager that all seventy-odd students leave, and a great deal of media coverage of the incident. The teenagers denied that they were expressing any racism or anti-Semitism and maintained that they were simply doing what they always do at the movies, which is to talk and express themselves. One 15-year-old girl described their col-

Figure 10. The Basketball Diaries *has been implicated in several real-world shootings in which the killers cited the inspirational nature of the film sequence where a high school kid (Leonardo Di Caprio) shoots his teacher and classmates. Note how the lighting and camera angle aestheticize the violence by accentuating the drama and making it visually striking.*

lective reaction: "It wasn't like people were laughing because people were dying. The woman who got shot fell funny and people just laughed."[73] For some of the viewers, no doubt, the laughter was a distancing response to alleviate tension, to insulate their feelings from the depicted violence, and, in a high school environment rife with peer pressure, to prevent peers from seeing that one is touched or sad and therefore emotionally vulnerable. At the same time, however, such laughter can signal a failure of empathy, an inability (or an unwillingness) to imaginatively place oneself inside the fiction and relate to the pain or violence on an immediately personal level. In some films, like *Taxi Driver*, the audiovisual structure of a scene might work to prevent a viewer's empathic response by stressing the artifice and spectacle of the violence, but here Spielberg evidently sought to show the violence within an appropriately moral and empathy-inducing framework. Viewer reactions were nevertheless somewhat unpredictable.

The Claremont High incident was not the only case of variant responses elicited by the film. *Washington Post* columnist Donna Britt encountered a similar incident when she went to see the film.[74] She reported that a group of middle-aged and elderly women were whooping and laughing during scenes that prompted flinching, gasps, and tears from the rest of the audience. A more extreme variant response occurred when an evidently deranged man in a San Diego theater shot the woman sitting in front of him during a scene in the film where Nazis were shooting Jewish victims in Krakow, Poland.[75] The 45-year-old gun-man said that he wanted to "test God" and protect Jews. These are vari-ant reactions because they are not the responses that Spielberg intended his viewers to have and that he, to the best of his not inconsiderable filmmaking talent, had worked to create.

Spielberg's inability to control the responses of his viewers, de-spite his skill as a filmmaker and evident desire to show violence that hurts and horrifies, is a significant failure. It is one that all filmmakers share, whatever their intentions in depicting ultraviolence. Coupled with the findings in the empirical literature about the effects of view-ing violence and with theories which hold that aggression, in many manifestations, is a socially learned response, the film industry's continuing investment in violent spectacle does not leave one very san-guinary about the social health of contemporary culture. Viewer reac-tions to screen violence are volatile, and filmmakers cannot reliably control these responses, that is, they cannot craft their scenes so as to eliminate the variant reactions. Furthermore, to compel viewers to watch, filmmakers routinely embed violence within an audiovisual de-sign that provides aesthetic pleasures. Screen violence is made attrac-tive, whether by dressing it up in special effects or by embedding it in scenarios of righteous (i.e., morally justified) aggression. Without these aesthetic pleasures, viewers are unlikely to consent to viewing grossly disturbing violence.

The filmmaker who wishes to use graphic violence to instruct or make a statement against violence pursues an elusive goal. The ef-fort is easily undermined by the medium's inherent aestheticizing of violence and by the prevalence of deviant viewer reactions, chief among these being the instigation of aggression as documented in the empiri-cal studies. Furthermore, popular film and culture, in general, exhibit a fascination with the spectacle and pleasures of violence. In this re-gard, the forum and context from which a filmmaker would speak is often counterproductive to the message. Working with graphic vio-lence, the filmmaker inherits the history of a stylistic whose conven-tionalized meanings are readily understood by contemporary viewers and are, in significant ways, counter to an antiviolence philosophy. These considerations suggest that a critique of violence may be best pursued on screen in its absence, that is, by not showing—at least not in graphic detail—the very phenomenon that a film would address. Otherwise, filmmakers risk that their moral efforts be undone by established characteristics of the medium in which they would work.

On the one hand, the policy implications of these considerations and the empirical findings are clear. As the current manifestation toward which cinema violence has been moving, graphic ultraviolence is not conducive to the long-term health of the social polity. However, efforts to censor program material create their own problems, and calls for the industry to regulate itself have been mostly ineffective. The CARA ratings have always showed greater leniency toward violence than toward sex, and graphic violence is now so endemic to the medium, such a pervasive feature of contemporary style, that filmmakers have become disconnected from the carnage on which they turn their cameras. In an odd but understandable turn of events, many filmmakers who purvey ultraviolence are emotionally disengaged from it and show it in a dispassionate manner. For them, it is a special effect and a box-office asset. This is quite evident in routine action films, but it sometimes afflicts even fine directors. Oliver Stone's *Natural Born Killers* (1994), for example, plays violence as a cartoon in a disconnected, postmodern style that romanticizes the serial killers it professes to critique. Its attentive and flamboyant depictions of violence make it a part of the violence-loving media it aims to target. Most of the ultraviolence in *Pulp Fiction* is played as comedy, with no grounding in suffering or pain. Cinematographer John Bailey has remarked that "the artifice of movie mayhem" has become "routine and unreal to us as filmmakers."[76]

This unreality is symptomatic of the social disconnect of many contemporary filmmakers. For them, violence is an image to be constructed, a special effect to be staged, but not a social effect that is produced. When characters die spectacularly bloody deaths in contemporary crime and action films, they are, for the individuals who make these films, just movie characters, without real-life correlates. In the culture of ultraviolence that now engulfs the medium, moviemakers operate in a kind of postmodern bubble, treating violence as an image and not as a social process. Furthermore, the sheer pervasiveness of media violence helps augment this sense of unreality. It has become an object for consumption, a familiar part of the social landscape as defined by movies and television. As German director Wim Wenders has said, "Violence appears in so many contexts where you cannot reflect on it any more, where you cannot experience it any other way than consuming."[77]

Violence has a legitimate place in art as part of the human experience and as one of the mysteries of life that haunts and fascinates. But viewers rarely experience screen violence in this fashion, treated in a serious and provocative way that invites reflection and contemplation (and, as noted, the medium of cinema does not make this kind of depiction easy to achieve). Instead, commercial films offer it as spectacle, an easy way to get to the viewer emotionally and to solve narrative issues. And it all becomes ever more unreal, ever more stylized and disconnected from a viewer's personal experience, except, as the empirical studies suggest, for its impact on the social psychology of the culture. There seems, at present, no way out from the blood and circus that much of present cinema has become, especially as the culture at large manifests such fascination (albeit horrified) with an ongoing spate of headline-grabbing homicides. The Littleton shootings were recent instances in a lengthy spate of murders in which the killers had feasted on media ultraviolence. In the words of a teenager sentenced to life for killing his mother, "The first stage you see a guy's head being blown off and you feel compassion. The second stage you see it again, you feel compassion, but it's not as strong as the first . . . the fifth stage, you want to do it but it's just a thought. The last stage you do it and you want to do it again."[78] Certainly this killer's words are self-serving. But they also speak to a worst-case, nightmare scenario about the connections between ultraviolent movies and real violence.

Once American cinema turned the corner toward graphic violence, there has been no going back. And the culture as a whole has accompanied cinema on this journey, becoming bloodier, ever more grim, and ever more confused about the accelerating spiral of movie-induced carnage.

The essays collected in this volume are drawn from a variety of sources that demonstrate the complexity of the topic and the manner in which it has cut across different realms of public discourse. These sources include the popular press, scholarly journal articles representing work in cinema studies and empirical social science, and testimony elicited by congressional committees investigating problems of violence in society and the media. By examining movie violence in three contexts—its history, its aesthetic characteristics and structure, and its potential effects upon individual and society—this volume presents the topic in its richness and complexity. As a result, readers will develop an understanding of cinema violence as a representational construct and a social phenomenon, a function of distinct historical periods, characteristics of film form, and ongoing intellectual and research paradigms.

The first five essays in this volume set the historical context.

They evoke the controversies that followed the explosion of graphic bloodshed in cinema during and after 1967 (the pivotal year that saw the release of *The Dirty Dozen, Bonnie and Clyde, A Fistful of Dollars,* and *For a Few Dollars More*). These films unleashed a stormy debate about the turn contemporary cinema had taken and the likely long-term effects of the new violence. The essays in this section are symptoms of that period and its controversy; they acquaint the reader with the immediate reactions of critics, reviewers, and others who were attempting to think through this confusing and seminal period in the history of American film and of the country itself.

After first labeling *Bonnie and Clyde* a trash film, the reviewer for *Newsweek* took the extraordinary step of publishing a second column on the film, this time retracting his earlier opinion and reassessing the picture and its violence in more favorable terms. In "The Thin Red Line," the reviewer, Joseph Morgenstern, defended the film by arguing that violent movies are a consequence of violent times (alluding to the diverse currents of late 1960s unrest). He added, though, an important qualification that resonates more powerfully twenty-some years later: "When artists are able to bring characters to life and keep them alive, they should not leave death to the special effects department." More often than not, this is exactly what movies have done—shown violent death as a special effect, as spectacle—and Morgenstern suggests that this is an abdication of the artist's responsibility. Although impressed with the artistic possibilities represented by *Bonnie and Clyde* and the new creative freedoms the industry was granting filmmakers, Morgenstern remained uneasy about the film's graphic violence, and his attitude was shared by many.

With less caution and ambivalence than Morgenstern displayed, Bosley Crowther, the film critic for the *New York Times,* expressed strong opposition to the increase of violence brought on by the pictures released in 1967. In a pair of columns, Crowther attacked the new violence and worried over its likely long-term effects on the culture. He felt that the explicitly detailed murders depicted in these pictures were gross, bloody, massive, and excessive. Furthermore, he believed that they expressed an attitude of "killing is fun," and he characterized this attitude as "an antisocial venom." Crowther's intensely negative reaction to these popular pictures quickly made him a target for criticism, but his worries were prescient. The questions he raised are with us still. Moreover, contrary to many critics and filmmakers (e.g., Sam Peckinpah and Arthur Penn) who argued that violent times justified the presentation of explicit movie violence, Crowther argued that violent times made it essential for the media to show balance and restraint. Rather than give new license to artists, periods of social unrest, for Crowther, ought to make them more prudent. Writing for *Variety*, the industry tradepaper, Ronald Gold summarized the reactions to Crowther's columns in the film industry and among movie reviewers and the widespread suggestions that Crowther was out of touch with contemporary film and the sensibilities of the audiences for these pictures.

The year that saw release of *The Dirty Dozen* and *Bonnie and Clyde*, and the one that followed, were among the most violent periods in modern American history. The Vietnam War continued to escalate, with American troop levels at 460,000, and massive antiwar protests in New York and Washington, D.C. Urban riots erupted in 128 cities during the first nine months of 1967, and in April and June of 1968, Martin Luther King Jr. and Robert Kennedy were murdered. The nation's turmoil led Congress to form a committee of inquiry into the sources producing the diverse skeins of domestic unrest. The National Commission on the Causes and Prevention of Violence heard testimony from a range of social scientists, political officials, and concerned citizens. Because of the upsurge in movie violence, the Commission examined, as part of its broad-ranging inquiries, whether Hollywood films might be playing a role in fomenting the contemporary unrest.

In December 1968, Jack Valenti, president of MPAA, testified before the Commission and defended the industry and its films from suggestions that it was peddling violence for a buck and that such violence might have undesirable social consequences. The MPAA was (and is) a buffer group, interceding between the industry and its public and promoting the industry's interests. In this context, Valenti's testimony is a masterpiece of rhetoric, treating the commissioners with great respect while defending Hollywood's right to make its pictures. Of special interest are the Commission's concerns that focus specifically on *Bonnie and Clyde* and Valenti's defense of graphic violence and the revolutionary new films and filmmakers that had been causing such controversy. He deftly insulated the industry and its films from the threat posed by the findings of empirical studies pointing to a connection between media violence and aggressive reactions among viewers. Valenti maintained that evaluating screen violence was an inevitably subjective undertaking and one not amenable to social science methods. Quantitative studies, he suggested, especially laboratory experiments, were flawed in design and conception. Thus, he claimed, social scientific findings about media effects were of limited use and that, in any case, the real question to worry over is that of censorship. Who decides the standards, and who applies them? As evidence that Hollywood took its social responsibilities seriously, he offered the industry's newly formulated ratings code. Much discussion focused on the 1966 revision of Hollywood's Production Code, and Valenti used the occasion of his testimony to introduce the newly created G-M-R-X classification scheme. This, he said, would for the first time prevent children from seeing films inappropriate for them. He might also have added that it significantly expanded the creative license of filmmakers, who could now make harder films for the R-rated adult audience, precisely the kinds of pictures that were embroiled in controversy.

The next six essays examine the aesthetics of ultraviolence. Hollywood cinematographer John Bailey (*The Big Chill* [1983], *In the Line of Fire* [1993], *Nobody's Fool* [1994]) explores the issues faced by filmmakers (or, at least, those issues that the honest ones think about) who craft screen violence. Bailey asks where the difference lies between the exploration of violence and its exploitation, and he examines the differences of style in two violent films, *Natural Born Killers* and *The Shawshank Redemption*. He finds that the camerawork in *Natural Born Killers* visualizes and makes exciting the sociopathic point of view of the killers, while the imagery in *Shawshank* humanizes the victims of violence and creates empathy for them. For Bailey, the distinction between exploration and exploitation turns on these differences, on the extent to which film style deglamorizes violence and focuses on its human consequences. He relates his own effort to grapple with these issues during the making of *China Moon*, a crime film that he directed. Bailey closes by asking that filmmakers consider their complicity in the images they create: "If our own sensibilities are askew, if we have no moral compass to guide us, what point of view are we going to create?"

David Thomson examines the ease and slickness of death as cinema portrays it. He discusses the distinctive mannerisms that stars as diverse as Humphrey Bogart, James Cagney, and Clint Eastwood brought to their screen encounters with death and dying, and he explores the fascination that staging deadly violence holds for filmmakers. Through a wealth of example, Thomson shows how easy death is in the movies—glamorized and 'slo-moed'—and how false to life. He finds that "something essential to the medium cleaves to . . . the chance to stare at death without honoring pain or loss." By contrast with its cinematic renditions, death in real life typically involves waiting and suffering, attributes that cinema has not often depicted. Thus does cinema become habituated to its own stylistic conventions: "When killing is so easy and death so brief, it becomes a way of life."

Devin McKinney proposes a schema for classifying movie violence: it is either "strong" or "weak." Weak violence, he suggests, is the most plentiful sort, and 'weakness' here is not to be understood as specifying a relative degree of explictness. The graphic ear-cutting scene in *Reservoir Dogs* is an example for McKinney of weak violence. This kind of violence carries few emotional consequences for the filmmaker who designs it, the characters who enact it, or the viewer who watches it. It is easily consumed and proposes no moral challenges for viewers who are asked, merely, to assent to it and, typically, to enjoy it. The action epics of Arnold Schwarzenegger fit this pattern, as do the killings in Paul Verhoeven's *Basic Instinct*. Indeed, McKinney finds a resurgence of weak violence in contemporary film: "The kind of disconnected, uncommitted movie mayhem that began with James Bond, came of age with the sociopathic crime dramas of the early 1970s, and served the reactionary agenda of the 1980s is once again ascendant." Strong violence, by contrast, opens an emotional trapdoor under the viewer, upsets one's moral equilibrium, and, above all, grasps the *consequences* of violent acts, for the characters on screen as for the viewer who watches. McKinney explicates this category with reference to *Bad Lieutenant, The Crying Game,* and *Henry: Portrait of a Serial Killer.* By emphasizing the importance of aesthetic designs that delineate consequences, McKinney's argument links with those of John Bailey and David Thomson. All propose that morally grounded designs are those that treat violence not simply as an image, but as a phenomenon and an experience that connects with life. For them, strong violence, violence responsibly rendered, designates the dilemmas of life and visualizes these, rather than hermetically and self-consciously referencing cinema and its stylistic conventions.

Vivian C. Sobchack finds that graphically violent movies perform a service for the viewer—they exorcise fears of chaos and senseless death. Discussing such early 1970s films as *A Clockwork Orange* and *Straw Dogs,* she suggests that the stylization of violence, achieved through slow motion and squib effects, elicits the viewer's real-world fears about chance encounters with violence while simultaneously alleviating those anxieties. Sobchack thus suggests that graphic screen violence performs a cathartic effect. Writing of *Bonnie and Clyde* and its seminal influence, she notes that "it was the first major film to allow us the luxury of inspecting what frightened us–the senseless, the unexpected, the bloody. And most important, it kindly stylized death for us; it created nobility from senselessness, it choreographed a dance out of blood and death, it gave meaning and import to our mortal twitchings." By choreographing violence in such a way as to impose an aesthetic order on the experience of violent death, films of graphic bloodshed impose this order upon the viewer's conceptual and emotional experience. Thus, Sobchack suggests that graphic violence performs a useful social function. Her essay and her reflections date from the early 1970s. In the essay's afterword, Sobchack reassesses these questions some twenty-five years later, in light of the intervening decades of movie violence. The contrast between her reflections past and present illuminates the trajectory that the nation's culture, as a whole, has traveled in relation to cinema violence.

Carol J. Clover explicates the sexual and gendered aspects of violence in horror films, specifically the slasher film. Since the 1980s, these grisly slaughter-fests had taken over the horror genre, offering viewers stalk-and-murder narratives overlaid with detailed imagery of butchery and mutilation. While most critics were quick to condemn these films as trash, Clover, instead, took a close view and found rich psychological material in the format. Her illuminating analysis clarifies the complex appeal of these films for viewers, amid all of the problematic and prurient violence.

In the concluding essay in this section, I examine the origins and aesthetic of slow-motion violence. Since *Bonnie and Clyde* and *The Wild Bunch,* this has become the predominant way of stylizing violent gun battles. Filmmakers insert slow-motion shots into extended montages of death and destruction. I explore how filmmakers (chiefly, Sam Peckinpah, who did more than any other director to popularize this aesthetic) orchestrate these scenes and the emotional and moral implications of these constructions.

Explorations of aesthetics inevitably open onto issues of effect. The remaining essays examine these issues. The essays by Leonard Berkowitz and Richard B. Felson offer somewhat contrasting portraits of the state of research on media violence. Berkowitz provides a detailed explanation of the role that cognitive factors (thoughts and ideas) play in viewer reactions to media violence. Readers should not be put off by the somewhat wordy title of this essay; the discussion is clearly presented and very straightforward. While arguing that the social costs of violent imagery in the mass media are real and may be deemed unacceptable, Berkowitz shows the complexity of media–viewer interactions. Specifically, he explicates the role of thought (induced by media programming) in activating bodily reactions. He terms this process the "spreading activation" of thoughts related to media images and content and which, under the right conditions, can dampen a viewer's inhibitions against acting aggressively. Berkowitz examines the factors that can trigger and facilitate this "spreading activation." His account shows that empirical research on media violence does not construct a mechanistic portrait of media messages and passively reacting viewers. Instead, while the bulk of the evidence clearly shows aggression-inducing characteristics of media programming, the processes involved are complicated and multifactoral.

While a general consensus prevails among social scientists about the aggression-inducing characteristics of movie and television content, some controversy exists about the strength and duration of these effects. In the final essay, sociologist Richard B. Felson undertakes a thorough review of the empirical literature and offers a more tentative assessment of media effects. He concludes that, while effects are present, they are likely to be weak and to affect only a small percentage of viewers, and are unlikely to be a significant factor in the high crime rate in this country.

The essays by Berkowitz and Felson give the reader an extensive account of the available literature and theory on the effects of media violence and a sampling of the controversy and range of opinion that bear on this issue. There is as yet no definitive resolution of the problem. The questions, though, remain urgent ones, from the standpoint of individual as well as social psychology. Neither Felson nor Berkowitz suggests that the media play a clearly causative role in fostering real-world aggression. But they do implicate film and television in the mix of social factors that incline individuals to behave violently. In light of the empirical work on media effects, the fascination with violence in popular culture should give us pause. It is an attribute unlikely to be conducive to the general well-being or social health of our society.

NOTES

1. Marcia Pally, "'Double' Trouble," *Film Comment* 20 (September–October 1984), p. 14.

2. A thorough review of this period can be found in Garth Jowett, *Film: The Democratic Art* (Boston: Little, Brown, 1976).

3. *Mass Media Hearings*, vol. 9A: *A Report to the National Commission on the Causes and Prevention of Violence* (Washington, D.C.: U.S. Government Printing Office, 1969), p. 193.

4. "'Brutal Films Pale Before Televised Vietnam'—Valenti," *Variety*, February 21, 1968, p. 2.

5. "Theatre Operators and Public Require Updating on Social Point of View," *Variety*, March 6, 1968, p. 7.

6. Quoted in Peter Wood, "How a Film Changes from an 'X' to an 'R,'" *New York Times*, July 20, 1980, sec. C.

7. "Pix Must 'Broaden Market,'" *Variety*, March 20, 1968, p. 1.

8. I examine these factors in *Savage Cinema: Sam Peckinpah and the Rise of Ultraviolent Movies* (Austin: University of Texas Press, 1998).

9. "Brutal Films Pale Before Televised Vietnam," p. 2.

10. Gary Crowdus and Richard Porton, "The Importance of a Singular, Guiding Vision: An Interview with Arthur Penn," *Cineaste* 20:2 (Spring 1993), pp. 8–9.

11. Robert J. Landry, "It's Murder, Italian Style," *Variety*, February 8, 1967, p. 7.

12. Review of *The Good, the Bad and the Ugly*, *Variety*, December 27, 1967, p. 6.

13. Bosley Crowther, "Movies to Kill People By," *New York Times*, July 9, 1967, sec. 2, p. 10.

14. Crowdus and Porton, p. 9.

15. "'Bonnie and Clyde's' Booming Repeats," *Variety*, February 14, 1968, p. 3.

16. "Hollywood: The Shock of Freedom in Films," *Time*, December 8, 1967, p. 73.

17. Phil Feldman memo, May 13, 1969, folder no. 46, Sam Peckinpah Collection, AMPAS Library, Los Angeles.

18. Wild Bunch—Bill Faralla, folder no. 43, letter of March 19, 1968, Sam Peckinpah Collection.

19. Wild Bunch reaction cards, folder no. 65, Sam Peckinpah Collection.

20. I explore Peckinpah's efforts in this regard in *Savage Cinema*.

21. Carol J. Clover, *Men, Women, and Chain Saws: Gender in the Modern Horror Film* (Princeton, N.J.: Princeton University Press, 1992), p. 41.

22. *Variety*, June 8, 1988, p. 24.

23. Roger Watkins, "'Demented Revenge' Hits World Screens," *Variety*, October 29, 1980, p. 3.

24. "Chi Tribune Blasts Gory X-Films in R-Rated Clothing," *Variety*, November 12, 1980, p. 6.

25. Ibid., p. 30.

26. Clover, p. 12.

27. Ruth A. Inglis, "Self-Regulation in Operation," in *The American Film Industry*, rev. ed., ed. Tino Balio (Madison: University of Wisconsin Press, 1985), p. 378.

28. Herbert Blumer, *Movies and Conduct* (New York: Macmillan, 1933), p. 74.

29. Mark Crispin Miller, "In Defense of Sam Peckinpah," *Film Quarterly* 28:3 (Spring 1975), p. 13.

30. "Films, Like TV, Lack Research on 'Violence,'" *Variety*, December 25, 1968, p. 5.

31. Walter Kaufmann, *Tragedy and Philosophy* (New York: Anchor Books, 1969), p. 34.

32. Dorothy L. Singer and Jerome L. Singer, "TV Violence: What's All the Fuss About?," *Television and Children* 7:2 (1984), p. 30.

33. Leonard Berkowitz, "Some Effects of Thoughts on Anti- and Prosocial Influences of Media Events: A Cognitive-Neoassociation Analysis," *Psychological Bulletin* 95, no. 3 (1984), p. 414.

34. Haejung Paik and George Comstock, "The Effects of Television Violence on Antisocial Behavior: A Meta-Analysis," *Communication Research*, 21, no. 4 (August 1994), pp. 516–46. For a different view of media effects, see Felson in this volume.

35. Eli A. Rubinstein, "Television Violence: A Historical Perspective," in *Children and the Faces of Television,* ed. Edward L. Palmer and Aimee Dorr (New York: Academic Press, 1980).

36. Surgeon General's Scientific Advisory Committee on Television and Social Behavior, *Television and Growing Up: The Impact of Televised Violence* (Washington, D.C.: U.S. Government Printing Office, 1972).

37. Seymour Feshback, "The Role of Fantasy in the Response to Television," *Journal of Social Issues* 32, no. 4 (1976), pp. 71–85; "Reality and Fantasy in Filmed Violence," in *Television and Social Behavior: A Technical Report to the Surgeon General's Scientific Advisory Committee on Television and Social Behavior,* ed. John P. Murray et al. (Washington, D.C.: U.S. Government Printing Office, 1972), pp. 318–45; "The Stimulating Versus Cathartic Effects of a Vicarious Aggressive Activity," *Journal of Abnormal and Social Psychology* 63, no. 2 (1961), pp. 381–85; "The Drive Reducing Function of Fantasy Behavior," *Journal of Abnormal and Social Psychology* 50 (1955), pp. 3–11. See also Gary A. Copeland and Dan Slater, "Television Violence and Vicarious Catharsis," *Critical Studies in Mass Communication* 2 (1985), pp. 352–62; Sidney A. Manning and Dalmas A. Taylor, "Effects of Viewed Violence and Aggression: Stimulation and Catharsis," *Journal of Personality and Social Psychology* 31, no. 1 (1975), pp. 180–88; Ann Roth Pytkowicz, Nathaniel N. Wagner, and Irwin G. Sarason, "An Experimental Study of the Reduction of Hostility Through Fantasy," *Journal of Personality and Social Psychology* 5, no. 3 (1967), pp. 295–303.

38. Feshback, "The Catharsis Hypothesis and Some Consequences of Interaction with Aggressive and Neutral Play Objects," *Journal of Personality* 24 (1956), pp. 449–62.

39. Leonard Berkowitz and Russell G. Geen, "Film Violence and the Cue Properties of Available Targets," *Journal of Personality and Social Psychology* 3, no. 5 (1966), pp. 525–30.

40. Albert Bandura, "Psychological Mechanisms of Aggression," in *Human Ethology,* ed. M. von Cranach et al. (New York: Cambridge University Press, 1979).

41. Albert Bandura, Dorothea Ross, and Sheila A. Ross, "Vicarious Reinforcement and Imitative Learning," *Journal of Abnormal and Social Psychology* 67, no. 6 (1963), pp. 601–7.

42. Ibid., p. 606.

43. Ibid.

44. Albert Bandura, Dorothea Ross, and Sheila A. Ross, "Imitation of Film-Mediated Aggressive Models," *Journal of Abnormal and Social Psychology* 66, no. 1 (1963), pp. 3–11.

45. Leonard Berkowitz and Edna Rawlings, "Effects of Film Violence on Inhibitions against Subsequent Aggression," *Journal of Abnormal and Social Psychology* 66, no. 5 (1963), pp. 405–12.

46. Ibid., p. 411.

47. Dolf Zillmann, "The Psychology of the Appeal of Portrayals of Violence," in Goldstein, *Why We Watch,* p. 202.

48. Ibid., p. 200.

49. Robert A. Baron, "Magnitude of Victim's Pain Cues and Level of Prior Anger Arousal as Determinants of Adult Aggressive Behavior," *Journal of Personality and Social Psychology* 17, no. 3 (1971), pp. 236–43; Glenn S. Sanders and Robert Steven Baron, "Pain Cues and Uncertainty as Determinants of Aggression in a Situation Involving Repeated Instigation," *Journal of Personality and Social Psychology* 32, no. 3 (1975), pp. 495–502.

50. D. Caroline Blanchard, Barry Graczyk, and Robert J. Blanchard, "Differential Reactions of Men and Women to Realism, Physical Damage, and Emotionality in Violent Films," *Aggressive Behavior* 12 (1986), pp. 45–55.

51. Ibid., p. 51.

52. Dolf Zillmann and James B. Weaver III, "Psychoticism in the Effect of Prolonged Exposure to Gratuitous Media Violence on the Acceptance of Violence as a Preferred Means of Conflict Resolution," *Personality and Individual Differences* 22, no. 5 (1997), pp. 613–27. On nontransient effects, see also Zillmann and Weaver, "Effects of Prolonged Exposure to Gratuitous Media Violence on Provoked and Unprovoked Hostile Behavior," *Journal of Applied Social Psychology* 29, no. 1 (1999), pp. 145–65.

53. Berkowitz, p. 411.

54. Russell Green, "Behavioral and Physiological Reactions to Observed Violence: Effects of Prior Exposure to Aggressive Stimuli," *Journal of Personality and Social Psychology* 40 (1981), pp. 868–75; M. Thomas, R. Horton, E. Lippincott, and R. Drabman, "Desensitization to Portrayals of Real-Life Aggression as a Function of Exposure to Television Violence," *Journal of Personality and Social Psychology* 35 (1977), pp. 450–58; Victor R. Cline, Roger G. Croft, and Steven Courrier, "Desensitization of Children to Television Violence," *Journal of Personality and Social Psychology* 27, no. 3 (1973), pp. 360–65.

55. Berkowitz, p. 418.

56. Dolf Zillmann, "Excitation Transfer in Communication-Mediated Aggressive Behavior," *Journal of Experimental Social Psychology* 7 (1971), pp. 419–34; P. H. Tannenbaum and Dolf Zillmann, "Emotional Arousal in the Facilitation of Aggression Through Communication," in *Advances in Experimental Social Psychology*, vol. 8, ed. Leonard Berkowitz (New York: Academic Press, 1975), pp. 149–92.

57. Wayne Wilson and Randy Hunter, "Movie-Inspired Violence," pp. 435–41.

58. *Mass Media Hearings,* vol. 9A: *A Report to the National Commission on the Causes and Prevention of Violence* (Washington, D.C.: U.S. Government Printing Office, 1969), p. 43.

59. Ibid., p. 207.

60. Sam Peckinpah Collection, Feldman memos, folder no. 46.

61. Sam Peckinpah Collection, *Wild Bunch* preview reaction cards, folder no. 65.

62. Review of *The Wild Bunch* in *The Nation,* July 14, 1969, p. 61.

63. Charles Higson, "The Shock of the Old," *Sight and Sound* 5, no. 8 (August 1995), p. 36.

64. P. F. Kluge, "Director Sam Peckinpah, What Price Violence," *Life* (August 11, 1972), p. 53.

65. Anthony DeCurtis, "What the Streets Mean: An Interview with martin Scorsese," in *Plays, Movies, and Critics,* ed. Jody McAuliffe (Durham, N.C.: Duke University Press, 1993), p. 211.

66. Goldstein's *Why We Watch* explores this issue and concludes with a series of unanswered questions.

67. The citation that McCauley provides for this information is unhelpful because it does not, in fact, contain information about these films. He cites J. Haidt, R. C. McCauley, and P. Rozin, "Individual Differences in Sensitivity to Disgust: A Scale Sampling Seven Domains of Disgust Elicitors," *Personality and Individual Differences* 16 (1994), pp. 701–13. McCauley discusses the research involving the films in "When Screen Violence Is Not Attractive," *Why We Watch*, pp. 144–62.

68. McCauley, "When Screen Violence Is Not Attractive," p. 161.

69. "Men Viewing Violence," Broadcasting Standards Commission, London, 1998.

70. Ibid., p. 41.

71. Zillmann, "The Psychology of the Appeal of Portrayals of Violence," p. 198.

72. Christine Spolar, "The Kids Who Laughed Till It Hurt," *Washington Post,* March 10, 1994, pp. C1, C4.

73. Ibid., p. C4.

74. Donna Britt, "Lights, Camera, Sad Reaction," *Washington Post*, March 15, 1994, pp. B1, B5.

75."Gunman Gets 6 Years for 'Schindler's List' Shooting," *Los Angeles Times*, August 10, 1994, p. B8.

76. John Bailey, "Bang Bang Bang Bang, Ad Nauseum," *American Cinematographer* 75:12 (December 1994), p. 26.

77. Manohla Dargis, "Sleeping with Guns," *Sight and Sound* 7, no. 5 (May 1997), p. 21.

78. "'Scream' Killer Fingers Film, TV," *The Hollywood Reporter*, July 25, 1999, online version.

The Historical Context
of Ultraviolence

Joseph Morgenstern

The Thin Red Line

Last week this magazine said that *Bonnie and Clyde,* a tale of two young bank robbers in the 1930s, turns into a "squalid shoot-'em for the moron trade" because it does not know what to make of its own violence. I am sorry to say I consider that review grossly unfair and regrettably inaccurate. I am sorrier to say I wrote it.

Seeing the film a second time and surrounded by an audience no more or less moronic than I, but enjoying itself almost to the point of rapture, I realized that *Bonnie and Clyde* knows perfectly well what to make of its violence, and makes a cogent statement with it—that violence is not necessarily perpetrated by shambling cavemen or quivering psychopaths but may also be the casual, easy expression of only slightly aberrated citizens, of jes' folks.

I had become so surfeited and preoccupied by violence in daily life that my reaction was as excessive as the stimulus. There are indeed a few moments in which the gore goes too far, becomes stock shockery that invites standard revulsion. And yet, precisely because *Bonnie and Clyde* combines these gratuitous crudities with scene after scene of dazzling artistry, precisely because it has the power both to enthrall and appall, it is an ideal laboratory for the study of violence, a subject in which we are all matriculating these days.

Violent movies are an inevitable consequence of violent life. They may also transmit the violence virus, but they do not breed it any more than the Los Angeles television stations caused Watts to riot. Distinctions can and must be made between violent films that pander and violent films that enlighten, between camp, comment, and utter cynicism. And there is nothing like the movies for giving us historical perspective on violence we have known, and in many cases loved.

No one but Charlie Chaplin's competitors ever deplored his

early comedies although they served up staggeringly large helpings of mayhem. Cruelty to animals, children, and adults was the crucial ingredient in W. C. Fields's social satire. No one ever accused Cagney of excess gentility in *Public Enemy*, but people consoled themselves in those days with the notion that violence was the particular province of a particular minority, namely, the violent. They called the group The Underworld, at least until 1939.

World War II brought back primitivism, which had been on the skids ever since 1918, and its popularity today has not discernibly declined. A fair amount of contemporary movie violence is still conventionally primitive, unadorned by anything but gangrenous nostalgia—*Battle of the Bulge*, for instance. Some movie violence is stylishly primitive—*St. Valentine's Day Massacre* pumps slugs into lugs by the thousands, but a few good performances lift the sleazy legend from the sewer to the gutter. Some is pretentiously primitive—*The Chase* was all awash with racial and social symbols yet seemed most pleased with itself when Marlon Brando's battered face was awash with ketchup. And some is ingeniously primitive—*The Dirty Dozen* spends more than two hours on an outlandishly detailed setup for a half-hour payoff in which the GI demolition squad really demolishes, the charges explode, the Kraut machine guns chatter, and the victims (including lots of screaming females) cry themselves a river of blood.

Such stuff as this is trash, and at least has the bad grace to give itself away. More serious complications arise when the overlay of comedy or comment is done more artfully. *A Fistful of Dollars* and its sequel, *For a Few Dollars More*, were synthetic Westerns made on the cheap in Italy and unmistakably brutal. But their director, Sergio Leone, had done his homework and studied the models he wanted to copy and/or parody. His primary motive clearly was profit, and therefore imitation, but that did not prevent him from adding a pinch of put-on and a dollop of dubious satire.

Yet violence can serve thoroughly satiric or artistic ends, and not only in Shakespeare, Marlowe, Buñuel, "Marat/Sade," or the coming film version of *In Cold Blood*. Violence was downright charming in *The Quiet Man*, delightful in *The Crimson Pirate*, enthralling in *Psycho* and *The Hill*, relevant in *Dutchman*. *West Side Story* might well have done with more of it to stiffen its spine, and so might *Up the Down Staircase*, which only tiptoed timorously around the crazy chaos of America's slum schools.

There is nothing timorous about *Bonnie and Clyde*, in which violence is at once a virtue and a vice. Director Arthur Penn and his col-

Figure 11. Using multiple cameras and slow motion, director Arthur Penn was the first American filmmaker to capture the spastic agonies of gunshot victims. Bonnie Parker (Faye Dunaway) expires in a hail of machine gun fire.

leagues perform poignant and intricate wonders with a Loony Toon gang of outlaws who bumble along from one bank job to another, from one blood bath to another, in an inchoate, uncomprehending, and fore-doomed attempt to fulfill their stunted selves. Both *Bonnie and Clyde* and *St. Valentine's Day Massacre* deal with the same slice of life, yet the characters in the latter are gun racks and the characters in *Bonnie* have a rushing of blood in their veins and a torrent of thought in their minds.

From time to time, however, all artistry falls by the wayside: when a cop trying to stop the getaway car is shot in the face, when a grocer is bludgeoned in a close-up, when a grenade demolishes a police tank, when one outlaw has his skull blown open and another has her eye shot out. These scenes are reprehensible not because they are ugly or shocking, but because they are familiar, gross, and demeaning. When artists are able to bring characters to life and keep them alive, they should not leave death to the special effects department.

There is, in the depiction of violence, a thin red line between the precisely appropriate and the imprecisely offensive. Sometimes a few too many frames of film may mean the difference between a shot that makes its point concisely and one that lingers slobberingly. These few frames or scenes in *Bonnie and Clyde* will hardly change the course of human events. When we talk about movies, we are not talking about urban renewal programs, nuclear nonproliferation treaties, or rat control bills. Art cannot dictate to life and movies cannot transform life, unless we want to retool the entire industry for the production of propaganda. But art can certainly reflect life, clarify and improve life; and since most of humanity teeters on the edge of violence every day, there is no earthly reason why art should not turn violence to its own good ends, showing us what we do and why. The clear danger, of course, is that violence begets violence in life and engenders confusion in art. It is a potent weapon, but it tends to aim the marksman.

Bosley Crowther

Movies to Kill People By

Something is happening in the movies that has me alarmed and disturbed. Moviemakers and moviegoers are agreeing that killing is fun. Not just old-fashioned, outright killing, either, the kind that is quickly and cleanly done by honorable law enforcers or acceptable competitors in crime. This is killing of a gross and bloody nature, often massive and excessive, done by characters whose murderous motivations are morbid, degenerate, and cold. This is killing of the sort that social misfits and sexual perverts are most likely to do. And the eerie thing is that moviegoers are gleefully lapping it up.

Not all moviegoers, thank goodness. There are plenty who disgustedly eschew this new flock of sadistic pictures that is coming to roost on our screens. But enough of them are eagerly swarming to see such slaughterhouse films as Robert Aldrich's *The Dirty Dozen* and Sergio Leone's *For a Few Dollars More* that it makes one tremble with amazement and wonder what this interest represents.

Take this picture *The Dirty Dozen*, which is a brazen and brutal account of how a group of American military prisoners, condemned for murder, rape, and other major crimes, are taken from a military prison in England shortly before D-Day in World War II and secretly trained as a team of commandos to mop up a chateau-full of Nazi officers on the eve of the assault on the Normandy coast.

It is not just a standard glorification of killing Nazis by brave American troops, which is a sad enough ethical perversion to practice and prolong on the screen. It is glorification of killing by hardened criminals who are willfully trained by a hard-bitten major (Lee Marvin) with an evident sadistic streak. And although most of these corrupt commandos are killed in the course of their slaughterhouse task, and thus are denied the enjoyment of the commutation of their sentences that has been promised them, they are elevated as heroes by the attitude that is blazingly assumed by Mr. Aldrich's direction of Nunnally Johnson and Lukas Heller's script.

What is more, the initial recalcitrance and arrogance of these brutes is given a tone of social defiance and individuality. The inculcation in them of a sort of hoodlum esprit de corps is developed as a feature of excitement that is obviously meant to stimulate glee. And the ultimate killing of the Nazis and their shrieking, cowering concubines is a superfluous amount of shooting and slashing and throwing of fire.

If one could find in the structure of this picture or in the way it was angled and staged the slightest hint of intentional, sardonic comment upon the fundamental nature of war—the slightest glimmer of revelation that all killing is essentially criminal—then the hideous brutality of it might be regarded as subtle irony, and the glorifying of its felons as a tragic travesty.

But there are no such hints or glimmers in it. It is a blatant and obvious appeal to the latent aggressiveness and sadism in undiscriminating viewers. And I would guess that the vast majority of the people who are seeing it at the Capitol and at the 34th Street East, where it is playing, are taking it for kicks and thrills and are coming away from it palpitating with a vicarious sense of enjoyment in war.

A similar sense of fun out of killing is being induced, I feel sure, by Mr. Leone's excessively violent *For a Few Dollars More*. This is another of those clever Italian-made Western films, shot in Spain, with a cast of actors speaking a babel of languages, but with English dialogue dubbed, and it follows the further adventures of the character created by Clint Eastwood in Mr. Leone's *A Fistful of Dollars*.

This gray-eyed, cool-cat gunman is a bounty killer here—that is, a self-commissioned huntsman whose prey are bandits with prices on their heads—and he is after a gang of Mexican bank robbers who are being stalked by another bounty killer, too. So the deadly confrontations are not only between the huntsman and the men he is out to bring back dead, but also between the two huntsmen, who clearly have no feeling for each other's lives.

Having found a market for bloodlust with his previous *Dollar* film, Mr. Leone is out to exploit it for all it's worth with this further killing spree. He fills the screen with violence, men stalking other men like animals—with blazing guns and whining bullets and bodies falling in spasm-twitching heaps. And he makes the deadlines of Mr. Eastwood—his urge and efficiency at knocking men off—a matter of cool bravado and glee-provoking triumph.

This film was a huge success in Europe before it opened here last week at the Trans-Lux West and other theaters, so the passion for this sort of thing is not exclusive to audiences in the United States. There have been previous films of this order, and there are going to be many more. Even though they merely purge aggressive spirits, which some people say is all they do, they seem to me as socially decadent and dangerous as LSD.

Bosley Crowther

Another Smash at Violence

There appears to have been some disagreement with the feeling of alarm I expressed at the increase of violence in movies a couple of weeks ago. One reader, who said she is a teacher—and a wife and mother—in Syracuse, was incensed that I should have used *The Dirty Dozen* as an example of excessive violence aimed, as I candidly calculated, to provide the general audience with kicks and thrills.

How could I be so callous as to criticize a picture that shows the "inner sensitivities" of criminals who are given a chance to redeem themselves by performing a "productive" mission (killing Germans), she wanted to know. My attitude is not shared by "people whose families may be involved in Vietnam," she assured me.

Several others repeated this notion, as though the fact that there is violence in the world is sufficient justification for exploding an irrational excess of it on the screen.

Another reader slapped my wrist soundly for not appreciating *For a Few Dollars More* because its cold-blooded cowboy bounty killer is as much of "an existentialist hero as Camus' Caligula." This literary-intellectual slotting of a fellow who guns people down with deliberate self-serving indifference elevates the splurge of blood and death in a viciously sadistic picture to the dignity of art, it seems.

"It is odd," continued this reader, "that one should show so much distaste for [this hero's] killing powers in a society which reads panegyrics to the Vietcong-killing power of the M-16 rifle."

Right there, with that extreme assumption, this reader and several others who wrote echoing his sweeping generalization put the case for restraint on the screen.

It is precisely because there are vast areas of violence and bloodshed in our world—because there are certain elements that foment and

From *The New York Times*, July 30, 1967. Copyright © 1967 by *The New York Times*. Reprinted by permission.

justify killing on the grounds of its ultimately leading to solutions of political and social ills—that our media of so-called entertainment should strive for balance and moral truth. It is precisely because there are panegyrists of killing that the exponents of life should cry out with distaste.

The fact that there are cold discussions of how efficiently a certain weapon kills, weekly publications of boxscores of casualties in Vietnam, enthusiastic glorifications of military conquerors in the Middle East, and irresponsible boastings and backslappings for violence in Newark and Detroit is not to say that many people—many good and humane people in this world—do not deplore these manifestations and yearn for their hastened cessation.

It is the fallacious idea that violent movies are playing an important cultural role as ironic reflection and commentators on these sad events or are offering release for anxieties and torn emotions with their excessive fantasies that some thoughtful critics and philosophers use to rationalize this trend.

Significantly, this idea is interestingly put in the new Peter Watkins picture, *Privilege*, which came to the Sutton last week. The calculated device of a pop singer to have himself tormented and tortured by fake police while he is agonizingly singing lurid folk songs crying for freedom is coolly justified by his managers as providing emotional release for the pent-up aggressions of his idolaters who agonize and moan with him. The hypocrisy of this thesis is indicated by the evidence of the hold that this illusory symbol of protest has on his followers and by how readily he can lead them to a religion of conformity, all to serve the purposes of a developing British dictatorship.

Such is the strange intoxication that this wave of violent movies can have for a public that is happily submissive to their wild and gory fantasies. They can lead the halfway preconditioned public to condone preposterous values and cruel deceits.

The fine French director, Claude Autant-Lara, observed several years ago, in commenting on the nature of war films for a volume published by Robert Hughes, that "by habituating the public to brutality in the exceptional as in the everyday war film, they (the war-mongers of the world) bring about the general acceptance of force as the only solution to any drastic situation—even in international problems."

By habituating the public to violence and brutality—by making these hideous exercises into morbid and sadistic jokes, as is done in *The Dirty Dozen*—these films of excessive violence only deaden their sensitivities and make slaughter seem a meaningless cliché. One reader wrote me she sat next to a 10-year-old boy at the above cited film. She asked him how he liked it. He looked at her blandly and shrugged.

I hate to have to be insistent and alarmist about these films. But when I see one such as Frank Sinatra's *The Naked Runner*, which posits the idea that a man might be righteously suborned by British Intelligence to assassinate a defector because he is going to bear military secrets to the "enemy," or another such as *The St. Valentine's Day Massacre*, which seems to take a morbid delight in reenacting in great detail the slaughter of Bugs Moran's Chicago gang in 1929, I feel again and again the penetration of an antisocial venom into my own flesh and I dread how widely such deliberate exploitation of the public's susceptibilities is poisoning and deadening our fiber and strength.

Ronald Gold

Crowther's 'Bonnie'-Brook: Rap at Violence Stirs Brouhaha

New York Times reviewer Bosley Crowther has long been the most influential critic in America, and during the course of his career he has been one of the industry's staunchest supporters and defenders. But almost as often he has been at odds with the Hollywood moguls, sometimes leading a crusade of his fellow scribes against the current tide of crass "commercialism."

Lately, Crowther has begun another crusade, against what he calls a "wave of violent movies." But this time he seems to have taken on not only the filmmakers, but his fellow critics, the bulk of whom have pointedly disagreed with his "violent" blasts at two recent pix, Robert Aldrich's *The Dirty Dozen* and Arthur Penn's *Bonnie and Clyde.*

Indeed some of them have gone so far as to suggest that his crusading spirit has clouded his perception, that he's been unable to separate a film's statement about violence from the thing itself—and, particularly in the case of *Bonnie,* that he has hurt the cause of serious filmmaking in America by shooting down a work of art.

Crowther's basic thesis, as he expressed it in the second of two Sunday pieces, ironically entitled "A Smash at Violence," is that "By habituating the public to violence and brutality . . . films of excessive violence only deaden their sensitivies and make slaughter seem a meaningless cliché." He added that "such deliberate exploitation of the public's susceptibilities is poisoning and deadening our fiber and strength," and he rejected the view that violence in the world is an excuse for it on the screen. "It is precisely because there are vast areas of violence and bloodshed in our world . . . that our media of so-called entertainment should strive for balance and moral truth," he said.

From *Variety*, August 30, 1967, pp. 5, 26. Reprinted by permission.

57

Some Don't Agree

While nobody has come out in favor of violence for its own sake, some of those who've been arguing with Crowther have thrown back at him his own arguments in favor of increased on-screen liberality in the area of sex. Indeed, Moira Walsh, critic for the Jesuit weekly *America* and reviewer for the National Catholic Office for Motion Pictures, sounds like an echo of the *Times* reviewer himself, when he defended such films as *The Pawnbroker, Who's Afraid of Virginia Woolf?* and *Blow-Up* from the onslaughts of the bluenoses.

"When I started looking at movies in a 'quasi-official' capacity," Miss Walsh said, "I was thoroughly indoctrinated with the prissy notion that 'common folk' should be protected from 'bad' and 'dangerous' ideas in films. By slow and painful steps I was disabused of this outlook. It simply cannot be squared with any coherent view of the realities of mid-20th-century life. . . . Without being dogmatic about it, I tend to the opinion that the hardest thing for a film to do is to change anyone's point of view; that films reflect the realities of the age far more than they influence them."

Rather than approaching the subject on this abstract level, most of Crowther's confreres who've chosen to take up his challenge (usually without mentioning him by name) have responded negatively to his dismissal of work by two highly respected filmmakers as nothing but crassly commercial trash, essentially "sympathetic" to violence and devoid of irony.

They've directly contradicted his view and, by implication, have accused Crowther of totally ignoring the technical felicities of the films at hand as well as the intentions of the men who made them.

In his review of *The Dirty Dozen,* for example, and in the Sunday piece which followed it, Crowther was unable to find "the slightest hint of intentional sardonic comment on the fundamental nature of war," and his overview of the film was that it is "a raw and preposterous glorification of a group of criminal soldiers" and "a studied indulgence of sadism that is morbid and disgusting beyond words."

Dirty Dozen

None of the other critics ignored the violence in *Dirty Dozen,* and some of them were quite unhappy about it too, accusing director and screen-

Figures 12 & 13. For 1960s audiences, one of the most shocking scenes in Bonnie and Clyde occurs following a bungled holdup, when Clyde shoots a bank official in the face at point blank-range. The victim hangs for a moment on the side of the car, his face pressed against the shattered glass.

writers of copping out in the final third of the film and spoiling the point. But all of them were prepared to see that there was a point—one which some of them emphasized later when taking up the discussion of violence.

"This particular film," said Judith Crist on the "Today" Show, "very clearly implies that it takes killers and psychopaths to do a successful job in war, which is a murderous and perhaps psychotic pastime." And Miss Walsh said *Dozen* contained "at least implicitly, the most uncompromising attack on the 'typical military mind' and exposition of the insanity and hell of war that I have ever encountered in a potentially popular 'mass audience' movie."

Accepting the picture on its own terms, most other critics also avoided Crowther's preoccupation with whether or not the central situation of *Dozen* (allegedly taken from an actual incident) was "a fictional supposition that is silly and irresponsible." And despite the *Times* man's accusation that "a raw and unmitigated campaign of sheer press-agentry has been trying to put across the notion that Warner Brothers' *Bonnie and Clyde* is a faithful representation of the desperado careers of Clyde Barrow and Bonnie Parker," they stayed away from the question of historical accuracy in their reviews of this pic too—most of them suggesting that what Penn had tried to create was a "folk ballad." (Warners claims it's never said anything different.)

While a number of the *Bonnie* reviews (including *Variety*'s own) thought Penn had been unsuccessful in welding comedy to tragedy, all without exception treated the concept respectfully, and all seemed to understand what was intended when, in Crowther's words, Penn went "out of his way to splash the comedy holdups with smears of the vivid blood."

Some, like Cue's William Wolf, called *Bonnie* "a major artistic accomplishment, but even those who turned thumbs down, like *New York Post*'s Archer Winston, said it had "qualities that can be praised extravagantly." And none duplicated Crowther's accusations that it had been "assembled in a helter-skelter fashion"; that its characters were "ridiculous, camp-tinctured travesties" or that it is "strangely antique, sentimental claptrap."

Penn's View

If one accepts the view that Penn had no intention of being either "antique" or "sentimental" and that both he and Aldrich were trying to make statements against violence, rather than in favor of it, how was Crowther able to view the films as he did?

One answer may be that he is not only concerned about, but in a sense shares the reactions of, that portion of the public which may be besieging the box office in search of kicks rather than illumination, and is more concerned with what it sees than what is implied. ("But will the picture do well because of its more probing aspects or because of the vivid violence with which it is filled?" asks the *Saturday Review*'s Hollis Alpert about *Bonnie and Clyde.*)

If this is so, then Crowther is in a better position than most to express concern about the effect of violent films on the public.

But what some in the trade are worried about is that these concerns over violence might spark a return to the genuinely "antique" days of filmmaking, when every "commercial" picture had to make an explicit statement of its point, rather than relying on the ability of its audience to see beneath the surface. And these folks have accused Crowther of making no effort to comprehend what the new breed of filmmakers is attempting—not only where violence is involved, but in other areas as well.

Offered as a recent example of what these people are talking about is Joseph Losey's *Accident,* which Crowther called "just a sad little story of a wistful don," and virtually everybody else referred to as "disturbing," "thought-provoking," or "a glacial dissection of human passion."

"We don't mind if Mr. Crowther doesn't like our picture," said one distributor this week. "What we're concerned about is that the *Times* readers may come away from his reviews with no idea of what it's supposed to be about."

Statement by Jack Valenti, MPAA President, before The National Commission on the Causes and Prevention of Violence

As you are aware and as we are, there are many disagreements today on the subject of violence. People say there is too much violence in the society and more than there used to be; there is disagreement about whether there is more violence in movies today than there was.

And there is disagreement among laymen as well as social scientists about the effect that violence in the media has, particularly on children.

The problem of violence was one of the principal matters that occupied my attention when I first became president of this Association. It is only one, I might say, because it's only one part of the human condition.

But I recognized immediately, from May 1966 when I became president of the MPAA, that for the filmmaker the treatment of violence in scenes and incidents of a story that he is trying to tell really involves the whole fundamental issue of the responsibility of the artist, the creative artist, not only toward his art but toward the society in which he lives.

And I think that as you talk to filmmakers you know that this issue confronts them almost in everything that they do. The question that confronts the artist is: How much is too much?

I have said on many occasions that what is important is for the

Statement issued by Jack Valenti on December 19, 1968.

creative man to be honest in his portrayals, to tell the story as he thinks it ought to be told. But the question is always: When does the balance tip from violence which is honest to portrayals which are excessive and overweighted with violence? In short, the whole question is: Where does one draw the line?

And I might interject here to the members of this honorable Commission that the next question is: Is there a man or an assembly or a group that is so divinely inspired that they can make those kinds of final judgments for others?

Almost everything I have said as president of the Association has been based on the theme that the screen must be free if it is going to flourish. There is no way to have a flourishing creativity in this land if you are going to put fetters on the creative man. But I have also said that this freedom must be responsible—must be responsible—lest liberty becomes license. I have said that to creative people countless times as I have tried to establish a rapport between what I am trying to do and the creative man in both Hollywood and New York and all over this country. Because this theme poses—and I think you must understand as I do—the artist and the ethical and the moral distinction between what a creative man must have for his art and what he must demand of himself. It is a mingling of inspiration and imagination and discipline.

That sounds a little esoteric and far-fetched, but it's really true to the responsible man of integrity who is creating motion pictures. Because even for this man, the conscientious man, this gray line—and that's all I can call it—the line between what is enough and what is too much—is so extraordinarily difficult to measure. It is so shadowy and dimly fit that it's very difficult to measure.

So that the essential point becomes not the inclusion of violence or the quantity of it or the nature of it but really how it is treated, how it is handled.

I don't have to tell you—I think it's almost a cliché to say—that throughout the whole history of drama, violence is a common ingredient. That goes without saying. The very nature of drama is conflict. New plays and old plays, ancient chants, litanies, the epic poems, and traditional literature of practically every country and civilization that you can name are rooted in violence because man's whole existence has been a story of conflict.

And I might add that we know, even to this very hour, that all civilizations have been alternately horrified and fascinated by death and violence. I didn't make it that way. That's the way it is.

So it's my judgment that violence should not be presented as a way of life—not at all—but for what it truly is, one of the facets in the complex fabric of the human condition.

Now, let me go to my second point. It is: What is the motion picture industry doing to fulfill its obligation of responsibility to the society in which it lives? I'm going to trace this for you very briefly. Since 1927 we have had codes, guides for producers, voluntary guides. And in 1930 we adopted the so-called Production Code, now very famous, which was a self-regulatory rubric through which producers, directors, and writers in a voluntary way tried to regulate themselves. This Code has been updated from time to time to change with the mores and the customs of the society, because all mores and customs change. And in 1966 we reaffirmed and we strengthened the Production Code.

The Production Code is operated separately but in tandem with an Advertising Code which does the same thing.

We try to avoid what we call a cumulative overemphasis on sex and violence, which are the two great facets of the human condition.

We recognize that sometimes incidents standing alone are quite permissible, but once they are allowed to accumulate they become almost intolerable. We understand this. And both in our Advertising Code and in our Production Code we are constantly trying to deal with this as we have been dealing with it for over thirty years.

There are objections; some say: "Well, that's very fine, Mr. Valenti, but you're dealing with it in general terms, and you're dependent on the subjective views of those people who are managing this Code."

The answer is that's very true, because the very nature of what we are doing is subjective. And I don't believe that you can base a decision as to whether a particular portrayal of violence is detailed or protracted or excessive on the number of killings or the number of blows or how many grams of blood were spilled.

The very nature of the problem makes it absolutely imperative that you deal with it, not numerically or quantitatively but subjectively or qualitatively. And these are the kinds of decisions, frail decisions, human decisions, that are made under this voluntary Code by people who are vastly experienced, not only in the appraisal of motion pictures but also in this very tenuous and sensitive relationship between the creative man and his monitor. It is a very difficult relationship.

The people on the Production Code operation are literate people, skilled people. While I would be the first to say that their judgments are no better or no worse than anyone else's, they are rooted in a better kind of experience.

Now, in addition to the Code, we have taken several other steps in dealing with the portrayal of violence. This spring, immediately following the tragic murder of Senator Kennedy, Louis Nizer, general counsel of this Association, and I traveled to Hollywood and called a special meeting with all heads of studios, with directors, writers, and actors, with producers. We urged upon them increased restraint and heightened responsibility in portraying violence.

The response was very heartening. Later on, more than 350 producers, writers, directors, and actors signed an open pledge that they would forgo scripts which had anything to do with aimless cruelty and senseless brutality. It is a voluntary act, of course, but I think it does testify to the accountability of creative people about their own responsibilities.

Now let me say a word about audiences. It has always been a great cliché in the motion picture business, that there was a single common denominator, a single audience, and that films were made for the 14-year-old level. You have heard that before. If this ever was true, it certainly isn't today.

The popular media, I don't have to tell you, produce a veritable tidal wave of products that almost drowns this country. Motion pictures do not appeal to a single audience. There is no mass audience today. The mass audience, in my judgment, just doesn't exist, if it ever did.

Today, we must understand the following: films explore more deeply into the human condition than they ever did before. A substantial number of films coming into this country are foreign in origin. There is a new breed of filmmaker. And mark you well this new filmmaker, because he's an extraordinary fellow. He's young. He's sensitive. He's dedicated. He's reaching out for new dimensions of expression. And he is not bound—not bound—by the conventions of a conformist past. I happen to think that's good. Moreover, this new style in filmmaking is matched by a new audience. It is seeking new fulfillment. Its members are better educated. . . .

Conscious of these findings and of the fact that the kind of society we live in today is different from the kind of society we used to live in, for the first time in the history of the motion picture industry we have developed a plan of rating films for audience suitability. It is a voluntary film rating system developed with the active assistance of theater owners and creative people and distributors and producers.

Its dominant, preeminent, overriding concern is for children. This is a rating system for parents and families. Films are rated not on their excellence or lack of it, not on their excitement or lack of it, but whether or not the content of the film is suitable for children. . . .

After November 1, all films released to the public will carry a rating. The first rating is "G"—suggested for general audiences. That rating means a parent may send his child in to that picture. There is no objectionable material in the film. However, this doesn't necessarily mean it is a children's film, because some of the most powerful and profoundly significant films of this generation would be G-films. One of the classic examples of such a film that, would surely have been a "G," had it been rated is *Man for All Seasons,* the great story of Sir Thomas More and the irreconcilable conflict of conscience between Sir Thomas More and his king.

The second rating is "M," suggested for mature audiences, mature young people, with parental discretion advised. What we're saying to a mother or father here is: "Look, don't take your child in to see this picture until you know more about it. For it may be—just may be—unsuitable for your child. There are no restrictions, but we want you to know more about it."

The third category is "R"—meaning restricted. Here for the first time there are restrictions on the audience. Children under 16, unless accompanied by a parent or an adult guardian, are barred from such pictures. These are adult films. However, there may be some adult films that a parent would want his child to see. The parent may want to go with his child so they can discuss it afterward together.

I can name a number of films of this nature that carry a message for young people but the parent ought to be there with him.

Figure 14. In 1968, the Motion Picture Association of America instituted its G-M-R-X ratings for film content. To satisfy the MPAA and earn an R rather than an X rating, producer Phil Feldman and editor Lou Lombardo had to abbreviate the throat-cutting scene in The Wild Bunch, *deleting a side-angle view of the blood spurt.*

The final category is "X," in which we say that this picture should not be shown to any child under 16, regardless of who accompanies him.

I think the filmmaker has to remember that discipline and restraint are part of the definition of true artistry and that therefore he must practice restraint.

It is my judgment that responsible filmmakers in this country, with whom I have been in contact, intend to do just this, but it would be dishonest to tell you that there won't be fringe operators on the periphery who are going to try to make a buck out of this thing. Of course there will be. But that's true in all professions and all enterprises, and even in families.

The third question is, How well will these ratings be enforced at the box office? I place my faith in the vast majority of responsible theater owners in this country. I place my faith and my hope in them, because I believe they will do it. They have told me that they will do it and I believe they will do it.

I have personally talked to more than seventy-five of the owners of the leading exhibitor chains in this country, probably representing four thousand to five thousand theaters, probably representing 80 to 85 percent of box office. These leaders of this industry have all told me that they will support and implement this program.

And, finally, how cooperative are the parents of this land? If the parents abandon their responsibility for the conduct of their child, it is very difficult for the motion picture industry to make up for that parental lack of responsibility.

Now for my third major point: Is the depiction of violence on the screen probably harmful to people, to children particularly? I'm not an expert. But what I have read tells me that the evidence is not conclusive. As we examine the writings of the past forty years of social scientists and others who are experienced observers, the best that can be said is that the opinions are ambivalent in intent . . . and contradictory and the differences among social scientists reach imposing levels. I am sure that you ladies and gentlemen, as you have examined the literature know that I'm not speaking in hyperbole. If there is one conclusion that appears to be warranted, it is simply this: most authorities are reluctant to conclude that the portrayal of violence in motion pictures results in harmful social behavior. That's one conclusion that I think is warranted.

Now, one of the things that makes it clear why experimentation in this area is so hard to design, hard to construct, is that it is morally unacceptable to induce delinquency experimentally in a child. It's wrong to do it. And it's the most serious barrier to experimentation.

There are additional reservations that I have about research in this area. I will list them very quickly.

First, fears that motion pictures may set off real-life acts of aggression, many times are based on very little solid evidence. Most of the time it's case histories of maladjusted people who are under treatment and this is not a valid kind of conclusion.

Second, alleged acts of aggression that happen in laboratory experiments are said to be brought on by what scientists call artificially induced preconditions. Therefore one begins to doubt the relationship to a real-life reaction in a live theater.

Number 3, very little is known of the effects in long-range behavior. In my personal judgment that is one of the key weaknesses in that whole scheme of social research.

And fourth, most clinical opinions are too heavily dependent on the deviant, the disturbed, the already mentally disfigured child.

You will find that the literature is filled with statements that well-adjusted children in a well-adjusted home life can't be harmed by anything shown on a motion picture screen.

The overwhelming evidence shows that the root causes of behavior are developed in the early years of the child and are primarily environmental, physical, and psychological, arising out of home and family life. This is a truth I'd stake my being on because I believe it.

Finally, you have a right to ask, "Well, all that is very fine, but what are your plans to be alert to the newest developments in the search for new social knowledge?"

First, I have been in consultation with an eminent social scientist on the West Coast, and I am concluding a similar arrangement with one on the East Coast, so that I can keep abreast of the latest developments in this rather fuzzily defined field.

Second, I have recently appointed to the Code and Rating Administration a woman who brings with her a very strong background in child psychology, family relations, and the behavioral sciences.

Basically, our approach to the problem is not to wait for scientific demonstration that some lurid depiction of violence is harmful to children. It may very well be, ladies and gentlemen, that this will never be proven. But my common sense tells me that the depiction of extreme violence or anything in the extreme is simply offensive to normal sensibilities. I don't need a scientist to tell me that. Whether or not it causes juvenile or adult delinquency, it's just offensive, and I am against it.

Therefore, if I had to pick a watchword, it would be "moderation." Our whole Code, all of our voluntary programs are based on that principle. "Nothing in excess," said the sign over the Delphic Oracle, and I think that ancient maxim is a good one here—moderation. . . .

Mr. Tone: Will you agree with me that when the members of MPAA adopted the 1966 Code they subscribed to this view: that motion pictures do have an effect on the moral standards and conduct of those who watch them, especially juveniles? Is that a fair statement?

Mr. Valenti: I'm not aware of such a statement.

Mr. Tone: Well, let's see whether I inferred too much. The 1966 Code does say under the heading "Particular Applications": "Crime shall never be presented in such a way as to throw sympathy with the crime as against law and justice or to inspire others with a desire for imitation."

It says: "Methods of crime shall not be explicitly presented or detailed in a manner calculated to glamorize crime or inspire imitation."

It says, under the heading "Reasons Supporting the Code": "The moral importance of entertainment is something which has been universally recognized. It enters intimately into the lives of men and women and affects them closely. It occupies their minds and affections during leisure hours and ultimately touches the whole of their lives. A man may be judged by his standard of entertainment as easily as by his standard of work. So correct entertainment raises the whole standard of the nation; wrong entertainment lowers the whole living conditions and moral ideals of the race."

Then it says (and this is the last passage I will read): "Hence, the important objective must be to avoid the hardening of the arteries, especially of those who are young and impressionable, to the thought and fact of crime. People can become accustomed even to murder, cruelty, brutality and repellant crimes if these are too frequently repeated."

Would you not say that the author of those statements believed that motion pictures could influence the conduct of the people who watch the pictures?

Mr. Valenti: Yes, I do. As a matter of fact, we have gone beyond that 1966 Code, way beyond it. Because we have now instituted something that the 1966 Code didn't have. That philosophy was related to a public feeling that anyone could go to any picture in this country. But today, for the first time, we are excluding children. We are excluding children from pictures we think are unsuitable for them. So I would say we have gone beyond the concept set by that statement.

Mr. Tone: I'm at the moment speaking only of the philosophy of the 1966 Code. And I recall your statement at the time the Code was announced in October, which I think is similar to your statement today: "There is no valid evidence at this time that proves movies have anything to do with antisocial behavior." Would you not say that that statement represents some change in viewpoint from the statement of principles in the 1966 Code? And if it does, I'm interested in how the motion picture industry's thinking has changed on that subject. What have the—

Mr. Valenti: Well, the principal change has been that the Association has a new president. Administrations may change and points of view—if indeed this is a change in point of view. That is a judgment.

I bear no responsibility for the 1966 Code, any more than the incoming president who bears responsibility for our nation would bear total responsibility for carrying forward something that his predecessor did—as long as it doesn't violate a principle. I truly believe that I have made the philosophy stronger by bringing it into an active program. To me this is far more important. It is well to say words, but I believe that to translate these words into an active program shows progress. That's why we have taken a philosophy and hardened it into an active program that keeps children under 16 out of certain movies. That in my judgment, Mr. Tone, is an advance. That's keeping in step with the changing mores and customs of a society and taking that which was first rooted in philosophy and constructing a living, breathing program through our new film rating system.

Mr. Tone: One more question before we get to the rating system specifically. You stated the children who are not disturbed, normal children who come from normal homes, are not likely to be affected by anything they see. Do you believe that motion picture producers have an obligation with respect to disturbed children or children who because of some problem or other could be affected by the amount of violence they see? Or do you believe that the advantages of creative freedom outweigh any obligation to such a small minority? What are your views?

Mr. Valenti: Mr. Counsel, my answer to that is quite obviously we can't make pictures at the level of the disturbed child. As Mr. Justice Marshall said in his 1968 decision, that would turn movies into a wasteland. We would make what he called inane movies. And I surely would agree with that. There is no rational person in the motion picture industry who would even suggest that we should make pictures aimed at the level of the disturbed child. You simply can't do it. Any more than you would write all books or portray all of life itself at this level. . . .

There are some people in America who have no patience or tolerance for the workings of a democratic society, and they would have the government intrude by law to control motion pictures in the belief that this is the way to control violence.

As a humble citizen of this land, I don't think there is any delusion so slippery or any act more perilous than the intrusion of the government into making such judgments for the communications media. Of course, I would hope that all thoughtful citizens would be opposed to that alternative.

The question that needs to be asked is: Can censorship cure the portrayal of violence in the media? That's the question everybody must ask. Some people would answer yes. I would have a larger question. I would ask: Can censorship curb violence in the society? I think it's a truism that movies are not beacons but rather mirrors of society. They don't lead; they follow the already established course.

That leads to another question and that is: How much is too much violence, Senator? How do you determine that?

And, then, the really tough question to be asked is: Who would make these judgments? Who would appoint them or who would anoint them? And by what omniscient or divine authority would they claim accurate judgment?

This is the crux. The more I get involved in even voluntary rating of pictures, the more convinced I am of the lunacy and the absurdity of governmental involvement in making such cultural judgments.

I promise you, ladies and gentlemen, all you have to do is read two leading critics and you will find one saying, "This is wonderful," another saying "It's pornography," and one saying, "This is the great moral play of our time," another saying, "It's cheap violence."

Who's right? This is the thing that causes me the greatest concern—knowing we are frail humans and yet we are making these difficult, even impossible, judgments. We do the best that we can. What's important is that it's voluntary.

Senator, I can only state this as my answer to your question regarding alternatives, which obviously must concern anybody looking at the problem: what we are doing now is not quite to our liking. What else can we do? It is a tormented question that is both attractive and repulsive to different people.

Figure 15. The graphic violence of Bonnie and Clyde *was tied to the social and political turmoil of the 1960s. Director Arthur Penn, for example, included a visual reference to the death of President Kennedy. When the Texas Rangers gun down Clyde, a piece of his head (like JFK's) flies off.*

I find sanction by law in this field odious beyond measure because, as I say, just trying to rate films voluntarily emphasizes how impossible it is to do.

Judge McFarland: Thank you very kindly. . . . Now, I'll have to admit my ignorance in not having seen this picture, *Bonnie and Clyde,* but I am told that it is replete with violence. How do you justify the amount of violence, if my information is correct, in that picture?

Mr. Valenti: Well, Senator, you are one of the few people in this country who seem not to have seen that picture, because it has gained wide audience.

Judge McFarland: A lot of them have.

Mr. Valenti: However, you bring out what I think is a legitimate question, and I will speak to that briefly. This picture, more than any other, I think, illuminates the great dichotomy of opinion that so bedevils this whole subject of rating films.

For example, I was being confirmed by the Senate in another job on the Corporation for Public Broadcasting, and a distinguished senator of the United States Senate took me to task on this picture. I will give you the same answer that I gave him, because I think it is germane, and it is simply this:

A number of people did think *Bonnie and Clyde* was a picture of extreme violence with a tendency to cause people to think kindly of bandits and robbers and hoodlums. And, as Congressman Boggs knows, I came from that part of the world, and as a young boy, I knew about Bonnie and Clyde, and I must say my great hero was not Bonnie or Clyde, but Frank Hamer, who doesn't come out too well in the picture.

But, on the other hand, may I point out something to you that you may not know? This picture, so disfigured by a number of critics, was chosen by the National Catholic Office for Motion Pictures as the best mature picture of 1967, they called it a "great morality play." I have said to some of my critics when they talk about *Bonnie and Clyde:* "Well, you've got to determine who you're going to follow, those people who criticize *Bonnie and Clyde,* or the Catholics who are probably the most indefatigable monitors of the motion picture screen and whose integrity is almost impeccable."

There is a good example of a great and prestigious group in America, beyond personal gain, that says this is a great motion picture. And there are others who say it's extremely violent. And I must also add that the Catholic Church is also a great critic of senseless violence on the screen, more than almost any other group that I know. I go along with the National Catholic Office of Motion Pictures. I think I would follow their judgment in this particular case.

Judge McFarland: Well, thank you very kindly. I must not take up more time. I know my colleagues have questions. But again I want to express my appreciation and say to you it's nice to see you and visit you even across the table.

Mr. Valenti: Thank you, Senator.

Judge McFarland: Although you have just been in your present position two and a half years, you certainly have the understanding of the problems confronting the motion picture industry as though you have been there for a much longer period.

Mr. Valenti: Thank you, Senator.

Judge Higginbotham: I would hate to think, Mr. Valenti, what a survey would show if we took a survey on this Commission as to how many have seen *Bonnie and Clyde. (laughter.)*

Congressman Boggs: Mr. Chairman, I did see *Bonnie and Clyde,* and the distinguished Justice anticipated some of my questions.

I might say that I am a great admirer of the witness. I have known him for many years and have been very closely associated with him. I am very happy to have him in his job. I think he does a very difficult and trying job.

But I was interested in the responses about *Bonnie and Clyde*. I might tell him that we had a murder in my town committed by an 18-year-old boy who had come out of *Bonnie and Clyde* one hour before. He killed a young man who was running a drive-in grocery store. And it was just a senseless murder. Now, whether or not what he saw in *Bonnie and Clyde* had any impact on the murder, I don't know. But I know that what I say to you is a fact—that he saw this movie which glorifies violence.

Those *Bonnie and Clyde* characters lived in my State. They were reprehensible criminals. There was nothing about them that was commendable. They killed in cold blood, as the movie depicts. . . . I can assure you that I share your fear of censorship. But oftentimes what brings repressive measures is abuse. . . .

And I read the Code here on page 4 of your statement where you set out five basic standards of the eleven. You say:

"The basic dignity and value of human life shall be respected and upheld." That certainly isn't true in that movie.

"Restraint shall be exercised in portraying the taking of life." God knows it isn't true in that one.

"Evil, sin, crime and wrongdoing shall not be justified." Well, I don't know what that means.

"Special restraint shall be exercised in portraying criminal or anti-social activities in which minors participate or are involved."

"Detailed and protracted acts of brutality, cruelty, physical violence, torture and abuse shall not be presented." That's the essence of that movie.

Now I presume that your whole emphasis is on self-policing. What happens when the self-policing doesn't work? You used the word "responsible operators." I understand that word perfectly. The average responsible citizen is not a criminal. We don't pass laws to deal with him. We finally get into the business of regulation and law passing and law enforcement because of the irresponsible. So what do you do about the irresponsible in your voluntary code? . . .

Valenti: There is no way to deal with the problem directly unless one chooses to make pictures aimed only for the disturbed youngster, aimed for the lowest-common-denominator audience. I don't have to tell this distinguished group what would happen to the level of art in the community, how all art, including movies, would cease to flourish. Art would become totally stagnant, and it would soon disappear.

The attempt we have made . . . with our rating system is, at least, to try to tell families what is in that picture vis-à-vis their children, so they don't wander into a theater without any knowledge whatsoever.

I think you are in a very difficult position when you try to make films that would exclude adults.

Now, the question was brought up: What do you do about a film that triggers a disturbed youngster? Well, anything might trigger such a person. You have to isolate him from life, I suppose. He may see something happen on a street corner. He may read something in a book. Somebody may speak harshly to him and he is triggered. So I find that not at all an argument for not making pictures that might trigger him.

To answer your question, I don't know of any way in a democratic society in which you can segregate pictures. I think the very fact you do have controversy about motion pictures is an indication of the interest, the hidden interest, that we find in it now.

The Aesthetics of
Ultraviolence

John Bailey, ASC

Bang Bang Bang Bang, Ad Nauseum

In September, over the three-day Labor Day weekend, I made a serious effort to catch up on the major summer films I had missed. I saw six films along with about two dozen trailers for the autumn releases. Not a single one of the trailers (not to mention the features themselves) was devoid of considerable firepower. I'm not speaking of just action excitement, but of a veritable litany of handgun and automatic weapons discharges, incendiary effects, stabbings, and throat slittings. There were also, of course, a few garrotings and numerous beatings of women. This is studio entertainment, after all.

But before your P.C. antennae start bobbing around, let me say this. I don't believe in censorship. It *does* violate basic freedoms, and it doesn't work. I don't support any alliterative watchdog group such as the Christian Coalition. I *do* support my own conscience.

We have all been deluged recently with magazine cover stories documenting, as individual and national tragedies, the 'senseless' murders on our streets and in our homes. We've digested heart-rending profiles of preteen murderers who could barely entertain the concept of mortality before they were swallowed up in the blitz of news that is attendant on an act as effortless as squeezing the trigger of a cheap handgun.

We're tired, angry, and frustrated by our seeming inability to have any influence over the ever-escalating statistics of real-life murder, rather than the artifice of movie mayhem that is so routine and unreal to us as filmmakers.

We've had plenty of finger-pointing and buck passing from Congress, the media, and the giant conglomerates that pass for studios and

From *American Cinematographer*, vol. 75, no. 12 (December 1994), pp. 26, 28–29. Reprinted by permission.

which crank out our "entertainment." Nobody's to blame. We're all at the video store.

I have been wanting to put down my thoughts on screen violence for some time, but I'm finding the path into the subject to be somewhat daunting, like Daedalus standing before his own creation, the Labyrinth. As a cinematographer I have tried to be responsible, or at least conscious, about the amount of, and approach to, violence in the films I have photographed. I think it became a crucial issue for me in the mid-1970s while I was still a camera operator.

I had accepted an offer to do an MOW with a cameraman who had been a very real mentor to me, a man whom I had assisted for some years. Accepting the job on short notice, I wasn't able to read the script in advance. I went into the production stone-cold.

At the start of the first day's shooting, machine gun-toting 'terrorists' charged the camera, herding a group of scantily clad beauty contestants into an abandoned Quonset hut, where they were soon to be held hostage. These very bad guys had just hijacked a beauty pageant. I swear, this really was the story line. Is it high-concept enough for you? Between grunts and vague threats of unmentionable sexual acts, these goons fired their guns into the tin ceiling. It was loud. It was dumb. I was ashamed.

Two days later I told the cinematographer that I couldn't continue the show (and I really did need the work). He felt I had left him in the lurch and promised that he would never work with me again. And he didn't. But, painful as it was, I think I crossed a personal Rubicon of self-respect that day and addressed a sense of my own part in the use and misuse of filmed violence. Even within the cartoon clichés of this forgettable film, an embryonic reference emerged that serves me to this day.

An ironic footnote to this tale is that a short time later [cinematographer] Nestor Almendros phoned me. I had met him in Paris in the late 1960s when, fresh out of film school, I made a pilgrimage to France to meet my idols, the cinematographers of the Nouvelle Vague. Nestor had called to ask me to be his camera operator on the upcoming *Days of Heaven*. Thus I ascended from the classic slough of despond to a friendship with one of the gentlest humanists who ever looked through a lens.

I don't mean this to be a cautionary tale about the efficacy of doing "the right thing." But I guess I do believe in some kind of just reward. I do believe there is strong correlation between our work, the kind of films that we choose to work on, those we refuse to do, and the people we become, certainly over the long haul.

It may seem I've diverged from the nominal topic of this essay, but there is for me an emotional "throughline" that remains intact. And that is pretty simple. As filmmakers, like any artists, we inhabit our work. Not only do we take it home at night, but often, especially when we are on location, our location *is* our home. We form and re-form ad hoc families and residences that are as real to us as our own spouses and children.

Because we live and work in such a violent society, it is natural that our films reflect and explore this violence. But often we only explore it deep enough to wallow in its muck. This is where the question of a demarcation arises. What is exploration and what is exploitation? And who decides?

I've always had difficulty with this question. It gets to the heart of the issue of censorship. Because one's intent and point of view are key factors, it is no easy subject to investigate. But recently I saw two films that so crystallized the matter that everything started to fall into place, and I found for myself a clear distillate of the dilemma.

I hope you have seen both *Natural Born Killers* and *The Shawshank Redemption.* They are magnificently made films, brilliantly conceived and photographed. They cast an unflinching look at the strains of violence in Americans and in our films. At times both films make you want to avert your eyes. Otherwise, they could not be more different.

The philosophical stand these two films take on the issue of violence may be fundamentally different. But just as telling and more germane to this essay is the photography of that violence.

Natural Born Killers is a manic, all-stops-out journey through the madness and darkness of the American obsession with violence as *acte gratuit,* an existential fury that defines all that is alien, angry, and antilife in our character. Its style is hyperkinetic and frenzied, mixing media and formats in a non-logical way that is said to have been determined at times by the flip of a coin. Its images seem to spin out of control, held in place only by an incantatory sound track, pivoting around the threnodic voice of Leonard Cohen.

The Shawshank Redemption is visually very measured and controlled, often almost processional. Its character and narrative skeins are nuanced and defined by circumspection, a tone set by the reflective timbre of Morgan Freeman's elegiac voice-over narration. The plot points are neatly resolved, although the ending may seem too attenuated to some. The depiction and eruption of violence is unflinching but distanced. None of this makes the film remote. In fact, it draws you in it and by the end the cumulative power of empathy is heroic.

The Shawshank Redemption observes moments of awful violence enacted upon the character played by Tim Robbins. And violence or the threat of it permeates many of the relationships in the film. But the point of view of the violence is external. It is an ugly fact of the characters' lives and its force is elemental and Darwinian. It is not heroic; it is not insightful; it is not stylized, slo-moed, or eroticized. The camera records, documents, then retreats and plays out the action in long-shot and in the shadows. The point of view is that of empathy for the victim. In short, it is human. And this is crucial to the transforming majesty of the film.

There is no doubt that the team of Oliver Stone and Robert Richardson have redefined many of the parameters of mainstream theatrical image-making. The raw power and immediacy of their films has been one of the defining markers of American cinema in the past decade. It has come at a price. The dragon has finally swallowed its own tail. Technique has become raison d'etre. And therein lies the cautionary tale.

Natural Born Killers places you inside the violence, makes you a part of it. Its point of view is that of the killers, not because of a clear

Figure 16. *Woody Harrelson as a multiple murderer in* Natural Born Killers. *The low-angle camera and the character's dramatically extended arm manifest the film's fascination with the lurid violence it purports to satirize and critique. It is very difficult for filmmakers to resist the attractions of aestheticizing violence.*

critical or moral perspective but because that's where the action is. The defining aesthetic is MTV. And if it is meant to be otherwise, if it is meant to be a de facto critique or satire of the American and media obsession with violence, I can only say that on this level it is, for me at least, a complete failure. The filmmaking tools which are wielded so artfully and with such panache distort the putative intent. The film eroticizes violence, wallows in it, and struggles to incite the viewer.

If you are an impressionable child, an angry adolescent, or an alienated sociopath, you will probably leave *Natural Born Killers* feeling jacked up. But if you are a rational adult you will feel drained, sullen, enervated. You leave *The Shawshank Redemption* feeling renewed, buoyant, sanguine. Both films spend a good part of their screen time inside the confines of a prison. Your experience of that space could not be more polarized by the two films.

The space and light of *Natural Born Killers* is that of a Sadean stage set replete with Grand Guignol effects, the whole grotesquerie awash in blazingly assaultive light and aggressive camera motion. The space and light of *Shawshank Redemption* is, like its narrative, almost classical. Roger Deakins and Frank Darabont brought close scrutiny and a sense of the importance of detail to their work. You have to watch this film closely. You have to live in its images. They don't beat you over the head. And because your head is left intact, you *experience* the film, not just watch it.

The restraint of Bresson's camera in *A Man Escaped* has no inherent moral force superior to the first-reel frenzy of Truffaut's *Jules and Jim*. Nor is *The Shawshank Redemption* with its formal pictorialism superior to the visual disjunction of *Natural Born Killers*. My point is not to negate one style of filmmaking in favor of another.

Nor do I wish to anathematize in toto the efficacy of violence in the arts. From the Greek tragedies, Jacobean drama, French theater of the Revolution, *German Sturm und Drang*, to Antonin Artaud and Peter Brook, the use of violence in theater has been the vehicle for probing the complexities and dysfunctions of the human condition and the means to catharsis and growth. Violence is as endemic to the human soul as is love. Both emotions are interwoven with the fear of and inevitability of death. Experiencing violence and death in our art is a very real way of affirming our life.

But we must know that there are dangerous shoals when we set out to conceptualize and visualize violence, especially in film. A camera may be a mechanical recording device but the eye behind it is artful and intentional—always. Storyboards are not comic strips. They are blue-prints for complex and powerful images. If "actions have consequences," so do images. We create images. We are conjurers. And, like it or not, we are teachers. Our images are more haunting and more influential than any of the words that will ever be written about them. If you can deny that fact, you can deny the movie memories of your own childhood.

Several years ago during pre-production of *China Moon* I had to deal with these issues as a director. There is a murder in the film: Made-line Stowe fires a handgun at close range into the head of her husband, Charles Dance. So, in the interest of responsible research, I found myself one afternoon on the police firing range in Lakeland, Florida, 9 mm semiautomatic pistol at the ready. I had never fired a handgun. I felt I needed to experience the sensation. The emotional shock of the first discharge far exceeded its ballistic "kick." The sense of power was instant and terrifying. I understood. That same week, also for research, I subjected myself to viewing the full autopsy of a local murder victim. I had never seen a human body rendered into parts. The sadness of this needless death and of my own empathic mortality haunted me for days.

I decided to film in a realistic way the scripted autopsy of the woman found murdered in her kitchen at the beginning of the film. I also filmed in detail Ed Harris's forensic investigation of the murder victim, with emphasis on the "bonding" between detective and deceased. Joe Laude, a homicide detective who served as our tech adviser, said that even in death the murder victim often "speaks" to him. And I photographed Charles Dance's murder as simply and as directly as I could. The second gunshot, the one to his head, was rigged with an elaborate prosthetic to cause a stream of blood to pulse out under pressure, just as I'd seen in documentary footage. It was graphic and shocking.

And it is not in the finished film. The close scrutiny of the autopsy, the even closer, humanizing look of the murder victim as Harris stares into her open eyes, and the shot in the head of Charles Dance all made the preview audience uncomfortable and was reported to have pulled down the survey scores. Some of the offending material quickly went onto the editing room floor; more fell victim to strategic compromises. At first, I felt completely co-opted, but then my own anxiety made me very tentative and uncertain about the choices I had made in being so direct—that is, so "uncinematic"—in the depiction of murder and its aftermath.

But the ensuing time has convinced me that it was correct to deglamorize the violence and to focus on its human consequences. In the end, my own complicity in agreeing to "tone down" the darkness of this film noir compromised the moral perspective I had intended. It had reduced the spiritual agony of Ed Harris, a once moral man now become accessory to murder, to the level that some in the audience would see as a man just trying to save his own skin. This was not the film Roy Carlson, the writer, and I had set out to make. While I remain proud of *China Moon* for many reasons, it is my own cautionary tale. Directing it, I learned much about the intersection of screen violence and box office. The final irony was that my effort to deal with violence and death responsibly proved not to be too violent but too much of a "downer."

I believe we have a great responsibility to the people who see the images we create. But we have as great a responsibility to ourselves. If our own sensibilities are askew, if we have no moral compass to guide us, what point of view are we going to create? Part of the responsibility we have to ourselves is to know and respect the trust we have been given to influence others.

Film is arguably the most influential of all of the arts; it is the art form of choice for young people. How we choose to show them those images of life and death, the emotive wallop they pack, and the imprint they make on their hearts and minds, are questions that we cannot keep in the shadows.

David Thomson

Death and Its Details

The seven screenwriters are decent men and women. Four of their children have been in Non-Violence Awareness programs. They are all devout in the faith that there are too many guns in America. Not to mention greater Los Angeles. They have written letters to senators urging resistance to National Rifle Association pressures. But they all have a problem with this script.

"What do we do with Arthur?"

"Arthur's a loose end."

"He did love Dolores."

"And he was useful in our second act bridge."

"Arthur was the second act bridge. Now he's spare."

"We kill him?"

"We have to. We leave him around the audience is wondering. How?"

"Arthur could get ill."

"Illness is a year, it's doctors."

"It's got to be quick. We're over two hours already."

"Suppose Roger shoots him? In a fit of hitherto repressed anger?"

"Love it. It makes Roger stronger, which is good for Angie."

"And it gets Roger put away, too."

"Ground clearing."

"We do it as a sudden epiphany. Ten-second scene."

"Bang bang, Arthur."

This is the way the world ends
Not with a bang but a whimper.
—T. S. Eliot, *The Hollow Men*

From *Film Comment*, vol. 29, no. 5, Sept.–Oct. 1993. Reprinted by permission.

Gittes pulls the car door open and Evelyn falls out. Her face is covered with blood. She is dead, shot through the back of the head, coming out through her left eye.
　　　—Robert Towne, *Chinatown*, the screenplay

The mass of men lead lives of quiet desperation.
　　　—Thoreau, *Walden*

Forget it, Jake. It's Chinatown!
　　　—Robert Towne, *Chinatown*

　　To illustrate the empire of bang-bang, let me list the deaths in *The Godfather*, the original and first part:

- Luca Brasi, one hand pinned to the bar counter with a knife, strangulation inflating his horrified dignity
- Paulie, the treacherous driver, plugged in the back of the head in a parked car, all in serene longshot, while Clemenza takes an easeful leak in the wheatfield
- Sollozzo, shot in the forehead so that an odd Indian castemark puts a dent in his pasta
- Police Chief McCloskey, shot in the throat and the forehead; these two men are left with their tipped-over table in the small Italian restaurant like lovers' clothes thrown off in haste—there *is* something orgasmic in this double murder, it's Michael getting laid
- Sonny, at the toll booth, with 612 bullets (you count them)
- Apollonia, eager to drive, blown up in the car, her persimmon breasts tossed to either end of the garden
- Vito Corleone, while playing in the tomato plants on a hot day with his grandson
- two Tattaglia brothers shotgunned in an elevator
- Moe Greene, having just put on his glasses, so blood can creep through a cracked lens
- a man in a revolving door
- a man and a woman astonished in bed, naked, and then quickly dead
- Barzini and Barzini's man, Barzini only after he has run to the top of some steps so that he may topple down again
- Tessio: we don't see Tessio's death, only his stooped figure being taken away and Abe Vigoda's dreadful glance

- and Carlo, Connie's husband, throttled in a car, his frantic feet kicking out the windscreen so that we can see he didn't even take care of his shoes

That's seventeen, to say nothing of a horse's head, a fish (to let us know where Luca Brasi sleeps), and at least three corpses in a montage. Not to mention Kay's hopes.

Over the years, I have taken it as an axiom that the American 18-year-old has seen twenty thousand acts of killing in movies and on TV. Most college freshmen with whom I shared this nodded like connoisseurs: few professors had taken their youth so seriously. Yet I am no longer sure how I ever knew this fact. Having totted up one movie (17 deaths in 171 minutes), I suspect the statistic is rather conservative. It would be as hard as counting the bullets in Sonny as it might be to keep tabs on the deaths in, say, *Sergeant York, Kriemhild's Revenge, The Wild Bunch,* Alan Clarke's *Elephant, Spartacus,* or *Tom and Jerry.* Let us agree that we have witnessed a lot of killings. By my age, 52, with more films endured than I can remember, I wouldn't doubt a hundred thousand. Yet in what I will call the rest of my life, I have seen just two dead bodies. From all I can gather, asking around, two is on the high side—enough to be thought a little morbid.

What a marvel that our bang-bang movies are so seldom chided for morbidity. Yet, as I recorded the deaths in *The Godfather,* I did feel infected or aroused by the sheer exuberance and stylistic slam of the movie. I recalled that aside from *Lolita:* "You can always count on a murderer for a fancy style." In turn that triggered the recollection of Francis Coppola admitting, long ago:

> You know, I took my kid to see a 45-minute assembly of some of the stuff of the old *Godfather* and I said what parts do you like better? He said, "I like when the guys get shot." Everyone is like that. Even when you're shooting the film. The second you're going to do a throatcutting or something, everyone including the crew crowds round.

He's right, of course (and he's no more bloodthirsty than most directors today). Kids—or boys—generally exult in the best balletic death scenes: it may be as close as they ever come to sissyness, preferring style over content. In the late 1940s and early 1950s, getting out of cinemas on Streatham High Road, I galloped to the prairies of Tooting Bee Common to reenact death scenes. My friends and I vied for the spectacular bits in these remakes: it was fine to be John Wayne on the bare

land that would become the Red River D ranch, but so much more lib-
erating to be Don Diego's man who is tumbled from the saddle by
Wayne's shot. Or Edmond O'Brien running through the streets of
D.O.A., clutching his bright stomach, loaded with irreversible poison,
running for his death. Or Elisha Cook Jr. in *Shane*, lifted off his feet and
thrown back in the mud by Jack Palance's guns. Cagney in *White Heat*,
seeming to go up like a rocket. There was a blooming in these deaths,
a jeté, reaching for beauty. We grazed our knees and dirtied our clothes
doing death falls. But we glowed in their rapture.

As time passed, I guessed some actors had the same fun and
release in extravagant death scenes. Cagney and Edward G. Robinson
were treasured for those cadenzas in which they occupied time and
space with their delirious dance of death. "Is this the end of Rico?"
Robinson asked in *Little Caesar*. Well, eventually. Was there anything
in movies so much in love with life as these whirling expirations? Slum
kids could at least look forward to the brilliant strut and fret of passing.

Cagney's stricken grace leaned toward the fits and fevers of
approaching rigor mortis. "Made it, Ma!" in *White Heat* was only a vet-
eran's fond tribute to the death throes from *Public Enemy, He Was Her
Man, Angels with Dirty Faces* (one of the first "showtime" deaths, proof

Figure 17. Ever the dynamo, James Cagney dispensed death while staying in constant motion. In
White Heat, *in one fluid move Cagney eats his lunch (a chicken leg) and "ventilates" a victim
stashed in a car trunk.*

that acting can get you over that hump), and *The Roaring Twenties*. Cagney yearned to throw himself about, to smell extinction, tousle his hair, and let his eyes see oblivion. He expanded on death scenes, he grew lithe and poetical. It was only then that he could disclose his passion for movement and his love of the precarious. Death gave this would-be real-life radical his greatest sense of insurrection.

If you doubt the nihilistic élan in Cagney's demises, then look at how bitterly Bogart went to his deaths. He never liked losing control. In such predicaments, we feel the truth in Louise Brooks's observation that "Humphrey" was a socially correct young man who liked to keep his cool and his distance. Bogart tensed up when he had to die: his body often folded in on itself, like hired evening dress packed in a suitcase. If he had to "act," in death, it was his worst acting. In *The Roaring Twenties* Bogart is intimidated, whipped, and mocked by Cagney, as if he were Liston being taught psychic danger by Cassius Clay. It's notable that in *High Sierra* Bogart's Roy Earle dies in extreme longshot, without benefit of triumphant staggering against the skyline. *High Sierra* was Raoul Walsh (who made *White Heat*), but *Sierra* is drugged by Bogart's depressive reticence. Bogart's glory learned a lot from *High Sierra*: it developed a smoldering, still fatalism, the chance for a few wry words before conclusions he had foreseen. But Cagney's death hound was always lit up by the surprise—the discovery!—of bullets.

We know of actors who held a nearly contractual right not to perish in fiction. To stay the hero, Wayne, Gary Cooper, and, more recently, Clint Eastwood walked up and down in the shadow of death, yet kept a beacon keylight on their ever more haggard faces. As one of those not swept away by *Unforgiven*, I note the greater historical and artistic plausibility if William Munny had died on his mission, rather than revert to that reassuring bringer of death. The film might then conclude with a simple scene of the forsaken Munny children, dying in their cabin from cholera or loneliness. But the Munny who had lost such edge and youth did pick up quickness at the end. Then he rode home in a grim spirit, condemning all the fates and movie conventions that had made him be lethal.

The comfort in Munny's regaining deadly impact surely extends to Eastwood himself. No matter how far this moviemaker has poked and prodded old genres, no matter his candor with age and fatigue lines, he cannot do without looking good and potent. He is—and he knows it—the last classic star. Thus, allegedly, he spent time researching Secret Service agentry for *In the Line of Fire*, but still indulged the cockamamy of a 60-year-old jogging along beside the limo and the sentimentality of a Service that keeps such maverick problem children on the payroll. Even then, the ludicrous fun of *In the Line of Fire* depends on John Malkovich's fastidious killer. He is a delicious tribute to the bliss of murderous daydreams. The fantasy appeal of *In the Line of Fire* is a balanced two-hander, but it is Malkovich who knows the whole thing is just a game. It is so often our killers now who are blessed with wisdom and insight. They are the only characters allowed to turn to philosophy or talk for the sake of talking.

It would not be out of order if Malkovich crooned into the phone, "Frank, don't be petulant, you know, and I know, we're just playing checkers for the audience, and they love to think about killing, and you're there just to waste me at the end so they feel okay about it. I've told you all along I'm ready to die for the picture—but, Frank, are you really ready to stop a bullet?"

And Clint is not: its thought seems indecent and un-American. On the other hand, Malkovich is a master of all those infinitesimal droops and melancholies that could while away a whole film with dying—"As I Lay Dying" seems to be the dream in Malkovich's remote eyes. Kirk Douglas in that ebullient youth of his seemed to crave horrid execution, agonies to prompt his throbbing cry, and movies where he could be mutilated, marred, and generally pecked at by those birds of story who knew his needs. Lee Marvin was made for the world-weariness that is a killer-for-hire only to stay awake. Thus, in Don Siegel's *The Killers*, the actor/assassin who is gradually clearing the film of life, mortally wounded himself, can say (to Angie Dickinson), "Lady, I'm just too tired. I haven't got the time." A career and an attitude are made lucid. James Mason was another actor born to see the sense in his own extinction—think of *Odd Man Out*, *North by Northwest*, and *Lolita*, or even *Heaven Can Wait*, where he is in charge of death's best hotel.

And who can mistake the self-discovery in William Holden, gazing down from the top of the pool in *Sunset Boulevard*, the hack who finally has a drop-dead story to peddle?

Death is so slick in film, it has become tongue-in-cheek. "If history has taught us anything," Michael Corleone will announce in *The Godfather Part II*, "it says you can kill anybody." That line portends the resolute evil with which Michael orders his older brother Fredo dead—in a rowboat on desolate Tahoe. It inspires confidence that any Hyman Roth can be taken out in broad daylight at an airport. And it tickles us to think that Michael may have assented to events in Dallas on November 22, 1963—as *In the Line of Fire* makes plain, killing a president is not that difficult.

But Michael's line signals a more pervasive mastery: that movie can kill whomever its weary, plot-crazed eye falls on. It can put Shelley Winters on the bottom of the lake in *The Night of the Hunter* (so that we marvel at the coup); it can consign Janet Leigh to the swamp after a scant forty minutes of *Psycho* (outraging stardom's expectations); it can make a studious tracking of so many serial killers for connoisseurs, so long as the killers are caught before the final crawl—except that after *The Silence of the Lambs* these killers may roam the earth if they are nicely spoken, have discerning tastes, and remember to call Clarice now and then.

There's a giggle in the end of *Silence of the Lambs* as Lecter goes a-roaming. There was a more smothered chuckle in the setup for *Sunset Boulevard*, a way in which contempt for Hollywood began to turn against the audience; there is malice and self-loathing in the camp superiority that betrays our disbelief. Long before the clamor to be on death's side in such titles as *Die Hard, Lethal Weapon, The Terminator,* and *Death Wish,* our movies had made deals with the glamour of death. The timing and polish of our well-made melodramas were like the ingenuity of Malkovich's gun in *In the Line of Fire.* They were to die for.

Deathliness is in the mise-en-scène. Think of the killings in *The Godfather:* Isn't the consciousness observing them that of a Corleone? These deaths are not messy or untidy. The attitude is proud, masterful, in love with meticulous detail. Nothing in the sensibility disturbs the remorseless efficiency of vengeance, or departs from the managerial pleasure in seeing intricate plans work sweetly.

There is gallows humor in the spatial tranquillity of Paulie's death—the wind-swept location; Paulie's stupid patience; Clemenza's ruminative urination; the far-away bump of the shot to match the lovely longshot: it is a kill-master's dream with Paulie the spare pin taken out by a dab hand. When Sollozzo and McCloskey get it, we are nearly palpitating with the urge to give it to them—one reason why "they" can kill anyone is because we are such willing, voyeur accomplices. Finally, when the total elimination of enemies is orchestrated with the rite of baptism, we might be witnessing the adorable fit of nuclear physics.

Is there irony in the magnificence? Is Michael being condemned? Watch the sequence again, and there is no escaping our deranged complicity in the lethal arrangement. There is such macabre comfort in feeling a part of the Corleones. The psychic infancy that dreads all strangers has been protected—they have got theirs, and our supreme plan has been vindicated. Michael is patriarch and paranoid, for surely, one day, he will have to eliminate every family member and anyone who knows.

It's during the grease-quiet, digestive mechanics of films like *The Godfather* that we may recall how frequently film has appealed to fascists. Not that I mean to suggest some directors are readier for the jackboot than others. No, the dilemma is tougher for those of us who love film: something essential to the medium cleaves to uncorrected powers, the magic of plot (or organization), and the chance to stare at death without honoring pain or loss. Still, for the moment let's pull back from that comprehensive unease and offer an intriguing disclaimer—roughly, that these corpses don't smell, none of these guys were ever "alive" anyway. They're 'toons, for crying out loud!

There is something childlike in the easy dispatch of so many people as quick as a wipe. My 4-year-old takes as much delight in hurling himself to many deaths, and in inflicting them with pointed finger and inner-mouth explosions, as ever I did. But did children have this game, or its risk, before moving pictures? Perhaps boys keep the game alive—and most things that depend on boyishness are becoming harder to sustain. Yet there are plenty of decent film critics, some of them women, who seem untroubled by the extended boyhood of, say, Sam Peckinpah and the very cinematic motto, "Kill anything that moves"— the line that introduces Peckinpah's credit on *The Wild Bunch*.

The deaths are easier to face when one gets in the habit of knowing movie deaths are akin to a bucket of dip cleaning out the premises. Dip, you may remember, is the green fluid that brings death or erasure to all 'toons in *Who Framed Roger Rabbit*. It works in the way water did on the Wicked Witch of the West in *The Wizard of Oz*— Christopher Lloyd's judge dies with the same cry of frustration, "What a world!", that Margaret Hamilton uttered in *Oz*.

Lloyd's judge actually dies twice. He is first flattened out by a steamroller: this is what reveals his secret looniness, although it is a cunning conceit of the Zemeckis film to say some characters are flatter than others in movie's two-dimensional illusion. Then the judge reinflates his own balloon and comes on wicked again—with gestures from *The Texas Chainsaw Massacre*—before dip takes him back to primordial ooze. He is too good a villain for one death. Zemeckis is so wantonly inventive in *Roger Rabbit* (and so inspired by other films), I could believe in the judge bouncing back as often as the cat in Tom and Jerry cartoons.

Did that cat ever die? Or were his lives infinite? He was reduced to fragments, blown to smithereens, electrocuted, pancaked—you

Figure 18. Martin Scorsese's films are often full of harsh, flamboyantly rendered physical violence. In Cape Fear, *the villain Max Cady (Robert De Niro) is subjected to an extended beating sequence, one of several mutilating ordeals the character undergoes.*

think of a way to go, Hanna-Barbera did it—and always there was the swift fade-out, fade-in, and puss was back again ready for worse. He was a character out of Bunuel. When killing is so easy and such fun, and death so brief, it becomes a way of life. And not just for card-carrying 'toons. We know how reluctant the film business is to let its most vital killers take retirement. At the end of *Halloween*, the demonstrably deceased Michael vanishes, so that he could return for sequels. As I tried to puzzle out why Scorsese had made *Cape Fear*, I noticed the clearly posed cue for Max Cady to grab back once more from the river, just as Carrie came out of the black earth of her own grave. The moment passed; it was presumably just a joke about such tricks. But Cady could have escaped—so burned, so crushed, and so drowned that he would be the harder to recognize next time.

    With death so climatic or constitutional, ghastliness becomes a subject for movies. Our watching from the dark, intensely "with" the images yet powerless to intervene in their progress, is a model for stories in which those left alive may keep some kind of community with lost ones. After all, the thrust of movies is so much more imaginary than actual. So there have been films in which ghosts come back, or the living make a journey to the realm of the dead. From *Nosferatu* and *A Matter of Life and Death* to Beatty's *Heaven Can Wait* and *Ghost*, movies have played with the undead (without having to hire other than the regular actors). Some of those films have resorted to "ghostly" special effects, superimposition, and so on. Yet, truly, no tricks are required. No one on screen has a real life or corporeality. The films keep playing long after the actors die. These are 'toons reread as appealing solids by our fond credulity.

Ghost hints at a way movies might—on the scent of Shirley MacLaine and Marianne Williamson—burrow into the self-help of projection. In several recent movies, there are wishful thinkings beyond the grave, psychic schmoozings: in *Field of Dreams*, Kevin Costner has the chance to meet his dead father again, so that the load of misunderstanding can be tolled away. That's not what I want an art form to offer. But that won't deter the development, and who knows if movie isn't less an art than just one of those fun boxes the Good Guys offer. We may not be far from a household video facility that could take all the hours of home movie of a loved one and then put that passed-away person into computer regeneration, so that those left behind have a house guest/ghost to chat with.

Already, TV commercials (today's pioneering) have worked this magic with the look and sound of dead stars. And there are rumors of Jurassic Parks in northern California where that readiness is poised for new feature films—with Bogart and Louise Brooks together again at last—if only the legal details can be worked out. The one interest in the actual *Jurassic Park* was that such ghosts shared a frame with the very pale humans Spielberg had time for. Most of the time, the seams didn't show. But suppose next that we could resurrect and write dialogue for Elvis and Marilyn? Or you could have your own home video tête-a-tête with the star/celebrity of your choice—the star as ultimate pet.

The bullet goes in, and life goes out. Movie prefers it as an instant, switchlike adjustment, without suffering or waiting. Yet so much of death is in those two grim departments. How do we stand up for the very few deaths, and corpses, we may meet in our lives? They are unscripted, no matter the anticipation; and they are not there for slo-mo analysis. Are there moments in films when we have a better than bang-bang understanding of what cessation means for the passer-on and those left behind? I can think of film deaths that move me, or give me a sharper sense of the precariousness of life. In every case I'm going to list, somehow, life remains the subject:

- the deaths in *The Missouri Breaks* are epic and lugubrious, undignified yet very skilled, but the best is Lee Clayton's, asleep after his horse pissed during his love song, then awake to the snap of bracken or sinews, his own vain efforts to breathe or stay calm at Tom Logan's dry inquiry, "You know what woke you up? Lee, you just had your throat cut."

- in *Pat Garrett and Billy the Kid,* Slim Pickens realizes he has a death wound while James Coburn is still fighting L. Q. Jones. But the music rises for his death, and leads him down to the river (Pickens has been building a boat to "drift out of this damn territory"). His woman, Katy Jurado, follows him and they gaze at each other by the water as he holds his startled face and his belly wound up to the evening light. And then we see that Coburn (Garrett) is watching the death and taking it in as evidence and responsibility. For he had hired Pickens away from the boat-building. And then there will be Garrett camped by another river, half an hour and months later in the film, as a vagrant family drifts by on a raft.

- in Renoir's *The River,* the little boy Bogey is entranced by the cobra at the end of the garden. He is warned. But he wants to charm the snake, and one afternoon he goes too close. We never see the cobra strike. There is just the boy's sprawled body. The loss comes not long after a siesta in which the several members of the household are seen sleeping, with the camera simmering on their breath. The boy dies, a new child is born. This easily sounds trite as a philosophy, but Renoir's structure, his camera, and the sense of breathing transform the quietism so that it becomes as steady and flowing as the river and the flooding sitar music.

- the moment when Isabelle dies in *Ambersons,* with the Major gazing into the fire, speaking of the sun as the source of life—Richard Bennett rambling very near his own death—and then the fateful word, the Major jerked out of his revery, ready to die, and the rapacious embrace that Fanny has for George. Family in a few seconds

- and the death of Tom Joslin in *Silverlake Life,* the documentary made by Joslin and his lover, Mark Massi, as they both faced the destiny of AIDS. In this case, it is the entire film, the ending of which never enjoys doubt. It takes a movie like this to remind us how gradually and faithfully death comes. Bodies diminish and waste, the lesions of sarcoma spread and join; courage and tact fail. Joslin sometimes rants out of fear and horror at what is happening to him. Months and years come down to ninety minutes or so of film, and we see Joslin seconds after he has died—a skull with skin, yet freed or deserted by life and the illness. We see so few authentic deaths on film, *Silverlake Life* can put you off movies.

I saw *Silverlake Life* on June 15 on PBS. Two days later I flew to England for my father's funeral. I was reading Philip Larkin on the plane because, for many Englishmen, Larkin has been like a life-sustaining illness: he had a sensibility I loathed, and a capacity with words that was piercing. And now, eight years after his death, Larkin is being revealed—in *Selected Letters* and a biography by Andrew Motion—as a furtive, less than honest man, darker and more afraid than he could admit. I felt there was some kind of kinship between Larkin and my father. My father left my mother when I was being born. He lived with another woman for over forty-five years. But he came home to us at weekends and Christmases, and he never once said anything about the double life. This is Larkin in *Aubade* (he never sold the movie rights):

> I work all day, and get half-drunk at night.
> Waking at four to soundless dark, I stare.
> In time the curtain-edges will grow light.
> Till then I see what's really always there:
> Unresting death, a whole day nearer now,
> Making all thought impossible but how
> And where and when I shall myself die.
> Arid interrogation: yet the dread
> Of dying, and being dead,
> Flashes afresh to hold and horrify.

Before London, I went to Dublin to see my oldest friend, Kieran Hickey. We met on the steps of the National Film Theatre in London thirty-three years ago. He was the first naturally eloquent person I had ever known—smart, gruff, lyrical, and caustic. He was a filmmaker, and a good one: he made documentaries and short fiction films in Ireland—*Faithful Departed, A Child's Voice, Exposure, Criminal Conversation, Attracta, The Rockingham Shoot.* I went to see him because he was set for double bypass surgery on June 28.

We had a fine weekend in Dublin, his house on the south side full of friends and all the things he collected. We watched a tape of *Bitter Victory*, letter-boxed yet incomplete, but with that scene where Richard Burton's officer remarks on his skill at killing the living and saving the dead. We watched Stephen Frears's wonderful *The Snapper*. Then I went to England for the funeral. My father was 84. He had had a stroke from which he never regained consciousness. I went to the funeral home to see him in his coffin before the cremation.

It was him, yet the fierceness had gone, and with it the last hope that he and I would ever talk about our history. You see, I had never quite been able to make him tell me; and instead there were ways in which I had imitated him. He was cremated and I came back to America.

Kieran had his operation. It was a complete success. The news from friends in Dublin could not have been more positive. Two weeks after the operation he was to be moved from the hospital to a nursing home for further convalescence. But in a matter of hours he developed a pulmonary embolism and died. The day after he died I got a card from him, written from the hospital —"My improvement is marked." You have to believe me: he would have chuckled and said, "Oh, dear, yes," for he loved irony.

The limit to death in most of our films is that it shows what poor attention they pay to life.

Devin McKinney

Violence: The Strong
and the Weak

For many of us, our earliest and most lasting moviegoing memories involve acts of violence. Whereas an older generation was marked by the murder of Bambi's mother, my epiphany came with seeing *Taxi Driver* at the age of 12 and being disturbed nearly to the point of physical sickness by its violence. But more intriguing to me now is the nightmare I awoke with two days later. Somewhere I realized that I had responded so viscerally not only because the violence felt physically real but because it was emotionally and morally complex: it brought up ambivalences and dreads that no amount of rationalization could overcome.

Time swings like a pendulum, and violence is once again an issue. Over the past few years a new ethos of violence has been accruing in the commercial cinema; directors have been attempting to take it further—but not necessarily deeper. More than ever, violence has emerged as thematic matter, the true meat even of movies that claim to be about something else. This has given a sharper edge to both "strong" and "weak" (as I'll call them) portrayals of violence, since both must compete in a media marketplace that is ever more vicious and in a social context that is ever more apathetic.

Of all that films contain, violence may be the most resistant to quantification. Only at its weakest does it yield to patterns and predictabilities. (Robin Wood conceded as much in his theory of the "incoherent text," a theory whose unvoiced admission is that many of the most violent and interesting films are so multilayered and resistant to singular meaning that their systematization can be built only on contradictions.) But perhaps some generalities can be discerned. Perhaps movie violence must contain multitudinous meanings if it hopes to avoid the prisons of ideology and cliché, if it seeks to draw anything more than a distant, formalized response, if it wants to outlast its moment. Perhaps it must bring the heart and mind together, and aim for the emotions as much as the viscera. And perhaps in order to entertain a discussion of "strong" violence versus "weak" violence, one has to accept the notion that some nightmares are worth having.

In an essay on "excessive" film types (weepie melodrama, pornography, horror), Linda Williams determined that essential to the allure of these "body" genres is their capacity to bring up unmitigated, unsocialized emotions—the extremes of feeling not elicited by pictures that take the straight and narrow path. Strong violence, while it often has the physical effect of the body genres, also acts on the mind by refusing it glib comfort and immediate resolutions. If successful socialization depends on a neutralizing of extremes, then violence of this kind amounts to a rent in the curtain of rationality, a glimpse of the ultimate questions one spends a lifetime denying. And it amounts to carnage that is haunting in the truest sense—that gives "meaning and import to our mortal twitchings," in Vivian Sobchack's fine phrase. This is a rarity on today's screen, but it shows up just often enough to make you feel its larger absence. It's the sort of violence that *Wild at Heart* pulsed with, that framed the good small thriller *One False Move,* and that Scorsese, despite the unwelcome gloss twinkling on his late work, can still deliver. It was the violence, not the time-saving homilies about fallen kings, that gave *JFK* its sense of loss. And it carried the climactic murder in *Casualties of War,* so surreally angled, to the level of catharsis.

Movie violence this strong communicates intensely the sense that a person who in one moment is fully alive has been reduced to God's garbage (as Joseph Heller perceived his doomed gunner, Snowden). It holds unspoken contingencies, and by its nature is crazed. It need not be particularly kinetic, but it shakes everything up, re-forming the entire fictive environment around itself.

Plainly the terrain mapped here is not an easy place to reach. Among recent films there are three in particular that in their impact—both immediate and residual—make the discrimination between strong and weak violence solid and meaningful. In each, the bloodshed has subtext, carries the weight of fear and mystery, and is piercing enough to shoot past the crap violence we all drink like beer.

If Neil Jordan's *The Crying Game* fits the present discussion, it isn't because its violence is plentiful or showy but because it exemplifies how strong violence can reshape both the entire context of a narrative and the audience's enunciation of the experience. The deaths that occur in this picture mark beginnings as well as endings, and open a world of new threats and possibilities. The nasty trick of fate that ends the life of a British soldier (Forest Whitaker) signals the beginning of a new life for his captor, an IRA terrorist (Stephen Rea), as does the murder committed by the Irishman's lover (Jaye Davidson) later on. In each case, violence is *committed*—as most movie violence is not—because it demands commitments of those still living.

This does not square with the conventions of movie violence, where the cataclysm of death constitutes no more than a momentary lull ending with a cutaway to the next sequence. Although stylistically well within a certain classical-realist tradition, *The Crying Game* breaks those bounds on the narrative level by according the consequences of violence a determining role. As much as anything, it is this grasp of consequence that distinguishes strong violence from weak.

The emotions we are enabled to feel by *The Crying Game* are ultimately comforting, affirmative, even warm—in the nonironic senses of those words. This does not, of course, detract from the film (whose warmth, in fact, is as central as its violence), but it does point out that strong violence is often put to the service of perceptions that are ugly and cold, and that it often etches a horrid picture. Abel Ferrara's savage cop movie, *Bad Lieutenant,* swan-dives into the waste of the excremental city, and whatever sympathy one extends to its eponymous antihero is repaid only after a punishing swim. Ferrara pursues the new, riskier violence in every respect, pushing a rigorous cum-stained filthiness against the keening excess of grand opera: the result is a Times Square men's room with the design of St. Patrick's Cathedral.

Harvey Keitel's doping, whoring, extorting L.T. is the film's center, and its metaphor: he is a walking, talking consequence. *Bad Lieutenant* is so single-minded and so steeped in the ubiquity of brutality that its violences come to feel organic to one another—symbolically, if not actually, intertwined. The L.T.'s act of autoeroticism—aided by two frightened girls in a car—echoes and counters the event that spurs his death-trip to redemption: the rape and vaginal mutilation of a nun by two boys. The skein of suggestions underlying these disparate acts of violence—active and passive subjugation of women, the priming of the male pump versus the attempted destruction of the female organ—is tight and intricate, with no vanishing point. That such echoes are heard at all implies that the film has deepened its grotesquerie by problematizing it, making it stand for more than a scream and a crotch shot.

And as relentless as it is, *Bad Lieutenant* has plenty of color; it's lined with rock 'n' roll; it moves. Other films don't. On one level,

John McNaughton's *Henry: Portrait of a Serial Killer* can be denigrated as a slack, unmodulated piece of filmmaking. But the truth of this judgment also underlines the fact that strong violence (like the features of Williams's "excessive" genres) is not always an experience defensible or divisible by aesthetic means. For though it may fail as an art object, *Henry* can't be dismissed.

Its tonelessness and sensual inertia apotheosize the particularly cruel, moribund tenor of violence in the 1980s. But unlike *American Psycho*, Bret Easton Ellis's portrait of a serial killer, *Henry* does not commit the imitative fallacy of depicting a barren mind through the barren accumulation of idiot minutiae, mistaking a willed emptiness for postmodern substance. It stands at just the right distance from its subject, never enforcing a sociologically judgmental thesis but nevertheless entailing that the killings be as grubbily, unexplosively real as kitchen-sink style can make them.

Perhaps the indirect success of *Henry* as a study in violence is that it comes to life only when witnessing death, and even then it comes only to a kind of life. The banality of its violence issues from a beclouding feeling of moral lassitude. There is a grinding insistence on murder as a mere relief of tension, a dully masturbatory act, and it infuses even the nonviolent scenes with a glowering menace. The life seen here is entirely of a piece with the death: there is no "real world," no normality to return to. What this means in practice is that although the presentation of violence is outwardly neutral, its effect is extreme. Unlike the common run of hermetic, low-budget bloodbaths, *Henry* puts its banality to a purpose. Its very monotony induces paranoia, hypersensitivity to what was once ordinary. Like all works of strong violence, it leaves an audience feeling dead inside, yet, somehow, more alive than it was two hours before.

The kind of disconnected, uncommitted movie mayhem that began with James Bond and that came of age with the sociopathic crime dramas of the early 1970s and served the reactionary agenda of the 1980s is once again ascendant. The increasingly visible violence of the global society virtually demands that its art be more violent, and already all the barricades seem to have been breached, no crimes left undepicted. But repetition always vitiates, particularly if it's the lowest-common-denominator variety habitually practiced by the movie industry. The paradoxes of strong violence are rich and mazelike, but weak violence thrives on a sterile contradiction: it reduces bloodshed to its barest components, then inflates them with hot, stylized air.

Figure 19. In Goodfellas *Tommy (Joe Pesci) is executed with a bullet to the head and a flamboyant blood spray. Note how director Martin Scorsese overtly plays this violence to the camera. The characters face the camera, and the composition gives the viewer the ideal vantage from which to watch the violence.*

Weak violence appears nearly everywhere in both popular and highbrow culture, and by its nature ridicules the powerful empathies that hard, personalized violence can make an audience feel. It's akin to what has been called camp, and it recalls John Fraser's account (in his touchstone work, *Violence in the Arts*) of camp aesthetics "draining off" the "charge of feeling and meaning" possible in a violent artwork. It informs not only the products of the Schwarzenegger school—which are merely bionic mutations of earlier action styles—but also works of some moment: Peter Greenaway's *The Cook, the Thief, His Wife and Her Lover;* parts of *Goodfellas;* Pedro Almodovar's postcommercial-breakthrough films; David Cronenberg's adaptation of *Naked Lunch;* much of Alan Parker's work; the French blockbuster *La Femme Nikita.* The violence of these pictures simply doesn't last; it gets left on the floor with the candy wrappers. It's too rationalized, too articulate— either in the limited sense of "nice" cinematic effects too well contrived to have any other content, or because the outrages are stapled, memo-like, to external signifiers that bury their very peculiar meanings. Either way, violence is used only as a device: something a crowd pays for when it goes in, but not when it comes out.

Although weak violence is marked by its lack of pluralities, the sensibilities that create it are various. Among the hacks of the world it is still the most popular pipeline to grim titillation, as witness Paul

Verhoeven's *Basic Instinct.* In building a dream world whose moral parameters are so easily drawn (straight = good, gay or bi = evil), Joe Eszterhas's screenplay abdicates any claim on psychological insight, and the director's angle on violence is a congruent refusal to believe that anything might be more than it appears. Like his demonized femme fatale, Verhoeven wields an ice pick—in the form of visual violence—and he uses it to pin his characters to the mat. Significantly, no pictorial reference is made to the accidental murders gratuitously committed by the hero cop, while the brutalities of the central lesbian are virtually turned into production numbers. The characters are not revealed by their acts, only summarily defined, and violence is used not as an entry to human depths but as a means of shutting them off.

But this sort of lacquered, discrete violence is no longer the exclusive province of the schlockmeisters. It also serves the needs of young, earnest filmmakers eager to showcase their formal skills, and who therefore seem worthier of considered attention because they're walking the art house walk. A paradigmatic case is Phil Joanou's *State of Grace,* a fitfully impressive, high-voltage melodrama about the stubborn dregs of New York's Irish mob. The picture follows its bumpy, overdeliberate, but generally absorbing course until a climactic massacre that comes charging right out of the movie past, impeccably choreographed to evoke the shades of Travis Bickle and the Wild Bunch. Joanou's marshaling of time and space is voluptuous and breathtaking, but the scene's brilliance is an affront. One is severed cleanly from the film's involving fiction—from a world where nearly everything seems real and vital to one where nothing does. Unlike the fierce, flatly observed throat-cutting earlier on, the bullets fired in this slow-motion shootout inflict no pain on a viewer; the blood-squibs explode with all the portent of popcorn.

Even more accomplished than *State of Grace* in its hollow treatment of violence is *Reservoir Dogs,* the debut of writer-director Quentin Tarantino. This high-gloss, low-budget job about the preparation for and disastrous fallout from a botched jewel heist is aggressively, conscientiously violent. In terms of perceptible intent, the tyro auteur seems involved in the playful crossbreeding of pop culture references from the past three decades with his own witty, state-of-the-art thriller technique. But despite its conscious avoidance of "relevance"—all its backward glances and retrograde finery—*Reservoir Dogs* is a pristine reflection of its socioartistic climate; this brutal exercise says much about the way we're absorbing violence today.

The picture's savagery is so assiduously appointed that it demands analysis as a thing in itself, a component of the work overarching all others—which is to say that the story usually serves the violence rather than the reverse. In theory, this is hardly a fatal flaw, and indeed, there is an initial passage whose strength leads one to expect that the subsequent violence will evolve into something more consummate. Speeding from the scene of the crime, the most psychologically complex of the thieves (Harvey Keitel) holds the hand of his friend (Tim Roth), who lies writhing in the back seat, slowly bleeding to death. The sequence is brought down to the tightly gripped hands and the strangled growls of the backseat passenger. It doesn't have many levels, but it does have some, and above all the scene is obstinate—it sinks in; and this at least bodes well for Tarantino's willingness to allow the violence a lifelike rhythm and character. But when the crew of hoods congregates in a warehouse to lick its wounds, the picture relaxes into its oddball formula and, despite its blood and curses, turns quisling, watering its frenzy with self-satisfied cool.

Figure 20. The notorious ear-cutting scene in Reservoir Dogs *is a moment of gratuitous screen violence. Failing to connect with any previous material in the film, it performs no narrative function. But it does offer a striking visual showcase for ultraviolence, in which the bloody effect becomes its own end and purpose.*

The film proclaims itself to be a jaunty, hyperbolic comedy of horrors that aspires to no particular realism or social import. It occurs in a comic-existential dead zone, and is as nonreferential to a reality outside itself as a (theoretically) mimetic work can be. Initially, it requires a stretch to allow that a gang of robbers—and self-designated "professionals" at that—would think it clever to outfit themselves in identical Blues Brothers costumes, or to go by ostentatiously colorful code names like "Mr. Pink" and "Mr. Orange." But *Reservoir Dogs* has approximately the same relation to true crime as *Mandingo* had to life in the antebellum South. This is a formalist filmmaker's logic, and it has only one self-apparent subject: the set-piece.

The set-piece that has drawn the most attention—perhaps because it draws the most attention to itself—is the one in which Mr. Blonde (Michael Madsen) gives the bloody business to a trussed-up policeman, all the while dancing the dance of the blissfully insane and swishing away with a razor to the accompaniment of a wonderful old Stealers Wheel tune. Although this may have seemed great on paper, the combination of pop music, self-infatuated dance, and offhand amputation inspires no clashing sensation in a viewer, perhaps because the incongruous ingredients are too obviously chosen for their effect of creative perversity. With every authorial impulse visible, the supposedly wild scene has an inapposite smoothness and objectivity, reinforced by a Formica-like sheen over the colors. When Blonde cuts off the cop's ear, it's not a determined act in any real sense but a show of flamboyance for its own hip, photogenic sake.

Where does a scene like this locate the audience? What is a viewer's level and kind of complicity, if any? On the surface (which is where weak violence phenomenalistically stays), one identifies with neither the victimizer (the infantile Blonde) nor the victim (the objectified cop), and is thus put in the position of the most passive, disinterested of observers. This is the limbo that weak violence inhabits: empathies are not engaged, commitments are not brought to bear, ambivalences are not acknowledged, neutrality is the currency.

Strong violence enables—and often entails—shifts in one's moral positioning. This is a part of its power, and a great deal of its threat. In fact, the realm of violence is one of the few aspects of film that can be legitimately called co-constructive. Movies, despite the penis-envious treatises of academically oriented critics, offer the viewer no degree of imaginative co-authorship comparable to that in literature. The image, after all, is right there before us, concrete block-like in its sensual solidity, ranging in opacity from a stiff Eisenstein tableau to Eric Rohmer's airy idylls. But when acts of strong violence are involved, a picture can (like Garry Wills's comment on *Oliver Twist*) open moral trapdoors under us, engendering an immediate and very subjective confrontation with the material. The most memorable of Hitchcock's murder scenes, for instance (the *Psycho* shower murder and its aftermath, the slow killing of the German agent in *Torn Curtain*), are at once acts of pure calculation and spontaneous disruptions of rational order; the calculation courts the audience's desires and the disruption serves to foreground those (discomfiting) desires. The audience is both acted upon and made to act by acknowledging its role in the fulfillment of a wish it barely knew it had: it is both victimizer and victim.

The new exploiters of violence use bloodshed as a kick, but in an agile, knowing, and self-consciously formal way. Verhoeven's kinky, whorey thriller is tarted and rouged with Hitchcock allusions, while Mr. Blonde's torture of the cop is meant not to horrify but to succeed as a ghastly entertainment, a bloody song and dance. It's a clean kick, and guilt-free, too: it obviates a viewer's self-disgust at getting off on sadism by positing figures who are plasticized and unreal to begin with, lacking even a certain crude B-movie immediacy. The gut-wrench one feels at

Figure 21. The action films starring Arnold Schwarzenegger popularized a smirking, wisecracking approach to ultraviolence. Schwarzenegger's heroes usually concluded their mayhem with a quip that took the bloodshed in the direction of comedy and "weak" violence.

the parboiled savageries of a *Basic Instinct* bears the same relation to real emotional empathy as the tears provoked by one of Douglas Sirk's moist epics: a conditioned reflex. But without emotional response, film violence trades flesh and blood for hamburger and ketchup.

If a film makes the decision to be violent, it shouldn't go about its business timidly: no art ever came of a hedged bet. But most of the violent pictures that cross the screen these days, however dangerous they appear, are as conservative at heart as a Disney fable. These films hedge their bets on the level of audience involvement by refusing a full commitment to their own content: they want to look at horror, but they don't want to feel it, smell it, take the chance of getting sick from it. By insuring itself in this way, a violent film can't help but resist a viewer's emotional investment, which, frustrated, displaces itself onto an academic admiration of style.

This consideration of involvement, finally, is perhaps the most important. All the other issues—consequences, multiplicity of meaning, arousal of empathy—are united by the questions that measure how successfully a group of film artists have involved their audience in the experience of violence. Do I care about this character? Will his or her passing leave a gap? Will I remember what I've seen?

More and more, violence—not merely as an aspect of art but as an everyday presence—seems to come equipped with its own escape hatch, its own assurance that involvement can be avoided. Those who communicate violence in its varied forms are eager to provide the means by which the receptor can reify it into a construct, something not messy and uncontrollable but regimented, with the workable outlines of fiction. A currently popular example is the phenomenon of "reality television," which in its seamier modes is like a Marxist's nightmare of capitalist decadence, or the bottoming-out of what Guy DeBord called "the society of the spectacle." Desperate for new and exciting diversions, millions gather around images of real-life violence edited and rechanneled as entertainment, images either caught in the flesh by video cameras or reenacted by those whom the violence befell, complete with stage blood and stage screams. "You'll think you're watching a disaster movie," one such show promises, hawking its enticing miseries, "but it's real."

As the violence of the world, the country, the city, and the street crowd closer, threatening to collapse whatever peaceful center one has tried to maintain, the more one is tempted to seek insulation wherever it can be found. There is a politics to all of this—or to be precise, a non-politics—and it cloaks itself in the absolving cleanliness of denial. Movies that offer the queasy pleasures of violence half-baked contribute just as much to the process of insulation as the remote control that shuts off the nightly news. Today's average violent movie doesn't ask suffering from those already inclined to stand aloof from it; it exacts none but monetary payment. Which brings me back to my childhood nightmare. The reclamation of that same empathy and receptivity is a project as old as human history, and when a film artist makes us cry over spilt blood it can start to seem like the project is worth it.

Vivian C. Sobchack

The Violent Dance:
A Personal Memoir
of Death in the Movies

Violence and death do not only sell movie tickets today; they also are the source of countless arguments, safely confined to paper, to panel discussions, to cocktail parties. What is all that technicolor blood doing to our youth? Are we a nation of voyeurs? Can the movies make us callous, unfeeling? Are the films innocent, merely presenting to us something which is already there? Is today's movie violence reflective of some phenomenon presently existent in our society (good, "honest," documentary revelation like *The French Connection*) or is it teaching us to regard blood and death with a blasé aplomb we would not otherwise acquire in our own insular lifetimes? Answers to these questions often boil down to whether one believes that cinema is reflective or affective, mimetic or cathartic. At any rate, issues such as these have been worried about and nosed over until one's response becomes, at best, gentle boredom and, at worst, calculated oversight.

Violence and death have always been with us in the darkness of the theater. They were there before I became a regular moviegoer in the late 1940s and will be there long after I have bloodlessly expired in bed or been juicily run down by an aggressive taxicab. They've always been there, as familiar as the smell of popcorn, and yet the violent deaths I remember from long ago—the deaths which have stuck to my ribs, so to speak—are rare. It certainly was not because I was shielded from the horrors of the screen. The first film I ever saw was *Bambi* and his mother's death before the forest fire was a movie experience I'll never

From *Journal of Popular Film* 3 (Winter 1974), pp. 2–14. Copyright © 1974 Heldref Publications. Reprinted with permission.
Afterword copyright © 1999 by Vivian Sobchack.

forget. Little sobs, including my own, rose in the audience; animated or not, the violence of that fire and the death of a mommy were real. Saturday and Sunday matinees followed—triple features plus ten cartoons—and the cinematic fare I grew up on consisted of little else but violence: Errol Flynn, Tyrone Power, Stewart Granger ran their enemies through and through, themselves suffered the rack, the Spanish Inquisition, and the slings and arrows of assorted outrageous fortunes; Joel McCrea, Randolph Scott, Audie Murphy said they hated guns but used them expertly, made their opponents dance to the graveyard or the scaffold in the name of decency and law and order; John Wayne and his battalions bombed, machine-gunned, and grenaded their way to Bataan and beyond, tearing themselves on barbed wire, dragging useless but precious left legs after them like so many sacks of mail from home.

Was it simply that as a child I had no intimations of my own mortality? Those deaths certainly never had the impact of the one in *Bambi*. (Perhaps I unconsciously believed that only mothers could die.) I watched those scenes of piracy and gunfighting and war with a great deal more forbearance than I gave to the gratuitous love scenes at which we all groaned in pubescent unison, but they didn't really touch me as did *Bambi* or the violent films I see today. Was it merely childish hubris that kept me essentially unmoved and only marginally fascinated by the deaths I saw in what were supposed to be fairly realistic movies? I think not. I feared and cowered before death in the horror films; I believed in Dracula and Frankenstein and Vincent Price. Death by fang, claw, and hot wax were very real to me while bullet holes and stab wounds never once caused my steps to quicken on my way home from the theater.

Perhaps the violent deaths I saw in those somewhat representational films were too realistic to move me to an awareness of my own fragile flesh. For one thing, they were often expertly concealed in a Breughel-like mise-en-scêne, similar to one of those puzzles we tried to solve on rainy days. There are twenty-three rabbits hidden in this picture. Find them! Death came swiftly, noisily, and in the midst of confusion—on the decks of pirate ships, in the circle of covered wagons, over the teeming battlefield. As in real life, no one told us precisely where to look and by the time we had found the locus of interest, a character or two had already neatly keeled over. The longshot, the panoramic view, kept death far from us and that was real. The bullet holes were too small to see well; the sword wounds were always on the side facing away from the camera. Sitting in the theatre, it was as realistically futile for us to crane our necks to see—really see—as it was when we passed an automobile accident in the car and my father refused to slow down in the name of good taste. In this sense those movies (and I'll include most of the domestic variety up through the mid-1960s) were indeed realistic. Real violence happened far away, neatly in the straight columns of a newspaper, safely confined in the geometric box of a television set.

As in the films I saw when I was growing up, real violence occurred quickly, giving neither the participants nor the spectators much time to abstract themselves from emotion, time to examine and explore and perhaps comprehend the internal mystery of the human body. Of course, in these films, we did have the drama of anticipating death, a drama usually not present in reality: the long ticking seconds before the shoot-out, the tense crawl over rough terrain. But death itself was quick, the camera didn't extend the last bleeding seconds of the antagonist's life nor did it linger on the carnage. Death was acknowledged in these films, but not inspected. Too few of us in the audience (our parents included) felt threatened enough by the presence of death and violence outside the theater to need the comfort of a microscopic inspection of it on the screen. Although it was talked about, violence was not yet an everyday occurrence, a civil occurrence; it was not yet a time when we feared not only the incomprehensibility of death but the incomprehensibility, the irrationality and senselessness of man as well. Death in the movies may have been quick, but it was dramatic, meaningful. Those who died did so for a reason. In those days, we didn't even think in terms of assassination (something that happened to Lincoln and livened our history books up a bit), or about junkies, madmen, snipers. We could be pretty certain (who even doubted it?) that the clean-cut kid next door was a clean-cut kid. Our relationship with violence and death in those Saturday movies was the same relationship we had with them in life. They happened to someone else and were mildly titillating, mildly disturbing.

Intimations of what was to come—given the right climate, the right circumstances and environment—were revealed in our youthful attitudes toward blood. In another sense, those movies were unrealistic; they didn't satisfy the very human curiosity that only children cared to voice in those safer times. They never told us what we wanted, albeit hesitantly, to know: the color and the texture of blood. All of us children, superficially satisfied with the realistic limitations of movie violence, worried over our cuts and picked our scabs and wondered at the rich red that coursed through our insides and occasionally came to the surface. Blood was something we were rarely given enough of on the screen—it oozed rather than spurted, it was most often black or a rusty Cine-color. Even in medium close-up (the man-to-man shoot-out or duel, the pink traceries of a whiplashing), I can't remember a single movie death which fired my imagination as much as the bright red blood from my own finger. Then as now, we humans attempted to hide from the frightening reality of our fragile innards by believing in the strength of plastic and supermarkets. Yet we were fascinated, as we have always been, by blood and tissue and bone. Snowden's secret (*Catch-22*) is everyone's secret. In the late 1940s, however, and in the 1950s and early 1960s it was a bit easier to keep that secret; everyone was comfortably mum.

Then, suddenly it seemed, in the mid-1960s, there was blood everywhere. We didn't have to go to war to find it—or stretch our necks to peer at it on the highway. Blood appeared in living color in more and more of our living rooms. And it was there all around us in the streets, is still there. Politicians became surprisingly more than caricatures; they became mortal. People who looked and lived exactly as we did shot at us from water towers, slit our throats, went berserk, committed murder next door. Even children died and supermarkets—meats neatly packaged and displayed to exorcise the taint of the slaughterhouse—were no longer havens of safety and sanity and civilization. No place, however ordinary, was safe; blood ran in busy streets, on university campuses, in broad daylight, everywhere. We were all threatened and terrified, all potential victims of our not so solid flesh and some unknown madman's whimsy.

Public figures splattered against our consciousness: John Kennedy, Martin Luther King Jr., Malcolm X, Robert Kennedy, Governor Wallace. Little men with strange other-worldly lights in their eyes took up arms against anonymity: Charles Whitman, Richard Speck, Richard Hickock, Perry Smith, Charles Manson. Students, police, and the National Guard fought it out on university campuses where the most burning issue when I went to college had been whether we had the right to wear Bermuda shorts to class. None of the blood spilt was picturesque or patriotic. Death by violence became a possibility for all of us because it lacked sense and meaning much of the time; there was no drama and catharsis. The blood in our lives had nothing of art or distance about it and we all felt personally threatened. Each one of us could die, each one of us could bleed, each one of us had to consciously acknowledge the secret which Snowden so shyly concealed in his flak suit—we all had pink and vulnerable guts.

One can hardly think that someone's careful calculations

somewhere in Hollywood read fear in all our faces and saw our hunger for the seeming security of knowledge, our yearning to find meaning in the senselessness of random violence. Films which had previously spoken to our unconscious desires and fears, like Topsy, "just growed." And in the fear-ridden 1960s and 1970s, it has been no different.

There always is, of course, a first film—the film which transcends its surface intentions and burns into us some unstated message with the intensity not of an arc lamp but of a laser. *Bonnie and Clyde,* released in 1967, was just such a film. Although it was not the first film to overtly bathe itself in blood, it was the first one to create an aesthetic, moral, and psychological furor. Uneven in tone yet brilliantly conceived, it fired our imaginations not merely because it was a good film, but because it was the first major film to allow us the luxury of inspecting what frightened us—the senseless, the unexpected, the bloody. And, most important, it kindly stylized death for us; it created nobility from senselessness, it choreographed a dance out of blood and death, it gave meaning and import to our mortal twitchings.

There has always been violence and death in the cinema. But the cinematic phenomenon in the films of our decade which is new and significant is the caressing of violence, the loving treatment of it by the camera. The most violent of deaths today is treated with the slow-motion lyricism of the old Clairol commercials in which two lovers glide to embrace each other. The once abrupt drop into nonbeing has become a balletic free fall. This, of course, is what has incensed those who fear for the nation's children and the nation's morality. Making death and violence "beautiful," they suggest, may seduce all of us into a cheerful acceptance of gore, may whet our aesthetic appetites for more and more artful and prolonged bloodletting, may even cause us to commit violence. After all, *The Wild Bunch* and their victims died so gracefully. Sonny's body was a poem in motion when he was machine-gunned to death in *The Godfather. A Clockwork Orange* kept our toes tapping to the tunes of rape and beatings. *The French Connection,* while certainly not musical, possessed a staccato tempo which was brutal and bloody.

I suppose that what bothers the moralists most is that these films are selling, are popular, are even critically acclaimed. The idea that we are a nation of voyeurs is indeed disturbing. Our Wednesday and Saturday night outings to see blood and gore while we eat buttered popcorn is disturbing. But then being human has always been disturbing. People are no more corrupt, no more voyeuristic than they were in the days of my childhood. But we are certainly more fearful. And it is this fear, rather than peeping Tom-ism, which has caused violence to almost literally blossom—like one of Disney's time-lapse flowers—on today's movie screens.

Fear has made even the most squeamish of us take our hands from our eyes. We still are afraid of violence and blood and death, but we are more afraid of the unknown—particularly when it threatens us personally and immediately. Even those of us who couldn't stand the sight of blood at one time find our desire to know and understand blood stronger than our desire not to see what frightens and sickens us. In a time when we seemed safe, not immediately threatened, we could ignore our fear and indulge our squeamishness. Today, this is hardly possible.

After many viewings of the film, I still cannot watch the scene in Dali and Bunuel's *Un Chien Andalou* in which a woman's eyeball is slit by a razor. I have read about it, heard about it, but I have not seen it. I cannot keep my eyes open; I have tried, but I physically and mentally cannot do it. The content of that scene is violent and bloody (although in black and white), and I am deeply afraid to watch it, to know it. On the other hand, I sat motionless and wide-eyed through *Straw Dogs*; my eyes refused to leave the screen for even a moment. I can remember my husband wanting to leave in the middle (he said his arm had fallen asleep and we had already watched *The French Connection*). I didn't want to go; I didn't want to miss anything. If that sounds voyeuristic, in essence it wasn't. I got no pleasure at all out of watching *Straw Dogs*. I felt extraordinarily tense, upset, sick. And yet I could not leave the theater until the film was over, even at the expense of a family argument. For some reason, it seemed to be a matter of life and death—mine—that I stay.

What is the difference between my responses to the two films? Both play upon hidden fear in the audience. Both have moments of extreme violence. Why should I be able to watch one, but not the other? The answer lies, I think, in the qualitative nature of the violence involved. I don't have the pressing need to see a woman's eyeball slit by a razor; seeing it will do nothing but disturb me. And this particular violent action—although terrifying with or without its Freudian implications—seems to have little to do with my life as I live it every day. I am not afraid of someone's slitting my eyeball while I passively submit. Watching that scene, in other words, is not going to instruct me; it is not going to reveal to me something that is terrible, but which I need to know. The nature of the violence in *Straw Dogs* is different. It may not be treated surrealistically, but it is not totally realistic either. (One

Vivian C. Sobchack

Figure 22. David Sumner (Dustin Hoffman) defends his home in the climax of Sam Peckinpah's treatise on violence, Straw Dogs.

remembers the little tailor in the fairy tale who wore a sash that proclaimed "Seven at One Blow.") Yet the violence in *Straw Dogs* touches contemporary nerves in a way that *Un Chien Andalou* doesn't. It involves the kind of violence that one fears now, today. Sickened, terrified, I *had* to watch the film. I had to learn and know what I fear and, however painful the experience was, for the moment I found a certain security in the fact that I had not backed away from instruction. In short, I was doing my homework—trying to learn how to survive. David in that movie was much like myself, the people around me. We all just wanted to mind our own business and yet found ourselves, our homes, our lives, threatened by people and things which plainly didn't make sense, weren't at all rational.

Popular films have always given us—the audience—what we want; otherwise they would not be popular. Today (just recently twenty-seven bodies were unearthed in Texas), we want to know blood and death. Although we retain little of the optimism which sprang from the Age of Reason, we still believe, even if it's half-heartedly and hopelessly, in knowledge, enlightenment. Knowledge is the magic which will save us; cataloguing will restore our crumbling sanity; inspection will cure our anxiety. Blood and tissue, death and killing, rape and beating don't please us, don't titillate us, can't be glibly compared to the centerfold of *Playboy*. Yet we have the clear and present need to know them, to have them made significant rather than senseless, to have them dramatized. Hence the slow motion, the lingering look at physical agony, the tongue-in-cheek treatment of brutality, the indecent amounts of blood. Our films are trying to make us feel secure about violence and death as much as it is possible; they are allowing us to purge our fear, to find safety in what appears to be knowledge of the unknown. To know violence is to be temporarily safe from the fear of it.

Of course, our belief in our sophistication, our comprehension of violence lasts about as long as it takes to walk from the theater to the subway or to the car—and sometimes not even that long. We quickly realize that the orgies of blood on the screen have told us nothing really *useful*. Our fear returns, and makes us return to the theatre to see more, hoping against hope that we will finally understand.

Our world has changed from the world of the 1940s, and 1950s, and early 1960s. And a world is changed by people. Yet the individual moviegoer today is not really much different than he was a decade ago. When I was a child, it was considered in bad taste to look at blood and talk about death. It wasn't "nice." Adults politely and tactfully avoided the issue because it was possible to avoid it; only we children, lacking manners, refused to hide our fascination with mortality. Today manners and niceness are too small a social device to cover up the fear and actuality of imminent violence.

At the drive-in, I can see my 3-and-a-half-year-old pajama-clad son become disturbed at the bloody and violent coming attractions, disturbed in a strange but very human way. He wants to know why and how. He stops eating his popcorn and wanting to drive the car. He leans forward from the back seat and carefully watches the screen. He becomes even more inquisitive than usual, running a high fever of fascination and questions. He is too young to be personally threatened by the particulars of the violence he sees (the death of Bambi's mommy would make him howl), but the blood on the screen seems to sing out to his blood. He may not know it, but he does have intimations of mortality. We, his parents, share his uneasiness, but don't tell him to hush. We don't tell him his curiosity is not nice. We sit there in the car, a contemporary family, united with all those other adults and children in their cars by a desire to know.

In the past we also wanted to know blood and violence but were afraid to ask, found it inconvenient, unnecessary for our day-to-day survival. Today, we are afraid not to ask. It seems our very lives depend upon the answers we get. The movies today merely reflect our search for meaning and significance—for order—in the essentially senseless. Drama can give us that meaning and order through form, through style. What frightens us in our daily lives is not only the possibility of personal violence, but the omnipresence of the chaos which surrounds contemporary violence, the fact that we may die for no other reason than that we were there to be killed.

The films today which stylize death and blood (and I can't think of many which don't) paradoxically reflect our fear of chaos but also create order. The senselessness and purposelessness, the randomness of real violence is certainly upheld in the content of current movies. In *The French Connection,* for example, a young mother walking her baby in the park is accidentally shot, commuters on a subway train find themselves the victims of something they cannot comprehend. Current films reflect our fear for our lives, our fear that no matter how uninvolved we may be, we are all potential victims of accident, that our deaths will horribly have no meaning at all. Yet the very presence of random and motiveless violence on the screen elevates it, creates some kind of order and meaning from it; accident becomes Fate. If we should get shot minding our own business, if we should be mowed down accidentally, at least we have seen it on the movie screen, have felt—along with a theatre full of people—for the hapless victim. And we also have realized that there was some reason even if the poor bystander who fell to the pavement didn't know it: the cop had to catch his crook. Even in films which are not lyrical in their presentation of violence and do not use the mannerisms of a Peckinpah, death—when it comes to Everyman—is given a nobility simply by its presence on the screen, its acknowledgment by the camera. These films reflect our fears, but also allay them.

All the current movies, then, which deal with violence say something important, if not particularly helpful. If we are to die for no apparent purpose, they seem to say, at least we will die with style, with recognition. We will create our own purpose and reason as we die; style will give our senseless death some sort of significance and meaning. The *form* of death in the movies today—the way the camera treats it—allows us to find some brief respite from our fears. The moment of death can be prolonged cinematically (through editing, slow motion, extreme close-ups, etc.) so that we are made to see form and order where none seems to exist in real life. The movement of the human body toward nonbeing is underlined, emphasized, dramatized and we all become Olympic participants of Olympian grace. We can also see ourselves on the fringes of the frame, falling by the wayside, but falling *in the movies.*

We may be horrified by the senselessness of violence and death, but we are also lulled and soothed by the possibility that there is—for all of us—a moment of truth, a moment of drama. We can believe, if only briefly, that even the most senseless and violent and horrible of deaths has at least a form, an internal order, and therefore a meaning. Those bloody and brutal films which appear on our theatre screens today perform, for us all, a kindness.

Afterword: The Postmorbid Condition

It is exceedingly strange to revisit something one has written twenty-five years ago. My son is now 29 and has his own car—and I no longer feel I have some desperate need or wish to see violence on the movie screen as I did when he was 3-and-a-half and the country had just begun to recognize explicitly that it was irreparably and irrevocably altered in the aftermath of "the sixties," Vietnam, and civil unrest. Perhaps this is because I'm a quarter of a century older and, facing my own fragile flesh and mortality, find violence on the screen so much "play-acting": that is, only a trivial figure of the larger annihilation that awaits each of us and looms larger on my existential horizon that it did when I was in my early 30s. Or, perhaps, I avoid violence in the movies because now, after various and intense experiences of physical pain, it affects me more strongly than it did before, writing itself on my body as it writes itself on the screen. Perhaps, however, my growing avoidance of screen violence (I would be dishonest if I called it "disinterest") also has much to do with changes in our culture's relationship to violence over the past quarter of a century and, correlatively and reciprocally, in the representation of violence in the movies themselves.

In the essay above, written so many years ago, I argued that screen violence in American films of the late 1960s and early 1970s was new and formally different from earlier "classical" Hollywood representations of violence. This new interest in violence and its new formal treatment not only literally satisfied an intensified cultural desire for "close-up" knowledge about the material fragility of bodies, but also—and more important—made increasingly senseless violence in the "civil" sphere sensible and meaningful by stylizing and aestheticizing it, thus bringing intelligibility and order to both the individual and social body's increasingly random and chaotic destruction. Indeed, I argued that random and senseless violence was elevated to meaning in these then "new" movies, its "transcendence" achieved not only by being up there on the screen, but also though long lingering gazes at carnage and ballets of slow motion that conferred on violence a benediction and the grace of a cinematic "caress."

Today, most American films have more interest in the presence
of violence than in its meaning. There are very few attempts to confer
order or perform a benediction upon the random and senseless death,
the body riddled with bullets, the laying waste of human flesh. (The
application of such order, benediction, and transcendental purpose is,
perhaps, one of the explicit achievements of Steven Spielberg's high-
tech but emotionally anachronistic *Saving Private Ryan*, and it is no
accident that its context is a morally intelligible World War II.) Indeed,
in today's films (and whatever happened started happening sometime
in the 1980s), there is no transcendence of "senseless" violence: it just
is. Thus, the camera no longer caresses it or transforms it into something with more significance than its given instance. Instead of caressing violence, the cinema has become increasingly *careless* about it:
either merely nonchalant or deeply lacking in care. Unlike medical
melodramas, those films that describe violent bodily destruction evoke
no tears in the face of mortality and evidence no concern for the fragility
of flesh. Samuel L. Jackson's violent role and religious monologues in
Quentin Tarantino's *Pulp Fiction* notwithstanding, we see no grace or
benediction attached to violence. Indeed, its very intensity seems
diminished: we need noise and constant stimulation and quantity to
make up for a lack of significant meaning.

Perhaps this change in attitude and treatment of violence is a
function of our increasingly *technologized* view of the body and flesh.
We see this view dramatized outside the theater in the practices and
fantasies of "maintenance" and "repair" represented by the "fitness
center" and cosmetic surgery. Inside the theater, we see it dramatized
in the "special effects" allowed by new technological developments and
in an increasingly hyperbolic and quantified treatment of violence and
bodily damage that is as much about "more" as it is about violence. It
seems to me that this quantitative move to "more" in relation to violence—more blood, more gore, more characters (they're really not people) blown up or blown away—began with the contemporary horror
film, with "slasher" and "splatter" films that hyperbolized violence
and its victims in terms of quantity rather than through exaggerations
of form. Furthermore, unlike in the "New Hollywood" films of the late
1960s and 1970s (here one thinks of Peckinpah or Penn), excessive violence in these "low" genre films, while eliciting screams also elicited
laughter, too much becoming, indeed, "too much": incredible, a "gross-
out," so "outrageous" and "over the top" that ironic reflexivity set in
(for both films and audiences) and the mounting gore and dead bodies

Figure 23. In Quentin Tarantino's Reservoir Dogs, *Mr. Orange (Tim Roth) spends the film bleeding out from a gunshot wound.*

became expected—and funny. (Here *Scream* and its sequel are recent examples.)

This heightened sense of reflexivity and irony that emerges from quantities of violence, from "more," is not necessarily progressive nor does it lead to a "moral" agenda or a critique of violence. (By virtue of its excesses and its emphasis on quantity and despite his intentions, Olive Stone's *Natural Born Killers* is quite ambiguous in this regard.) Indeed, in its present moment, this heightened reflexivity and irony merely leads to a heightened sense of representation: that is, care for the film as experience and text, perhaps, but a lack of any real concern for the bodies blown away (or up) upon the screen. In recent "splatter" films, in Tarantino films like *Reservoir Dogs* and *Pulp Fiction,* and in quite a number of action thrillers, bodies are more carelessly *squandered* than carefully stylized. Except, of course, insofar as excess, as hyperbole, itself constitutes stylization. Thus, most of the violence we see on the screen today suggests Grand Guignol rather than Jacobean tragedy. However, in our current cultural moment, tiredly described as "postmodern" but filled with new forms of violence like "road rage," the exaggeration and escalating quantification of violence and gore are a great deal less transgressive than they were—and a great deal more absurd. Thus, Tarantino has said on various occasions that he doesn't take violence "very seriously" and describes it as "funny" and "outrageous."

This hyperbolic escalation and quantification of violence also has become quite common to the action picture and thriller, where the body count only exceeds the number of explosions and neither matters very much to anyone: here violence and the laying waste of bodies seems more "naturalized": that is, it regularly functions to fill up screen space and time in lieu of narrative complexity, and to make the central character look good by "virtue" of his mere survival (see, for example, *Payback*). Again, there seems no moral agenda or critique of violence here—only wisecracks and devalution uttered out of the sides of a Bruce Willis-type mouth. Indeed, here is the careless violence and laconic commentary of comic books (where the panels crackle with zaps and bullets and explosions and the body count is all that counts).

On a more progressive note, I suppose it is possible to see this new excessive and careless treatment of violence on screen as a satiric form of what Russian literary theorist Mikhail Bakhtin has called "grotesque realism." That is, excessive representations of the body and its messier aspects might be read as containing critical and liberatory potential—this, not only because certain social taboos are broken, but also because these excessive representations of the grotesquerie of being embodied are less "allegorical" and fantastic than they are exaggerations of concrete conditions in the culture of which they are a part. In this regard, and particularly relevant to "indie" crime dramas and the action thriller (a good deal of it science-fictional), much has been written recently about the "crisis of the body" and a related "crisis of masculinity." Both of these crises are no longer of the *Bonnie and Clyde* or *Wild Bunch* variety: they are far too much inflected and informed by *technological* concerns and confusions and a new sense of the body as a technology, altered by technology, enabled by technology, and disabled by technology. Indeed, along with the Fordist assembly line and its increasing production of bodies consumed as they are violently "wasted" on the screen, comes the production of bodies as both technological *subjects* and *subjected to* technology: enhanced and extended, but also extinguished by Ouzis, bombs, whatever the latest in firepower. Thus, we might argue, the excessive violence we see on the screen, the carelessness and devaluation of mere human flesh, is both a recognition of the high-tech, powerful, and uncontrollable subjects we (men, mostly) have become through technology—and an expression of the increasing frustration and rage at what seems a lack of agency and effectiveness as we have become increasingly controlled by and subject to technology.

This new quantification of and carelessness toward violence on the screen also points to other aspects of our contemporary cultural context. We have come both a long way and not so far from the assassins, serial killers, and madmen who made their mass presence visibly felt in the late 1960s and early 1970s. They, like the bodies wasted on the screen, have proliferated at an increasingly faster and decreasingly surprising rate. They and the violence that accompanies them are now a common, omnipresent phenomenon of daily life—so much so that, to an unprecedented degree, we are resigned to living with them in what has become an increasingly uncivil society. "Senseless" and "random" violence pervades our lives and is barely remarkable or specific any longer—and while "road rage" and little children killed by the stray bullets of gang bangers do elicit a moral *frisson*, for the most part we live in and suspect the absence of a moral context in this decade of extreme relativism. Violence,

Figure 24. John Travolta and Samuel L. Jackson are buddies and professional killers in Pulp Fiction, *which takes a cartoonish approach to graphic violence, using a character's exploding head as the basis for an extended comic sketch.*

like "shit," happens—worth merely a bumper sticker nod that reconciles it with a general sense of helplessness (rather than despair).

No longer elevated through balletic treatment or narrative purpose, violence on the screen is sensed—indeed, appreciated—as senseless. But then so is life under the extremity of such technologized and uncivil conditions. Indeed, what has been called the "postmodern condition" might be more accurately thought of as the "postmortem condition." There's a kind of meta-sensibility at work here: life, death, and the movies are a "joke" or an "illusion" and everyone's in on it. Violence on the screen and in the culture is not related to a moral context, but to a proliferation of images, texts, and spectacle. And, given that we cannot contain or stop this careless proliferation, violence and death both on the street and in *Pulp Fiction* become reduced to the practical—and solvable—problem of cleanup.

Pain, too, drops out of the picture. The spasmodic twitching that ends *Bonnie and Clyde* has become truly lifeless. The bodies now subjected to violence are just "dummies": multiple surfaces devoid of subjectivity and gravity, "straw men," if you will. "Wasting" them doesn't mean much. Hence, the power (both appealing and off-putting) of those few films that remind us that bodily damage hurts, that violently wasting lives has grave consequences. Hence, the immense popularity of *Saving Private Ryan*, a movie in which the massive quantity of graphic physical damage and the violent "squandering" of bodies and lives is "redeemed" to social purpose and meaning, its senselessness made sensible by its (re)insertion in a clearly defined (and clearly past) moral context. Hence, also, the popular neglect of *Beloved* or *Affliction*, movies in which violence is represented "close up" as singularly felt: graphically linked to bodily pain and its destruction of subjectivity. In these films, violence is not dramatized quantitatively or technologically and thus becomes extremely difficult to watch: that is, even though an image, understood by one's own flesh as *real*.

I am not sure how to end this particular postmortem on my original essay. I still can't watch the eyeball being slit in *Un Chien Andalou*. But, as with *Straw Dogs* and *The French Connection*, I could and did watch all the violence in *Pulp Fiction*. Nonetheless, there's been a qualitative change as well as a quantitative one: while I watched those earlier violent films compulsively, with some real need to know what they showed me, I watch the excesses of the current ones casually, aware they won't show me anything real that I don't already know.

Carol J. Clover

Her Body, Himself:
Gender in the Slasher Film

On the high side of horror lie the classics: F. W. Murnau's *Nosferatu* (1922), *King Kong* (1933), *Dracula* (1931), *Frankenstein* (1931), and various works by Alfred Hitchcock, Carl Theodor Dreyer, and a few others—films that by virtue of age, literary ancestry, or fame of director have achieved reputability within the context of disreputability. Farther down the scale fall the productions of Brian De Palma, some of the glossier satanic films *(Rosemary's Baby* [1968], *The Omen* [1976], *The Exorcist* [1973]), certain science-fiction hybrids *(Alien* [1979], *Aliens* [1986], *Blade Runner* [1982]), some vampire and werewolf films *(Wolfen* [1981], *An American Werewolf in London* [1981]), and an assortment of other highly produced films, often with stars *(Whatever Happened to Baby Jane?* [1962], *The Shining* [1980]). At the very bottom, down in the cinematic underbrush, lies—horror of horrors—the slasher (or splatter or shocker) film: the immensely generative story of a psycho killer who slashes to death a string of mostly female victims, one by one, until he is himself subdued or killed, usually by the one girl who has survived.

Drenched in taboo and encroaching vigorously on the pornographic, the slasher film lies by and large beyond the purview of the respectable (middle-aged, middle-class) audience. It has also lain by and large beyond the purview of respectable criticism. Staples of drive-ins and exploitation houses, where they "rub shoulders with sex pictures and macho action flicks," these are films that are "never ever written up."[1] Books on horror film mostly concentrate on the classics, touch on the middle categories in passing, and either pass over the slasher in silence or bemoan it as a degenerate aberration.[2] The one full book on the category, William Schoell's *Stay Out of the Shower*, is immaculately unintelligent.[3] Film magazine articles on the genre rarely get past technique, special effects, and profits. The Sunday *San Francisco Examiner* relegates reviews of slashers to the syndicated "Joe Bob Briggs, Drive-In Movie Critic of Grapevine, Texas," whose lowbrow, campy tone ("We're talking two breasts, four quarts of blood, five dead bodies . . . Joe Bob says check it out") establishes what the paper and others like it deem the necessary distance between their readership and that sort of film.[4] There are of course the exceptional cases: critics or social observers who have seen at least some of these films and tried to come to grips with their ethics or aesthetics or both. Just how troubled is their task can be seen from its divergent results. For one critic, *The Texas Chainsaw Massacre* (1974) is "the *Gone with the Wind*, of meat movies."[5] For another it is a "vile little piece of sick crap . . . nothing but a hysterically paced, slapdash, imbecile concoction of cannibalism, voodoo, astrology, sundry hippieesque cults, and unrelenting sadistic violence as extreme and hideous as a complete lack of imagination can possibly make it."[6] Writes a third: "[Director Tobe] Hooper's cinematic intelligence becomes more apparent in every viewing, as one gets over the initial traumatizing impact and learns to respect the pervasive felicities of camera placement and movement."[7] The Museum of Modern Art bought the film in the same year that at least one country, Sweden, banned it.

Robin Wood's tack is less aesthetic than anthropological: "However one may shrink from systematic exposure to them [slasher films], however one may deplore the social phenomena and ideological mutations they reflect, their popularity . . . suggests that even if they were uniformly execrable they shouldn't be ignored."[8] We may go a step farther and suggest that the qualities that locate the slasher film outside the usual aesthetic system—that indeed render it, along with pornography and low horror in general, the film category "most likely to be betrayed by artistic treatment and lavish production values"[9]—are the very qualities that make it such a transparent source for (sub)cultural attitudes toward sex and gender in particular. Unmediated by otherworldly fantasy, cover plot, bestial transformations, or civilized routine, slasher films present us in startlingly direct terms with a world in which male and female are at desperate odds but in which, at the same time, masculinity and femininity are more states of mind than body. The premise of this essay, then, is that the slasher film, not despite but exactly because of its crudity and compulsive repetitiveness, gives us a clearer picture of current sexual attitudes, at least among the segment of the population that forms its erstwhile audience, than do the legitimate products of the better studios.

Before we turn to the generic particulars, however, let us review some of the critical and cinematic issues that attend the study of the sensation genres in general and horror in particular. We take as our point of departure not a slasher film but Brian de Palma's art-horror film *Body Double* (1984). The plot—a man witnesses and after much struggle solves the mysterious murder of a woman with whom he has become voyeuristically involved—concerns us less than the three career levels through which the hero, an actor named Jake, first ascends and then descends. He aspires initially to legitimate roles (Shakespeare), but it becomes clear during the course of a method-acting class that his range of emotional expression is impaired by an unresolved childhood fear. For the moment he has taken a job as vampire in a "low-budget, independent horror film," but even that job is threatened when, during a scene in which he is to be closed in a coffin and buried, he suffers an attack of claustrophobia and must leave the set. A plot twist leads him to the underworld of pornography, where he takes on yet another role, this time in a skin flick. Here, in the realm of the flesh with a queen of porn, the sexual roots of Jake's paralysis—fear of the (female) cavern—are exposed and finally resolved. A new man, he returns to *A Vampire's Kiss* to master the burial scene, and we are to understand that Shakespeare is the next stop.

The three cinematic categories are thus ranked by degree of sublimation. On the civilized side of the continuum lie the legitimate genres; at the other end, hard on the unconscious, lie the sensation or "body" genres, horror and pornography, in that order. For De Palma, the violence of horror reduces to and enacts archaic sexual feelings. Beneath Jake's emotional paralysis (which emerges in the "high" genre) lies a death anxiety (which is exposed in the burying-alive of horror), and beneath *that* anxiety lies a primitive sexual response (which emerges, and is resolved, in pornography). The layers of Jake's experience accord strikingly, and perhaps not coincidentally, with Freud's archaeology of "uncanny" feelings. "To some people," Freud wrote, "the idea of being buried alive by mistake is the most uncanny thing of all. And yet psychoanalysis has taught us that this terrifying phantasy is only a transformation of another phantasy which originally had nothing terrifying about it at all, but was qualified by a certain lasciviousness—the phantasy, I mean," of intrauterine existence [*der Phantasie vom Leben im Mutterleib*]."[10] Pornography thus engages directly (in pleasurable terms) what horror explores at one remove (in painful terms) and legitimate film at two or more. Beneath the "legitimate" plot of *The Graduate* (1967), in which Ben must give up his relationship with a friend's mother in order to marry and take his proper social place, lies the plot of *Psycho* (1960), in which Norman's unnatural attachment to his own mother drives him to murder women to whom he is attracted; and beneath *that* plot lies the plot of the porn film *Taboo* (1980), in which the son simply has sex with his mother ("Mom, am I better than Dad?"). Pornography, in short, has to do with sex (the act) and horror with gender.

It is a rare Hollywood film that does not devote a passage or two—a car chase, a sex scene—to the emotional/physical excitement of the audience. But horror and pornography are the only two genres specifically devoted to the arousal of bodily sensation. They exist solely to horrify and stimulate, not always respectively, and their ability to do so is the sole measure of their success: they "prove themselves upon our pulses."[11] Thus in horror-film circles, "good" means scary, specifically in a bodily way (ads promise shivers, chills, shudders, tingling of the spine; Lloyds of London insured audiences of *Macabre* [1958] against death by fright);[12] and *Hustler's Erotic Film Guide* ranks pornographic films according to the degree of erection they produce (one film is ranked a "pecker popper," another "limp"). The target is in both cases

Figure 25. *Joe Spinell plays a serial killer in* Maniac, *which devotes lingering and graphic attention to the savagery he inflicts on his victims. The special effects makeup by Tom Savini details gunshot wounds to the head, garrotings, and scalping. No manner of death was now off-limits for the commercial cinema.*

the body, our witnessing body. But *what* we witness is also the body, another's body, in experience: the body in sex and the body in threat. The terms *flesh film* (*skin flicks*) and *meat movies* are remarkably apt.

Cinema, it is claimed, owes its particular success in the sensation genres (witness the early and swift rise of vampire films) to its unprecedented ability to manipulate point of view. What written narrative must announce, film can accomplish silently and instantaneously through cutting. Within the space of seconds, the vampire's first-person perspective is displaced by third-person or documentary observation. To these simple shifts can be added the variables of distance (from the panorama of the battlefield to the close-up of an eyeball), angle, frame tilt, lighting effects, unsteadiness of image, and so on—again, all subject to sudden and unannounced manipulation.[13] *Friday the 13th* (1980) locates the I-camera with the killer in pursuit of a victim; the camera is hand-held, producing a jerky image, and the frame includes in-and-out-of-focus foreground objects (trees, bushes, window frames) behind which the killer (I-camera), is lurking—all accompanied by the sound of heartbeats and heavy breathing. "The camera moves in on the screaming, pleading victim, 'looks down' at the knife, and then plunges it into the chest, ear, or eyeball. Now that's sick."[14]

Lagging behind practice is a theoretical understanding of effect. The processes by which a certain image (but not another) filmed in a certain way (but not another) causes one person's (but not another's) pulse to race finally remains a mystery—not only to critics and theorists but even, to judge from interviews and the trial-and-error (and baldly imitative) quality of the films themselves, by the people who make the product. The process of suture is sensed to be centrally important in effecting audience identification, though just how and why is unclear.[15] Nor is identification the straightforward notion some critics take it to be.[16] Where commentators by and large agree is in the importance of the "play of pronoun function."[17] If the fantastic depends for its effect on an uncertainty of vision, a profusion of perspectives, and a confusion of subjective and objective, then cinema is preeminently suited to the fantastic. Indeed, to the extent that film can present "unreal" combinations of objects and events as "real" through the camera eye, the "cinematic process itself might be called fantastic."[18] The "cinefantastic" in any case succeeds, far more efficiently and effectively and on a far greater scale than its ancestral media, in the production of sensation.

The fact that the cinematic conventions of horror are so easily and so often parodied would seem to suggest that, individual variation notwithstanding, its basic structures of apperception are fixed and fundamental. The same is true of the stories they tell. Students of folklore or early literature recognize in the slasher film the hallmarks of oral story: the free exchange of themes and motifs, the archetypal characters and situations, the accumulation of sequels, remakes, imitations. This is a field in which there is in some sense no original, no real or right text, but only variants; a world in which, therefore, the meaning of the individual example lies outside itself. The "art" of the horror film, like the "art" of pornography, is to a very large extent the art of rendition, and it is understood as such by the competent audience.[19] A particular example may have original features, but its quality as a horror film lies in the ways it delivers the cliché. James B. Twitchell rightly recommends an "ethnological approach, in which the various stories are analyzed as if no one individual telling really mattered. . . . You search for what is stable and repeated; you neglect what is 'artistic' and 'original.' This is why, for me, auteur criticism is quite beside the point in explaining horror. . . . The critic's first job in explaining the fascination of horror is not to fix the images at their every appearance but, instead, to trace their migrations to the audience and, only then, try to understand why they have been crucial enough to pass along."[20] That auteur criticism is at least partly beside the point is clear from interviews with such figures as John Carpenter (*Halloween* [1978], *The Fog* [1980])—interviews that would seem to suggest that, like the purveyors of folklore, the makers of film operate more on instinct and formula than conscious understanding. So bewildered was Hitchcock by the unprecedented success of *Psycho* that he approached the Stanford Research Institute about doing a study of the phenomenon.[21]

What makes horror "crucial enough to pass along" is, for critics since Freud, what has made ghost stories and fairy tales crucial enough to pass along: its engagement of repressed fears and desires and its reenactment of the residual conflict surrounding those feelings. Horror films thus respond to interpretation, as Robin Wood puts it, as "at once the personal dreams of their makers and the collective dreams of their audiences—the fusion made possible by the shared structures of a common ideology."[22] And just as attacker and attacked are expressions of the same self in nightmares, so they are expressions of the same viewer in horror film. Our primary and acknowledged identification may be with the victim, the adumbration of our infantile fears and desires, our memory sense of ourselves as tiny and vulnerable in the face of the enormous Other; but the Other is also finally another part of ourselves, the projection of our repressed infantile rage and desire (our blind drive to annihilate those toward whom we feel anger, to force satisfaction from those who stimulate us, to wrench food for ourselves if only by actually devouring those who feed us) that we have had in the name of civilization to repudiate. We are both Red Riding Hood *and* the Wolf; the force of the experience, the horror, comes from "knowing" both sides of the story—from giving ourselves over to the cinematic play of pronoun functions. It is no surprise that the first film to which viewers were not admitted once the theater darkened was *Psycho*. Whether Hitchcock actually meant with this measure to intensify the "sleep" experience is unclear, but the effect both in the short run, in establishing *Psycho* as the ultimate thriller, and in the long run, in altering the cinema-going habits of the nation, is indisputable. In the current understanding, horror is the least interruptable of all film genres. That uninterruptability itself bears witness to the compulsive nature of the stories it tells.

Whatever else it may be, the slasher film is clearly "crucial enough to pass along." Profits and sequels tell much of the story. *Halloween* cost $320,000 to make and within six years had grossed over $75 million; even a highly produced film like *The Shining* has repaid itself tenfold.[23] *The Hills Have Eyes* (1977), *The Texas Chainsaw Massacre*, and *Alien* (a science-fiction/slasher hybrid) are [as of 1987] at Part Two. *Psycho* and *A Nightmare on Elm Street* are at Part Three. *Halloween* is at Part Four, and *Friday the 13th* is at Part Six. These are better taken as remakes than sequels; although the subsequent part purports to take up where the earlier part left off, it in most cases simply duplicates with only slight variation the plot and circumstances—the formula—of its predecessor. Nor do different titles indicate different plots; *Friday the 13th* is set at summer camp and *Halloween* in town, but the story is much the same, compulsively repeated in those ten films and in dozens like them under different names. The audience for that story is by all accounts largely young and largely male—most conspicuously groups of boys who cheer the killer on as he assaults the victims, then reverse their sympathies to cheer the survivor on as she assaults the killer.[24] Our question, then, has to do with that particular audience's stake in that particular nightmare, with what in the story is "crucial" enough to warrant the price of admission and what the implications are for the current discussion of women and film.

Carol J. Clover

The Slasher Film

The immediate ancestor of the slasher film is Hitchcock's *Psycho* (1960). Its elements are familiar: the killer is the psychotic product of a sick family but still recognizably human; the victim is a beautiful, sexually active woman; the location is not-home, at a Terrible Place; the weapon is something other than a gun; the attack is registered from the victim's point of view and comes with shocking suddenness. None of these features is original, but the unprecedented success of Hitchcock's particular formulation, above all the sexualization of both motive and action, prompted a flood of imitations and variations. In 1974, a film emerged that revised the *Psycho* template to a degree and in such a way as to mark a new phase: *The Texas Chainsaw Massacre*, directed by Tobe Hooper. Together with *Halloween*, it engendered a new spate of variations and imitations.

The plot of *The Texas Chainsaw Massacre* is simple enough: five young people are driving through Texas in a van; they stop off at an abandoned house and are murdered one by one by the psychotic sons of a degenerate local family; the sole survivor is a woman. The horror, of course, lies in the elaboration. Early in the film the group picks up a hitchhiker, but when he starts a fire and slashes Franklin's arm (having already slit open his own hand), they kick him out. The abandoned house they subsequently visit, once the home of Sally's and Franklin's

Figure 26. Suddenly looming into view, Leatherface claims his first victim in The Texas Chainsaw Massacre.

grandparents, turns out to be right next door to the house of the hitch-hiker and his family: his brother Leatherface; their father; an aged and only marginally alive grandfather; and their dead grandmother and her dog, whose mummified corpses are ceremonially included in the family gatherings. Three generations of slaughterhouse workers, once proud of their craft but now displaced by machines, have taken up killing and cannibalism as a way of life. Their house is grotesquely decorated with human and animal remains—bones, feathers, hair, skins. The young people drift apart in their exploration of the abandoned house and grounds and are picked off one by one by Leatherface and Hitchhiker. Last is Sally. The others are attacked and killed with dispatch, but Sally must fight for her life, enduring all manner of horrors through the night. At dawn she manages to escape to the highway, where she is picked up by a passing trucker.

Likewise, the nutshell plot of *Halloween:* a psychotic killer (Michael) stalks a small town on Halloween and kills a string of teenage friends, one by one; only Laurie survives. The twist here is that Michael has escaped from the asylum in which he has been incarcerated since the age of 6, when he killed his sister minutes after she and her boyfriend parted following an illicit interlude in her parents' bed. That murder, in flashback, opens the film. It is related entirely in the killer's first person (I-camera) and only after the fact is the identity of the perpetrator revealed. Fifteen years later, Michael escapes his prison and returns to kill Laurie, whom he construes as another version of his sister (a sequel clarifies that she is in fact his *younger* sister, adopted by another family at the time of the earlier tragedy). But before Michael gets to Laurie, he picks off her high school friends: Annie, in a car on her way to her boyfriend's; Bob, going to the kitchen for a beer after sex with Lynda; Lynda, talking on the phone with Laurie and waiting for Bob to come back with the beer. At last only Laurie remains. When she hears Lynda squeal and then go silent on the phone, she leaves her own babysitting house to go to Lynda's. Here she discovers the three bodies and flees, the killer in pursuit. The remainder of the film is devoted to the back-and-forth struggle between Laurie and Michael. Again and again he bears down on her, and again and again she either eludes him (by running, hiding, breaking through windows to escape, locking herself in) or strikes back (once with a knitting needle, once with a hanger). In the end, Dr. Loomis (Michael's psychiatrist in the asylum) rushes in and shoots the killer (although not so fatally as to prevent his return in the sequels).

Before we turn to an inventory of generic components, let us add a third, more recent example: *The Texas Chainsaw Massacre, Part 2* (1986). The slaughterhouse family (now named the Sawyers) is the same, although older and, owing to their unprecedented success in the sausage business, richer.[25] When Mr. Sawyer begins to suspect from her broadcasts that a disk jockey named Stretch knows more than she should about one of their recent crimes, he dispatches his sons Leatherface and Chop Top (Hitchhiker in the earlier film) to the radio station late at night. There they seize the technician and corner Stretch. At the crucial moment, however, power fails Leatherface's chainsaw. As Stretch cowers before him, he presses the now still blade up along her thigh and against her crotch, where he holds it unsteadily as he jerks and shudders in what we understand to be orgasm. After that the sons leave. The intrepid Stretch, later joined by a Texas Ranger (Dennis Hopper), tracks them to their underground lair outside town. Tumbling down the Texas equivalent of a rabbit hole, Stretch finds herself in the subterranean chambers of the Sawyer operation. Here, amid all the slaughterhouse paraphernalia, the Sawyers live and work. The walls drip with blood. Like the decrepit mansion of the first film, the residential parts of the establishment are quaintly decorated with human and animal remains. After a long ordeal at the hands of the Sawyers, Stretch manages to scramble up through a culvert and beyond that up onto a nearby pinnacle, where she finds a chainsaw and wards off her final assailant. The Texas Ranger evidently perishes in a grenade explosion underground, leaving Stretch the sole survivor.

The spiritual debt of all the post-1974 slasher films to *Psycho* is clear, and it is a rare example that does not pay a visual tribute, however brief, to the ancestor—if not in a shower stabbing, then in a purling drain or the shadow of a knife-wielding hand. No less clear, however, is the fact that the post-1974 examples have, in the usual way of folklore, contemporized not only Hitchcock's terms but also, over time, their own. We have, in short, a cinematic formula with a twenty-six-year history, of which the first phase, from 1960 to 1974, is dominated by a film clearly rooted in the sensibility of the 1950s, while the second phase, bracketed by the two *Texas Chainsaw* films of 1974 and 1986, responds to the values of the late 1960s and early 1970s. That the formula in its most recent guise may be in decline is suggested by the campy, self-parodying quality of *The Texas Chainsaw Massacre, Part 2*, as well as the emergence, in legitimate theater, of the slasher satire *Buckets of Blood* (1991). Between 1974 and 1986, however, the formula evolved and flourished in ways of some interest to observers of popular culture, above all those concerned with the representation of women in film. To apprehend in specific terms the nature of that mutation, let us, with *Psycho* as the benchmark, survey the genre by component category: killer, locale, weapons, victims, and shock effects.

Killer

The psychiatrist at the end of *Psycho* explains what we had already guessed from the action: that Norman Bates had introjected his mother, in life a "clinging, demanding woman," so completely that she constituted his other, controlling self. Not Norman but "the mother half of his mind" killed Marion—had to kill Marion—when he (the Norman half) found himself aroused by her. The notion of a killer propelled by psychosexual fury, more particularly a male in gender distress, has proved a durable one, and the progeny of Norman Bates stalk the genre up to the present day. Just as Norman wears his mother's clothes during his acts of violence and is thought, by the screen characters and also, for a while, by the film's spectators to be his mother, so the murderer in the *Psycho* imitation *Dressed to Kill* (1980), a transvestite psychiatrist, seems until his unveiling to be a woman; like Norman, he must kill women who arouse him sexually. Likewise, in muted form, Hitchhiker/Chop Top and Leatherface in the *Texas Chainsaw* films: neither brother shows overt signs of gender confusion, but their cathexis to the sick family—in which the mother is conspicuously absent but the preserved corpse of the grandmother (answering the treated body of Mrs. Bates in *Psycho*) is conspicuously present—has palpably arrested their development. Both are in their 20s (30s, in the later film), but Hitchhiker/Chop Top seems a gangly kid and Leatherface jiggles in baby fat behind his butcher's apron. Like Norman Bates, whose bedroom displays his childhood toys, Hitchhiker/Chop Top and Leatherface are permanently locked in childhood. Only when Leatherface "discovers" sex in *The Texas Chainsaw Massacre, Part 2* does he lose his appetite for murder. In *Motel Hell* (1980), a send-up of modern horror with special reference to *Psycho* and *The Texas Chainsaw Massacre*, we are repeatedly confronted with a portrait of the dead mother, silently presiding over all manner of cannibalistic and incestuous doings on the part of her adult children.

No less in the grip of boyhood is the killer in *The Eyes of Laura Mars* (1978). The son of a hooker, a hysterical woman gone for days at a time, the killer has up to now put his boyish anger to good use in police work—the film makes much of the irony—but the sight of Laura's violent photographs causes it to be unleashed in full force. The killer in *Hell Night* (1981) is the sole member of his family to survive, as a child, a murderous rampage on the part of his father; the experience condemned him to an afterlife as a murderer himself. In *Halloween* the killer *is* a child, at least in the first instance: Michael, at the age of 6, is so enraged at his sister (evidently for her sexual relations with her boyfriend) that he stabs her to death with a kitchen knife. The remainder of the film details his return rampage at the age of 21, and Dr. Loomis, who has overseen the case in the interim, explains that although Michael's body has attained maturity, his mind remains frozen in infantile fury. In *It's Alive* (1974), the killer is literally an infant, evidently made monstrous through intrauterine apprehension of its parents' ambivalence (early in the pregnancy they considered an abortion).

Even killers whose childhood is not immediately at issue and who display no overt gender confusion are often sexually disturbed. The murderer in *A Nightmare on Elm Street* is an undead child molester. The killer in *Slumber Party Massacre* (1982) says to a young woman he is about to assault with a power drill: "Pretty. All of you are very pretty. I love you. Takes a lot of love for a person to do this. You know you want it. You want it. Yes." When she grasps the psychodynamics of the situation in the infamous crotch episode *of Texas Chainsaw, Part 2*, Stretch tries a desperate gambit: "You're really good, you really are good," she repeats; indeed, immediately after ejaculation Leatherface becomes palpably less interested in his saw. The parodic *Motel Hell* spells it out. "His pecker don't work; you see when he takes off his overalls—it's like a shriveled prune," Bruce says of his killer-brother Vincent when he learns of Terry's plans to marry him. Terry never does see, for on her wedding night he attempts (needless to say) not sex but murder. Actual rape is practically nonexistent in the slasher film, evidently on the premise— as the crotch episode suggests—that violence and sex are not concomitants but alternatives, the one as much a substitute for and a prelude to the other as the teenage horror film is a substitute for and a prelude to the "adult" film (or the meat movie a substitute for and prelude to the skin flick).[26] When Sally under torture (*The Texas Chainsaw Massacre*) cries out, "I'll do anything you want," clearly with sexual intention, her assailants respond only by mimicking her in gross terms; she has profoundly misunderstood the psychology.

Female killers are few and their reasons for killing significantly different from men's. With the possible exception of the murderous mother in *Friday the 13th*, they show no gender confusion. Nor is their motive overtly psychosexual; their anger derives in most cases not from childhood experience but from specific moments in their adult lives in which they have been abandoned or cheated on by men (*Strait-jacket* [1964], *Play Misty for Me* [1971], *Attack of the 50-Foot Woman* [1958]). (Films like *Mother's Day* [1980], *Ms. 45* [1980], and *I Spit on Your Grave* [1978] belong to the rape-revenge category.) *Friday the 13th* is something of an anomaly. The killer is revealed as a middle-aged woman whose son, Jason, drowned years earlier as a consequence of negligence on the part of the camp counselors. The anomaly is not sustained in the sequels (Parts Two to Six), however. Here the killer is Jason himself, not dead after all but living in a forest hut. The pattern is a familiar one; his motive is vengeance for the death of his mother, his excessive attachment toward whom is manifested in his enshrining of her severed head. Like Stretch in the crotch episode of *Texas Chainsaw, Part 2*, the girl who does final combat with Jason in *Friday the 13th Part 2* (1981) sees the shrine, grasps its significance (she's a psych major), and saves herself by repeating in a commanding tone, "I am your mother, Jason; put down the knife." Jason, for his part, begins to see his mother in the girl (I-camera) and obeys her.

In films of the *Psycho* type (*Dressed to Kill, The Eyes of Laura Mars*), the killer is an insider, a man who functions normally in the action until, at the end, his other self is revealed. *The Texas Chainsaw Massacre* and *Halloween* introduced another sort of killer: one whose only role is that of killer and one whose identity as such is clear from the outset. Norman may have a normal half, but these killers have none. They are emphatic misfits and emphatic outsiders. Michael is an escapee from a distant asylum; Jason subsists in the forest; the Sawyer sons live a bloody subterranean existence outside town. Nor are they clearly seen. We catch sight of them only in glimpses—few and far between in the beginning, more frequent toward the end. They are usually large, sometimes overweight, and often masked. In short, they may be recognizably human, but only marginally so, just as they are only marginally visible—to their victims and to us, the spectators. In one key aspect, however, the killers are superhuman: their virtual indestructibility. Just as Michael (in *Halloween*) repeatedly rises from blows that would stop a lesser man, so Jason (in the *Friday the 13th* films) survives assault after assault to return in sequel after sequel. Chop Top in

Texas Chainsaw, Part 2, is so called because of a metal plate implanted in his skull in repair of a head wound sustained in the truck accident in the earlier film. It is worth noting that the killers are normally the fixed elements and the victims the changeable ones in any given series.

Terrible Place

The Terrible Place, most often a house or tunnel in which the victims sooner or later find themselves, is a venerable element of horror. The Bates mansion is just one in a long list of such places—a list that continues, in the modern slasher, with the decaying mansion of *The Texas Chainsaw Massacre,* the abandoned and haunted mansion of *Hell Night,* the house for sale but unsellable in *Halloween* (also a point of departure for such films as *Rosemary's Baby* and *The Amityville Horror* [1979]), and so on. What makes these houses terrible is not just their Victorian decrepitude but the terrible families—murderous, incestuous, cannibalistic—that occupy them. So the Bates mansion enfolds the history of a mother and son locked in a sick attachment, and so the mansion/labyrinth of the *Texas Chainsaw* movies shelters a lawless brood presided over by the decaying corpse of the grandmother. Jason's forest hut (in the *Friday the 13th* sequels) is no mansion, but it houses another mummified mother (or at least her head), with all the usual candles and dreadful paraphernalia. The terrors of the *Hell Night* mansion stem, we learn, from an early owner's massacre of his children. Into such houses unwitting victims wander in film after film, and it is the conventional task of the genre to register in close detail those victims' dawning understanding, as they survey the visible evidence, of the human crimes and perversions that have transpired there. That perception leads directly to the perception of their own immediate peril.

In *The Texas Chainsaw Massacre, Part 2,* house and tunnel elide in a residential labyrinth underground, connected to the world above by channels and culverts. The family is intact, indeed it thrives, but for reasons evidently having to do with the nature of their sausage business has moved residence and slaughterhouse underground. For Stretch, trying desperately to find a way out, it is a ghastly place: dark, full of blind alleys, walls wet with blood. Likewise the second basement of the haunted mansion in *Hell Night:* strewn with decaying bodies and skeletons, lighted with masses of candles. Other tunnels are less familial: the one in *Body Double* that prompts Jack's claustrophobic faint, and the horror-house tunnel in *He Knows You're Alone* (1980) in which the killer lurks. The morgue episode in the latter film, certain of the hospital scenes in *Halloween II* (1981), and the bottom-cellar scenes from various films may be counted as Terrible Tunnels: dark, labyrinthine, exitless, usually underground and palpably damp, and laced with heating ducts and plumbing pipes. In *Hell Night*, as in *Texas Chainsaw, Part 2*, Terrible House (the abandoned mansion) and Terrible Tunnel (the second basement) elide.

The house or tunnel may at first seem a safe haven, but the same walls that promise to keep the killer out quickly become, once the killer penetrates them, the walls that hold the victim in. A phenomenally popular moment in post-1974 slashers is the scene in which the victim locks herself in (a house, room, closet, car) and waits with pounding heart as the killer slashes, hacks, or drills his way in. The action is inevitably seen from the victim's point of view; we stare at the door (wall, car roof) and watch the surface break with first the tip and then the shaft of the weapon. In Hitchcock's *The Birds* (1963), it is the birds' beaks we see penetrating the door. The penetration scene is commonly the film's pivot moment; if the victim has up to now simply fled, she has at this point no choice but to fight back.

Weapons

In the hands of the killer, at least, guns have no place in slasher films. Victims sometimes avail themselves of firearms, but like telephones, fire alarms, elevators, doorbells, and car engines, guns fail in the squeeze. In some basic sense, the emotional terrain of the slasher film is pretechnological. The preferred weapons of the killer are knives, hammers, axes, ice picks, hypodermic needles, red-hot pokers, pitchforks, and the like. Such implements serve well a plot predicated on stealth, the unawareness of later victims that the bodies of their friends are accumulating just yards away. But the use of noisy chainsaws and power drills and the nonuse of such relatively silent means as bow and arrow, spear, catapult, and even swords would seem to suggest that closeness and tactility are also at issue.[27] The sense is clearer if we include marginal examples like *Jaws* (1975) and *The Birds*, as well as related werewolf and vampire genres. Knives and needles, like teeth, beaks, fangs, and claws, are personal, extensions of the body that bring attacker and attacked into animalistic embrace.[28] In *I Spit on Your Grave*, the heroine forces a rapist at gunpoint to drop his pants, evidently meaning to shoot him in genitals. But she changes her mind, invites him home for what he all too readily supposes will be a voluntary follow-up of the earlier gang rape. Then, as they sit together in a bubble bath, she castrates him with a knife. If we wondered why she threw away the pistol, now we know: all phallic symbols are not equal, and a hands-on knifing answers a hands-on rape in a way that a shooting, even a shooting preceded by a humiliation, does not.[29]

Beyond that, the slasher evinces a fascination with flesh or meat itself as that which is hidden from view. When the hitchhiker in *The Texas Chainsaw Massacre* slits open his hand for the thrill, the onlookers recoil in horror-all but Franklin, who seems fascinated by the realization that all that lies between the visible, knowable outside of the body and its secret insides is one thin membrane, protected only by a collective taboo against its violation. It is no surprise that the rise of the slasher film is concomitant with the development of special effects that let us see with our own eyes the "opened" body.

Victims

Where once there was one victim, Marion Crane, there are now many: five in *The Texas Chainsaw Massacre*, four in *Halloween*, fourteen in *Friday the 13th Part III* (1982), and so on. (As Schoell puts it, "Other filmmakers figured that the only thing better than one beautiful woman being gruesomely murdered was a whole series of beautiful women being gruesomely murdered.")[30] Where once the victim was an adult, now she is typically in her teens (hence the term *teenie-kill pic*). Where once she was female, now she is both girl and boy, although most often and most conspicuously girl. For all this, her essential quality remains the same. Marion is first and foremost a sexual transgressor. The first scenes show her in a hotel room dressing at the end of a lunch hour, asking her lover to marry her. It is, of course, her wish to be made an honest woman that leads her to abscond with $40,000, an act that leads her to the Bates motel in Fairvale. Here, just as we watched her dress in the opening sequences, we now watch her undress. Moments later, nude in the shower, she dies. A classic publicity poster for *Psycho* shows Janet Leigh with a slightly uncomprehending look on her face sitting on the bed, dressed in a bra and half-slip, looking backward in such a way as to outline her breasts. If it is the task of promotional materials to state in one image the essence of a film, those breasts are what *Psycho* is all about.

In the slasher film, sexual transgressors of both sexes are scheduled for early destruction. The genre is studded with couples trying to find a place beyond purview of parents and employers where they can have sex, and immediately afterward (or during) being killed. The theme enters the tradition with the Lynda–Bob subplot of *Halloween*. Finding themselves alone in a neighborhood house, Lynda and Bob make hasty use of the master bedroom. Afterward, Bob goes downstairs for a beer. In the kitchen he is silently dispatched by the killer, Michael, who then covers himself with a sheet (it's Halloween), dons Bob's glasses, and goes upstairs. Supposing the bespectacled ghost in the doorway to be Bob, Lynda jokes, bares her breasts provocatively, and finally, in irritation at "Bob's" stony silence, dials Laurie on the phone. Now the killer advances, strangling her with the telephone cord, so that what Laurie hears on the other end are squeals she takes to be orgasmic. *Halloween II* takes the scene a step farther. Here the victims are a nurse and orderly who have sneaked off for sex in the hospital therapy pool. The watching killer, Michael again, turns up the thermostat and, when the orderly goes to check it, kills him. Michael then approaches the nurse from behind (she thinks it's the orderly) and strokes her neck. Only when he moves his hand toward her bare breast and she turns around and sees him does he kill her.

Other directors are less fond than John Carpenter of the mistaken-identity twist. Denise, the English vamp in *Hell Night*, is simply stabbed to death in bed during Seth's postcoital trip to the bathroom. In *He Knows You're Alone*, the student having the affair with her professor is stabbed to death in bed while the professor is downstairs changing a fuse; the professor himself is stabbed when he returns and discovers the body. The postcoital death scene is a staple of the *Friday the 13th* series. Part Three offers a particularly horrible variant. Invigorated by sex, the boy is struck by a gymnastic impulse and begins walking on his hands; the killer slices down on his crotch with a machete. Unaware of the fate of her boyfriend, the girl crawls into a hammock after her shower; the killer impales her from below.[31] Brian De Palma's *Dressed to Kill* presents the infamous example of the sexually desperate wife, first seen masturbating in her morning shower during the credit sequence, who lets herself be picked up later that day in a museum by a man with whom she has sex first in a taxi and later in his apartment. On leaving his place in the evening, she is suddenly attacked and killed in the elevator. The cause-and-effect relationship between (illicit) sex and death could hardly be more clearly drawn. *All* of the killings in *Cruising* (1980) occur during (homo)sexual encounters; the difference here is that the killer is one of the participants, not a third party.

Killing those who seek or engage in unauthorized sex amounts to a generic imperative of the slasher film. It is an imperative that crosses gender lines, affecting males as well as females. The numbers are not equal, and the scenes not equally charged; but the fact remains that in most slasher films after 1978 (following *Halloween*), men and boys who go after "wrong" sex also die. This is not the only way males die; they also die incidentally, as girls do, when they get in the killer's way or try to stop him, or when they stray into proscribed territory. The victims in *Hell Night* and in the *Texas Chainsaw Massacre* and *Friday the 13th* films are, respectively, those who trespass in Garth Manor, those who stumble into the environs of the slaughterhouse family, and those who become counselors at a cursed camp, all without regard to sex. Boys die, in short, not because they are boys but because they make mistakes.

Some girls die for the same mistakes. Others, however, and always the main one, die—plot after plot develops the motive—because they are female. Just as Norman Bates's oedipal psychosis is such that only female victims will do, so Michael's sexual anger toward his sister (in the *Halloween* series) drives him to kill her—and after her a string of sister surrogates. In much the same way, the transsexual psychiatrist in *Dressed to Kill* is driven to murder only those women who arouse him and remind him of his hated maleness. In *The Eyes of Laura Mars*, the killer's hatred of his mother drives him to prey on women specifically—and, significantly, one gay male. *He Knows You're Alone* features a killer who in consequence of an earlier jilting preys exclusively on brides-to-be. But even in films in which males and females are killed in roughly even numbers, the lingering images are inevitably female. The death of a male is always swift; even if the victim grasps what is happening to him, he has no time to react or register terror. He is dispatched and the camera moves on. The death of a male is moreover more likely than the death of a female to be viewed from a distance, or viewed only dimly (because of darkness or fog, for example), or indeed to happen offscreen and not be viewed at all. The murders of women, on the other hand, are filmed at closer range, in more graphic detail, and at greater length.

The pair of murders at the therapy pool in *Halloween II* illustrates the standard iconography. We see the orderly killed in two shots: the first at close range in the control room, just before the stabbing, and the second as he is being stabbed, through the vapors in a medium-long-shot; the orderly never even sees his assailant. The nurse's death, on the other hand, is shot entirely in medium close-up. The camera studies her face as it registers first her unwitting complicity (as the killer strokes her neck and shoulders from behind), then apprehension, and then, as she faces him, terror; we see the knife plunge into her repeatedly, hear her cries, and watch her blood fill the therapy pool. This cinematic standard has a venerable history, and it remains intact in the slasher film. Indeed, "tits and a scream" are all that is required of actresses auditioning for the role of victim in *Co-Ed Frenzy*, the fictive slasher film whose making constitutes the frame story of *Blow Out* (1981). It is worth noting that none of the actresses auditioning has both in the desired amount and that the director must resort to the use of doubles: one for the tits, one for the screams.

Final Girl

The image of the distressed female most likely to linger in memory is the image of the one who did not die: the survivor, or Final Girl. She is the one who encounters the mutilated bodies of her friends and perceives the full extent of the preceding horror and of her own peril; who is chased, cornered, wounded; whom we see scream, stagger, fall, rise, and scream again. She is abject terror personified. If her friends knew they were about to die only seconds before the event, the Final Girl lives with the knowledge for long minutes or hours. She alone looks death in the face; but she alone also finds the strength either to stay the killer long enough to be rescued (ending A) or to kill him herself (ending B). She is inevitably female. In Schoell's words: "The vast majority of contemporary shockers, whether in the sexist mold or not, feature climaxes in which the women fight back against their attackers—the wandering, humorless psychos who populate these films. They often show more courage and levelheadedness than their cringing male counterparts."[32] Her scene occupies the last ten to twenty minutes (thirty in the case of *The Texas Chainsaw Massacre*) and constitutes the film's emphatic climax.

The sequence first appears in full-blown form (ending A) in *The Texas Chainsaw Massacre* with Sally's spirited self-defense and eventual rescue. Her brother and companions were dispatched suddenly and uncomprehendingly, one by one, but Sally survives the ninth round—long enough to see what has become of her fellows and what is in store for her, long enough to meet and even dine with the whole slaughterhouse family, long enough to undergo all manner of torture (including the ancient grandfather's effort to strike a fatal hammer blow on the temple as they bend her over a washtub), and long enough to bolt and rebolt, be caught and recaught, plead and replead for her life, and eventually

escape to the highway. For nearly thirty minutes of screen time—a third
of the film—we watch her shriek, run, flinch, jump through windows,
and sustain injury and mutilation. Her will to survive is astonishing; in
the end, bloody and staggering, she finds the highway, Leatherface and
Hitchhiker in pursuit. Just as they bear down on her, a truck comes up
and crushes Hitchhiker. Minutes later a pickup driver plucks Sally up
and saves her from Leatherface. The final shots show us Leatherface
from her point of view (the bed of the pickup): standing on the highway,
wounded (having gashed open his abdomen during the truck episode)
but upright, waving the chainsaw crazily over his head.

Halloween's Final Girl is Laurie. Her desperate defense is
shorter in duration than Sally's but no less fraught with horror. Limp-
ing from a knife wound in the leg, she flees to a garden room and breaks
in through the window with a rake. Neighbors hear her scream for help
but suspect a Halloween prank and shut the blinds. She gets into her
own babysitting house—by throwing a potted plant at a second-story
window to rouse the children—just as the killer descends. Minutes
later he comes through the window and they grapple; she manages to
fell him with a knitting needle and grabs his butcher knife—but drops
it when he seems dead. As she goes upstairs to the children, the killer
rises, takes the knife, and goes after her. She takes refuge in a closet,
lashing the two doorknobs together from the inside. As the killer
slashes and stabs at the closet door—we see this from her inside perspective—she bends a hanger into a weapon and, when he breaks the
door down, stabs him in the eye. Again thinking him vanquished, she
sends the children to the police and sinks down in pain and exhaustion.
The killer rises again, but just as he is about to stab her, Dr. Loomis,
alerted by the children, rushes in and shoots the killer.

Given the drift in just the four years between *The Texas Chainsaw Massacre* and *Halloween*—from passive to active defense—it is no
surprise that the films following *Halloween* present Final Girls who not
only fight back but do so with ferocity and even kill the killer on their
own, without help from the outside.[33] Valerie in *Slumber Party Massacre* (a film directed by Amy Jones and scripted by Rita Mae Brown)
takes a machete-like weapon to the killer, striking off the bit from his
drill, severing his hand, and finally impaling him. Alice assaults and
decapitates the killer of *Friday the 13th.* Pursued by the killer in *Hell
Night,* Marti pries the gate key from the stiff fingers of a corpse to let
herself out of the mansion grounds to safety; when the car won't start,
she repairs it on the spot; when the car gets stuck in the roadway, she
inside and killer on top, she releases it in such a way as to cast the killer

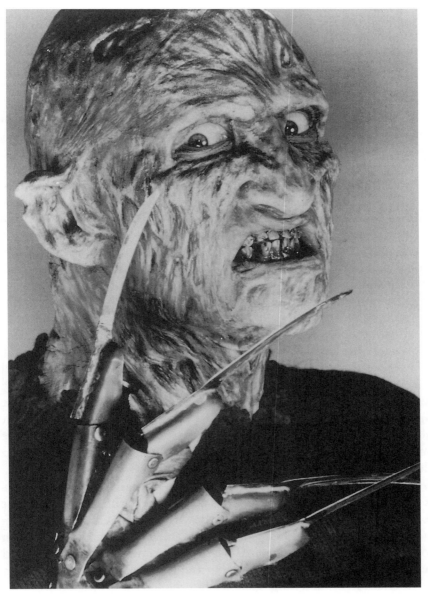

Figure 27. Freddy Kreuger stalked and slashed his way through the popular Nightmare on Elm Street *films. Unlike other killers in the slasher cycle, Kreuger leavened his sadism with an urbane wit.*

on the gate's upper spikes. The grittiest of the Final Girls is Nancy of *A Nightmare on Elm Street*. Aware in advance that the killer will be paying her a visit, she plans an elaborate defense. When he enters the house, she dares him to come at her, then runs at him in direct attack.

As they struggle, he springs the contraptions she has prepared; he is stunned by a swinging sledgehammer, jolted and half incinerated by an electrical charge, and so on. When he rises yet again, she chases him around the house, bashing him with a chair.[34]

In *The Texas Chainsaw Massacre, Part 2*, the Final Girl sequence takes mythic measure. Trapped in the underground slaughterhouse, Stretch repeatedly flees, hides, is caught, tortured (at one point forced to don the flayed face of her murdered technician companion), and nearly killed. She escapes with her life chiefly because Leatherface, having developed an affection for her after the crotch episode, is reluctant to ply his chainsaw as the tyrannical Mr. Sawyer commands. Finally Stretch finds her way out, leaving the Texas Ranger to face certain death below, and clambers up a nearby pinnacle, Chop Top in pursuit. At the summit she finds the mummified grandmother, ceremoniously enthroned in an open-air chamber, and next to her a functional chainsaw. She turns the saw on Chop Top, gashing open his abdomen and tossing him off the precipice. The final scene shows her in extreme longshot, in brilliant sunshine, waving the buzzing chainsaw triumphantly overhead. (It is a scene we are invited to compare to the final scene of the first film, in which the wounded Leatherface is shown in longshot at dawn, staggering after the pickup on the highway waving his chainsaw crazily over *his* head.) In the 1974 film the Final Girl, for all her survivor pluck, is, like Red Riding Hood, saved through male agency. In the 1986 sequel, however, there is no male agency; the figure so designated, the Texas Ranger, proves so utterly ineffectual that he cannot save himself, and much less the girl. The comic ineptitude and failure of would-be "woodsmen" is a repeated theme in the later slasher films. In *Slumber Party Massacre*, the role is played by a woman—although a butch one (the girls' basketball coach). She comes to the slumber party's rescue only to fall victim to the drill herself. But to focus on just who brings the killer down, the Final Girl or a male rescuer, is—as the easy alternation between the two patterns would seem to suggest—to miss the point. The last moment of the Final Girl sequence is finally a footnote to what went before, to the quality of the Final Girl's fight, and more generally to the qualities of character that enable her, of all the characters, to survive what has come to seem unsurvivable.

The Final Girl sequence too is prefigured, if only rudimentarily, in *Psycho*'s final scenes, in which Lila (Marion's sister) is caught reconnoitering in the Bates mansion and nearly killed. Sam (Marion's boyfriend) detains Norman at the motel while Lila snoops about (taking note of Norman's toys). When she perceives Norman's approach, she flees to the basement. Here she encounters the treated corpse of Mrs. Bates and begins screaming in horror. Norman bursts in and is about to strike when Sam enters and grabs him from behind. Like her generic sisters, then, Lila is the spunky inquirer into the Terrible Place—the one who first grasps, however dimly, the past and present danger, the one who looks death in the face, and the one who survives the murderer's last stab. There the correspondences end, however. The *Psycho* scene turns, after all, on the revelation of Norman's psychotic identity, not on Lila as a character—she enters the film midway and is sketchily drawn—and still less on her self-defense.

The Final Girl of the slasher film is presented from the outset as the main character. The practiced viewer distinguishes her from her friends minutes into the film. She is the girl scout, the bookworm, the mechanic. Unlike her girlfriends (and Marion Crane), she is not sexually active. Laurie (*Halloween*) is teased because of her fears about dating, and Marti (*Hell Night*) explains to the boy with whom she finds herself sharing a room that they will have separate beds. Although Stretch (*Texas Chainsaw, Part 2*) is hardly virginal, she is not available, either; early in the film she pointedly turns down a date, and we are given to understand that she is, for the present, unattached and even lonely. So too Stevie of Carpenter's *The Fog*, like Stretch a disk jockey. Divorced mother and a newcomer in town, she is unattached and lonely but declines male attention. The Final Girl is also watchful to the point of paranoia; small signs of danger that her friends ignore she takes in and turns over. Above all, she is intelligent and resourceful in extreme situations. Thus Laurie even at her most desperate, cornered in a closet, has the wit to grab a hanger from the rack and bend it into a weapon; Marti can hot-wire her getaway car, the killer in pursuit; and the psych major of *Friday the 13th Part 2*, on seeing the enshrined head of Mrs. Voorhees, can stop Jason in his tracks by assuming a stridently maternal voice. Finally, although she is always smaller and weaker than the killer, she grapples with him energetically and convincingly.

The Final Girl is boyish, in a word. Just as the killer is not fully masculine, she is not fully feminine—not, in any case, feminine in the ways of her friends. Her smartness, gravity, competence in mechanical and other practical matters, and sexual reluctance set her apart from the other girls and ally her, ironically, with the very boys she fears or rejects, not to speak of the killer himself. Lest we miss the point, it is

Figures 28 & 29. *The shower murder of Marion Crane in Alfred Hitchcock's* Psycho *exerted a seminal influence over the subsequent slasher horror cycle.*

spelled out in her name: Stevie, Marti, Terry, Laurie, Stretch, Will. Not only the conception of the hero in *Alien* and *Aliens* but also her name, Ripley, owes a clear debt to slasher tradition.

   With the introduction of the Final Girl, then, the *Psycho* formula is radically altered. It is not merely a question of enlarging the figure of Lila but of absorbing into her role, in varying degrees, the functions of Arbogast (investigator) and Sam (rescuer) and restructuring the narrative action from beginning to end around her progress in relation to the killer. In other words, *Psycho*'s detective plot, revolving around a revelation, yields in the modern slasher film to a hero plot, revolving around the main character's struggle with and eventual triumph over evil. But for the femaleness, however qualified, of that main character, the story is a standard one of tale and epic.

Shock

One reason that the shower sequence in *Psycho* has "evoked more study, elicited more comment, and generated more shot-for-shot analysis from a technical viewpoint than any other in the history of cinema" is that it suggests so much but shows so little.[35] Of the forty-odd shots in as many seconds that figure the murder, only a single fleeting one actually shows the body being stabbed. The others present us with a rapid-fire concatenation of images of the knife-wielding hand, parts of Marion, parts of the shower, and finally the bloody water as it swirls down the drain. The horror resides less in the actual images than in their summary implication.

Although Hitchcock is hardly the first director to prefer the oblique rendition of physical violence, he may, to judge from current examples, be one of the last. For better or worse, the perfection of special effects has made it possible to show maiming and dismemberment in extraordinarily credible detail. The horror genres are the natural repositories of such effects; what can be done is done, and slashers, at the bottom of the category, do it most and worst. Thus we see a head being stepped on so that the eyes pop out, a face being flayed, a decapitation, a hypodermic needle penetrating an eyeball in close-up, and so on.

With this new explicitness also comes a new tone. If the horror of *Psycho* was taken seriously, the "horror" of the slasher films is of a rather more complicated sort. Audiences express uproarious disgust ("Gross!") as often as they express fear, and it is clear that the makers of slasher films pursue the combination. More particularly, spectators fall silent while the victim is being stalked, scream out at the first stab, and make loud noises of revulsion at the sight of the bloody stump. The rapid alternation between registers—between something like "real" horror on one hand and campy, self-parodying Horror on the other—is by now one of the most conspicuous characteristics of the tradition. In its cultivation of intentionally outrageous excess, the slasher film intersects with the cult film, a genre devoted to such effects. Just what this self-ironizing relation to taboo signifies, beyond a remarkably competent audience, is unclear—it is yet another aspect of the phenomenon that has lain beyond criticism—but for the time being it stands as a defining characteristic of the lower genres of popular culture.

The Body

On the face of it, the relation between the sexes in slasher films could hardly be clearer. The killer is with few exceptions recognizably human and distinctly male; his fury is unmistakably sexual in both roots and expression; his victims are mostly women, often sexually free and always young and beautiful ones. Just how essential this victim is to horror is suggested by her historical durability. If the killer has over time been variously figured as shark, fog, gorilla, birds, and slime, the victim is eternally and prototypically the damsel. Cinema hardly invented the pattern. It has simply given visual expression to the abiding proposition that, in Poe's famous formulation, the death of a beautiful woman is the "most poetical topic in the world."[36] As slasher director Dario Argento puts it, "I like women, especially beautiful ones. If they have a good face and figure, I would much prefer to watch them being murdered than an ugly girl or a man."[37] Brian De Palma elaborates: "Women in peril work better in the suspense genre. It all goes back to the *Perils of Pauline*. . . . If you have a haunted house and you have a woman walking around with a candelabrum, you fear more for her than you would for a husky man."[38] Or Hitchcock, during the filming of *The Birds:* "I always believe in following the advice of the playwright Sardou. He said 'Torture the women!' The trouble today is that we don't torture women enough."[39]

What the directors do not say, but show, is that "Pauline" is at her very most effective in a state of undress, borne down upon by a blatantly phallic murderer, even gurgling orgasmically as she dies. The case could be made that the slasher films available at a given neighborhood video rental outlet recommend themselves to censorship under the Dworkin–MacKinnon guidelines at least as readily as the hard-core films the next section over, at which that legislation is aimed; for if some victims are men, the argument goes, most are women, and the women are brutalized in ways that come too close to real life for comfort. But what this line of reasoning does not take into account is the figure of the Final Girl. Because slashers lie for all practical purposes beyond the purview of legitimate criticism and, to the extent that they have been reviewed at all, have been reviewed on an individual basis, the phenomenon of the female victim-hero has scarcely been acknowledged.

It is, of course, "on the face of it" that most of the public discussion of film takes place—from the Dworkin–MacKinnon legislation to Siskel and Ebert's reviews to our own talks with friends on leaving the movie house. Underlying that discussion is the assumption that the sexes are what they seem; that screen males represent the Male and screen females the Female; that this identification along gender lines authorizes impulses toward sexual violence in males and encourages impulses toward victimization in females. In part because of the massive authority cinema by nature accords the image, even academic film criticism has been slow—slower than literary criticism—to get beyond appearances. Film may not appropriate the mind's eye, but it certainly encroaches on it; the gender characteristics of a screen figure are a visible and audible given for the duration of the film. To the extent that the possibility of cross-gender identification has been entertained, it has been in the direction female-with-male. Thus some critics have wondered whether the female viewer, faced with the screen image of a masochistic/narcissistic female, might not rather elect to "betray her sex and identify with the masculine point of view."[40] The reverse question—whether men might not also, on occasion, elect to betray their sex and identify with screen females—has scarcely been asked, presumably on the assumption that men's interests are well served by the traditional patterns of cinematic representation. Then too there is the matter of the "male gaze." As E. Ann Kaplan sums it up: "Within the film text itself, men gaze at women, who become objects of the gaze; the spectator, in turn, is made to identify with this male gaze, and to objectify the women on the screen; and the camera's original 'gaze' comes into play in the very act of filming."[41] But if it is so that all of us, male and female alike, are by these processes "made to" identify with men and "against" women, how are we then to explain the appeal to a largely male audience of a film genre that features a female victim-hero? The slasher film brings us squarely up against a fundamental question of film analysis: Where does the literal end and the figurative begin; how do the two levels interact and what is the significance of the particular interaction; and to which, in arriving at a political judgment (as we are inclined to do in the case of low horror and pornography), do we assign priority?

A figurative or functional analysis of the slasher begins with the processes of point of view and identification. The male viewer seeking a male character, even a vicious one, with whom to identify in a sustained way has little to hang on to in the standard example. On the good side, the only viable candidates are the schoolmates or friends of the girls. They are for the most part marginal, undeveloped characters; more to the point, they tend to die early in the film. If the traditional horror film gave the male spectator a last-minute hero with whom to identify, thereby "indulging his vanity as protector of the helpless female,"[42] the slasher eliminates or attenuates that role beyond any such function; indeed, would-be rescuers are not infrequently blown away for their efforts, leaving the girl to fight her own fight. Policemen, fathers, and sheriffs appear only long enough to demonstrate risible incomprehension and incompetence. On the bad side, there is the killer. The killer is often unseen, or barely glimpsed, during the first part of the film, and what we do see, when we finally get a good look, hardly invites immediate or conscious empathy. He is commonly masked, fat, deformed, or dressed as a woman. Or "he" *is* a woman: woe to the viewer of *Friday the 13th* who identifies with the male killer only to discover, in the film's final sequences, that he was not a man at all but a middle-aged woman. In either case, the killer is himself eventually killed or otherwise evacuated from the narrative. No male character of any stature lives to tell the tale.

The one character of stature who does live to tell the tale is of course female. The Final Girl is introduced at the beginning and is the only character to be developed in any psychological detail. We understand immediately from the attention paid it that hers is the main story line. She is intelligent, watchful, level-headed; the first character to sense something amiss and the only one to deduce from the accumulating evidence the patterns and extent of the threat; the only one, in other words, whose perspective approaches our own privileged understanding of the situation. We register her horror as she stumbles on the corpses of her friends; her paralysis in the face of death duplicates those moments of the universal nightmare experience on which horror frankly trades. When she downs the killer, we are triumphant. She is by any measure the slasher film's hero. This is not to say that our attachment to her is exclusive and unremitting, only that it adds up and that in the closing sequence it is very close to absolute.

An analysis of the camerawork bears this out. Much is made of the use of the I-camera to represent the killer's point of view. In these passages—they are usually few and brief, but powerful—we see through his eyes and (on the sound track) hear his breathing and heartbeat. His and our vision is partly obscured by bushes or window blinds in the foreground. By such means we are forced, the argument goes, to identify with the killer. In fact, however, the relation between camera point of view and the processes of viewer identification are poorly understood; the fact that Steven Spielberg can stage an attack in *Jaws* from the shark's point of view (underwater, rushing upward toward the swimmer's flailing legs) or Hitchcock an attack in *The Birds* from the bird's-eye perspective (from the sky, as they gather to swoop down on the streets of Bodega Bay) would seem to suggest either that the viewer's identificatory powers are unbelievably elastic or that point-of-view shots can sometimes be pro forma.[43]

But let us for the moment accept the equation point of view = identification. We are linked, in this way, with the killer in the early part of the film, usually before we have seen him directly and before we have come to know the Final Girl in any detail. Our closeness to him wanes as our closeness to the Final Girl waxes—a shift underwritten by story line as well as camera position. By the end, point of view is hers: we are in the closet with her, watching with her eyes the knife blade stab through the door; in the room with her as the killer breaks through the window and grabs at her; in the car with her as the killer stabs through the convertible top; and so on. With her, we become if not the killer of the killer then the agent of his expulsion from the narrative vision. If, during the film's course, we shifted our sympathies back and forth and dealt them out to other characters along the way, we belong in the end to the Final Girl; there is no alternative. When Stretch eviscerates Chop Top at the end of *Texas Chainsaw, Part 2*, she is literally the only character left alive, on either side.

Audience response ratifies this design. Observers unanimously stress the readiness of the "live" audience to switch sympathies in midstream, siding now with the killer and now, and finally, with the Final Girl. As Schoell, whose book on shocker films wrestles with its own monster, "the feminists," puts it:

> Social critics make much of the fact that male audience members cheer on the misogynous misfits in these movies as they rape, plunder, and murder their screaming, writhing female victims. Since these same critics walk out of the moviehouse in disgust long before the movie is over, they don't realize that these same men cheer on (with renewed enthusiasm, in fact) the heroines, who are often as strong, sexy, and independent as the [earlier] victims, as they blow away the killer with a shotgun or get him between the eyes with a machete. All of these men are said to be identifying with the maniac, but they enjoy *his* death throes the most of all, and applaud the heroine with admiration.[44]

What filmmakers seem to know better than film critics is that gender is less a wall than a permeable membrane.[45]

No one who has read "Red Riding Hood" to a small boy or participated in a viewing of, say, *Deliverance* ([1972], an all-male story that women find as gripping as men) or, more recently, *Alien* and *Aliens,* with whose spaceage female Rambo, herself a Final Girl, male viewers seem to engage with ease, can doubt the phenomenon of cross-gender identification.[46] This fluidity of engaged perspective is in keeping with the universal claims of the psychoanalytic model: the threat function and the victim function coexist in the same unconscious, regardless of anatomical sex. But why, if viewers can identify across gender lines and if the root experience of horror is sex blind, are the screen sexes not interchangeable? Why not more and better female killers, and why (in light of the maleness of the majority audience) not Pauls as well as Paulines? The fact that horror film so stubbornly genders the killer male and the principal victim female would seem to suggest that representation itself is at issue—that the sensation of bodily fright derives not exclusively from repressed content, as Freud insisted, but also from the bodily manifestations of that content.

Nor is the gender of the principals as straightforward as it first seems. The killer's phallic purpose, as he thrusts his drill or knife into the trembling bodies of young women, is unmistakable. At the same time, however, his masculinity is severely qualified: he ranges from the virginal or sexually inert to the transvestite or transsexual, is spiritually divided ("the mother half of his mind"), or even equipped with vulva and vagina. Although the killer of *God Told Me To* (a.k.a. *Demon* [1979]) is represented and taken as a male in the film text, he is revealed, by the doctor who delivered him, to have been sexually ambiguous from birth: "I truly could not tell whether that child was male or female; it was as if the sexual gender had not been determined . . . as if it were being developed."[47] In this respect, slasher killers have much in common with the monsters of classic horror—monsters who, in Linda Williams's formulation, represent not just "an eruption of the normally repressed animal sexual energy of the civilized male" but also the "power and potency of a *non-phallic* sexuality." To the extent that the monster is constructed as feminine, the horror film thus expresses female desire only to show how monstrous it is.[48] The intention is manifest in *Aliens,* in which the Final Girl, Ripley, is pitted in the climactic scene against the most terrifying "alien" of all: an egg-laying Mother.

Nor can we help noticing the "intrauterine" quality of the Terrible Place, dark and often damp, in which the killer lives or lurks and whence he stages his most terrifying attacks. "It often happens," Freud wrote, "that neurotic men declare that they feel there is something uncanny about the female genital organs. This *unheimlich* place, however, is an entrance to the former *Heim* [home] of all human beings, to the place where each one of us lived once upon a time and in the beginning. . . . In this case too then, the *unheimlich* is what once was *heimisch*, familiar; the prefix *'un'* [*'un-'*] is the token repression."[49] It is the exceptional film that does not mark as significant the moment that the killer leaps out of the dark recesses of a corridor or cavern at the trespassing victim, usually the Final Girl. Long after the other particulars have faded, the viewer will remember the images of Amy assaulted from the dark halls of a morgue (*He Knows You're Alone*), Sally or Stretch facing dismemberment in the ghastly dining room or underground labyrinth of the slaughterhouse family (the *Texas Chainsaw* films), or Melanie trapped in the attic as the savage birds close in (*The Birds*). In such scenes of convergence the Other is at its bisexual mightiest, the victim at her tiniest, and the component of sado-masochism at its most blatant.

The gender of the Final Girl is likewise compromised from the outset by her masculine interests, her inevitable sexual reluctance (penetration, it seems, constructs the female), her apartness from other girls, sometimes her name. At the level of the cinematic apparatus, her unfemininity is signaled clearly by her exercise of the "active investigating gaze" normally reserved for males and hideously punished in females when they assume it themselves. Tentatively at first and then aggressively, the Final Girl looks *for* the killer, even tracking him to his forest hut or his underground labyrinth, and then *at* him, therewith bringing him, often for the first time, into our vision as well.[50] When, in the final scene, she stops screaming, looks at the killer, and reaches for the knife (sledgehammer, scalpel, gun, machete, hanger, knitting needle, chainsaw), she addresses the killer on his own terms. To the critics' objection that *Halloween* in effect punished female sexuality, director John Carpenter responded: "They [the critics] completely missed the boat there, I think. Because if you turn it around, the one girl who is the most sexually uptight just keeps stabbing this guy with a long knife. She's the most sexually frustrated. She's the one that killed him. Not because she's a virgin, but because all that repressed energy starts coming out. She uses all those phallic symbols on the guy. . . . She and the killer have a certain link: sexual repression."[51]

For all its perversity, Carpenter's remark does not underscore the sense of affinity, even recognition, that attends the final encounter. But the "certain link" that puts killer and Final Girl on terms, at least briefly, is more than "sexual repression." It is also a shared masculinity, materialized in "all those phallic symbols"—and it is also a shared femininity, materialized in what comes next (and what Carpenter, perhaps significantly, fails to mention): the castration, literal or symbolic, of the killer at her hands. His eyes may be put out, his hand severed, his body impaled or shot, his belly gashed, or his genitals sliced away or bitten off. The Final Girl has not just manned herself; she specifically unmans an oppressor whose masculinity was in question to begin with. By the time the drama has played itself out, darkness yields to light (often as day breaks) and the close quarters of the barn (closet, elevator, attic, basement) give way to the open expanse of the yard (field, road, lakescape, cliff). With the Final Girl's appropriation of "all those phallic symbols" comes the queuing, the dispelling, of the "uterine" threat as well. Consider again the paradigmatic ending of *Texas Chainsaw, Part 2*. From the underground labyrinth, murky and bloody, in which she faced saw, knife, and hammer, Stretch escapes through a culvert into the open air. She clambers up the jutting rock and with a chainsaw takes her stand. When her last assailant comes at her, she slashes open his lower abdomen—the sexual symbolism is all too clear—and flings him off the cliff. Again, the final scene shows her in extreme longshot, standing on the pinnacle, drenched in sunlight, buzzing chainsaw held overhead.

The tale would indeed seem to be one of sex and parents. The patently erotic threat is easily seen as the materialized projection of the dreamer's (viewer's) own incestuous fears and desires. It is this disabling cathexis to one's parents that must be killed and rekilled in the service of sexual autonomy. When the Final Girl stands at last in the light of day with the knife in her hand, she has delivered herself into the adult world. Carpenter's equation of the Final Girl with the killer has more than a grain of truth. The killers of *Psycho, The Eyes of Laura Mars, Friday the 13th*, Parts Two through Six, and *Cruising*, among others, are explicitly figured as sons in the psychosexual grip of their mothers (or fathers, in the case of *Cruising*). The difference is between past and present and between failure and success. The Final Girl enacts in the present, and successfully, the parenticidal struggle that the killer himself enacted unsuccessfully in his own past—a past that constitutes the film's backstory. She is what the killer once was; he is what she could become should she fail in her battle for sexual selfhood. "You got a choice, boy," says the tyrannical father of Leatherface in *Texas Chainsaw, Part 2*, "sex or the saw; you never know about sex, but the saw—the saw is the family."

But the tale is no less one of maleness. If the early experience of the oedipal drama can be—is perhaps ideally—enacted in the female form, the achievement of full adulthood requires the assumption and, apparently, brutal employment of the phallus. The helpless child is gendered feminine; the autonomous adult or subject is gendered masculine; the passage from childhood to adulthood entails a shift from feminine to masculine. It is the male killer's tragedy that his incipient femininity is not reversed but completed (castration) and the Final Girl's victory that her incipient masculinity is not thwarted but realized (phallicization). When De Palma says that female frailty is a predicate of the suspense genre, he proposes, in effect, that the lack of the phallus, for Lacan the privileged signifier of the symbolic order of culture, is itself simply horrifying, at least in the mind of the male observer. Whereas pornography (the argument goes) resolves that lack through a process of fetishization that allows a breast or leg or whole body to stand in for the missing member, the slasher film resolves it either through eliminating the woman (earlier victims) or reconstituting her as masculine (Final Girl). The moment at which the Final Girl is effectively phallicized is the moment that the plot halts and horror ceases. Day breaks, and the community returns to its normal order.

Casting psychoanalytic verities in female form has a venerable cinematic history. Ingmar Bergman has made a career of it, and Woody Allen shows signs of following his lead. One immediate and practical advantage, by now presumably unconscious on the part of makers as well as viewers, has to do with a preestablished cinematic "language" for capturing the moves and moods of the female body and face. The cinematic gaze, we are told, is male, and just as that gaze "knows" how to fetishize the female form in pornography (in a way that it does not "know" how to fetishize the male form),[52] so it "knows," in horror, how to track a woman ascending a staircase in a scary house and how to study her face from an angle above as she first hears the killer's footfall. A set of conventions we now take for granted simply "sees" males and females differently.

To this cinematic habit may be added the broader range of emotional expression traditionally allowed women. Angry displays of force may belong to the male, but crying, cowering, screaming, fainting, trembling, begging for mercy belong to the female. Abject terror, in short, is gendered feminine, and the more concerned a given film with that condition—and it is the essence of modern horror—the more likely the femaleness of the victim. It is no accident that male victims in slasher films are killed swiftly or offscreen, and that prolonged struggles, in which the victim has time to contemplate her imminent destruction, inevitably figure females. Only when one encounters the rare expression of abject terror on the part of a male (as in *I Spit on Your Grave*) does one apprehend the full extent of the cinematic double standard in such matters.[53]

It is also the case that gender displacement can provide a kind of identificatory buffer, an emotional remove, that permits the majority audience to explore taboo subjects in the relative safety of vicariousness. Just as Bergman came to realize that he could explore castration anxiety more freely via depictions of hurt female bodies (witness the genital mutilation of Karin in *Cries and Whispers* [1972]), so the makers of slasher films seem to know that sadomasochistic incest fantasies sit more easily with the male viewer when the visible player is female. It is one thing for that viewer to hear the psychiatrist intone at the end of *Psycho* that Norman as a boy (in the backstory) was abnormally attached to his mother; it would be quite another to see that attachment dramatized in the present, to experience in nightmare form the elaboration of Norman's (the viewer's own) fears and desires. If the former is playable in male form, the latter, it seems, is not.

The Final Girl is, on reflection, a congenial double for the adolescent male. She is feminine enough to act out in a gratifying way, a way unapproved for adult males, the terrors and masochistic pleasures of the underlying fantasy, but not so feminine as to disturb the structures of male competence and sexuality. Her sexual inactivity, in this reading, becomes all but inevitable; the male viewer may be willing to enter into the vicarious experience of defending himself from the possibility of symbolic penetration on the part of the killer, but real vaginal penetration on the diegetic level is evidently more femaleness than he can bear. The question then arises whether the Final Girls of slasher films —Stretch, Stevie, Marti, Will, Terry, Laurie, and Ripley—are not boyish for the same reason that the female "victims" in Victorian flagellation literature—"Georgy," "Willy"—are boyish: because they are transformed males. The transformation, Steven Marcus writes, "is itself both a defense against and a disavowal of the fantasy it is simultaneously expressing"—namely, that a "little *boy* is being beaten . . . by another man."[54] What is represented as male-on-female violence, in short, is figuratively speaking male-on-male sex. For Marcus, the literary picture of flagellation, in which *girls* are beaten, is utterly belied by the descriptions (in *My Secret Life*) of real-life episodes in which the persons being beaten are not girls at all but "gentlemen" dressed in women's clothes ("He had a woman's dress on tucked up to his waist, showing his naked rump and thighs. . . . On his head was a woman's cap tied carefully round his face to hide whiskers") and whipped by prostitutes. Reality, Marcus writes, "puts the literature of flagellation out of the running . . . by showing how that literature is a completely distorted and idealized version of what actually happens."[55] Applied to the slasher film, this logic reads the femaleness of the Final Girl (at least up to the point of her transformation) and indeed of the women victims in general as only apparent, the artifact of heterosexual deflection. It may be through the female body that the body of the audience is sensationalized, but the sensation is an entirely male affair.

At least one director, Hitchcock, explicitly located thrill in the equation victim = audience. So we judge from his marginal jottings in the shooting instructions for the shower scene in *Psycho*: "The slashing. An impression of a knife slashing, as if tearing at the very screen, ripping the film."[56] Not just the body of Marion is to be ruptured, but also the body on the other side of the film and screen: our witnessing body. As Marion is to Norman, the audience of *Psycho* is to Hitchcock; as the audiences of horror film in general are to the directors of those films, female is to male. Hitchcock's "torture the women" then means, simply, torture the audience. De Palma's remarks about female frailty likewise contemplate a male-on-"female" relationship between director and viewer. Cinefantastic horror, in short, succeeds in the production of sensation to more or less the degree that it succeeds in incorporating its spectators as "feminine" and then violating that body—which recoils, shudders, cries out collectively—in ways otherwise imaginable, for males, only in nightmare. The equation is nowhere more plainly put than in David Cronenberg's *Videodrome* (1983). Here the threat is a mind-destroying video signal and the victims television viewers. Despite the (male) hero's efforts to defend his mental (and physical) integrity, a deep, vaginalike gash appears on his lower abdomen. Says the media conspirator as he thrusts a videocassette into the victim's gaping wound, "You must open yourself completely to this."

If the slasher film is "on the face of it" a genre with at least a strong female presence, it is in these figurative readings a thoroughly strong male exercise, one that finally has very little to do with femaleness and very much to do with phallocentrism. Figuratively seen, the Final Girl is a male surrogate in things oedipal, a homoerotic stand-in, the audience incorporate; to the extent she "means" girl at all, it is only for purposes of signifying phallic lack, and even that meaning is nullified in the final scenes. Our initial question—how to square a female victim-hero with a largely male audience—is not so much answered as it is obviated in these readings. The Final Girl is (apparently) female not despite the maleness of the audience, but precisely because of it. The discourse is wholly masculine, and females figure in it only insofar as they "read" some aspect of male experience. To applaud the Final Girl as a feminist development, as some reviews of *Aliens* have done with Ripley, is, in light of her figurative meaning, a particularly grotesque expression of wishful thinking.[57] She is simply an agreed-upon fiction, and the male viewer's use of her as a vehicle for his own sado-masochistic fantasies an act of perhaps timely dishonesty.

For all their immediate appeal, these figurative readings loosen as many ends as they tie together. The audience, we have said, is predominantly male; but what about the women in it? Do we dismiss them as male-identified and account for their experience as an "immasculated" act of collusion with the oppressor?[58] This is a strong judgment to apply to large numbers of women; for while it may be that the audience for slasher films is mainly male, that does not mean that there are not also many female viewers who actively like such films, and of course there are also women, however few, who script, direct, and produce them. These facts alone oblige us at least to consider the possibility that female fans find a meaning in the text and image of these films that is less inimical to their own interests than the figurative analysis would have us believe. Or should we conclude that males and females read these films differently in some fundamental sense? Do females respond to the text (the literal) and males the subtext (the figurative)?[59]

Some such notion of differential understanding underlies the homoerotic reading. The silent presupposition of that reading is that male identification with the female as female cannot be, and that the male viewer/reader who adjoins feminine experience does so only by homosexual conversion. But does female identification with male experience then similarly indicate a lesbian conversion? Or are the processes of patriarchy so one-way that the female can identify with the male directly, but the male can identify with the female only by trans-sexualizing her? Does the Final Girl mean "girl" to her female viewers and "boy" to her male viewers? If her masculine features qualify her as a transformed boy, do not the feminine features of the killer qualify him as a transformed woman (in which case the homoerotic reading can be maintained only by defining that "woman" as phallic and retransforming her into a male)? Striking though it is, the analogy between the Victorian flagellation story's Georgy and the slasher film's Stretch falters at the moment that Stretch turns on her assailant and unmans him. Are we to suppose that a homoerotic beating fantasy suddenly yields to what folklorists call a "lack-liquidated" fantasy? Further, is it simple coincidence that this combination tale—trials, then triumph—bears such a striking resemblance to the classic (male) hero story? Does the standard hero story featuring an anatomical female "mean" differently from one featuring an anatomical male?

As Marcus perceived, the relationship between the Georgy stories of flagellation literature and the real-life anecdote of the Victorian gentleman is a marvelously telling one. In his view, the maleness of the latter must prove the essential or functional maleness of the former. What his analysis does not come to full grips with, however, is the clothing the gentleman wears—not that of a child, as Marcus's "childish" reading of the scene contemplates, but explicitly that of a woman.[60] These women's clothes can of course be understood, within the terms of the homoerotic interpretation, as a last-ditch effort on the part of the gentleman to dissociate himself from the (incestuous) homosexuality implicit in his favored sexual practice. But can they not just as well, and far more economically, be explained as part and parcel of a fantasy of literal femaleness? By the same token, cannot the femaleness of the gentleman's literary representatives—the girls of the flagellation stories—be understood as the obvious, even necessary, extension of the man's dress and cap? The same dress and cap, I suggest, haunt the margins of the slasher film. This is not to deny the deflective convenience, for the male spectator (and filmmaker), of a female victim-hero in a context so fraught with taboo; it is only to suggest that the femaleness of that character is also conditioned by a kind of imaginative curiosity about the feminine in and of itself.

So too the psychoanalytic case. These films do indeed seem to pit the child in a struggle, at once terrifying and attractive, with the parental Other, and it is a rare example that does not directly thematize parent–child relations. But if Freud stressed the maternal source of the *unheimlich*, the Other of our films is decidedly androgynous: female/feminine in aspects of character and place (the "intrauterine" locale) but male in anatomy. Conventional logic may interpret the killer as the phallic mother of the transformed boy (the Final Girl), but the text itself does not compel such a reading. On the contrary, the text at every level presents us with hermaphroditic constructions—constructions that draw attention to themselves and demand to be taken on their own terms.

For if we define the Final Girl as nothing more than a figurative male, what do we then make of the context of the spectacular gender play in which she is emphatically situated? In his essay on the uncanny, Freud rejected out of hand Jentsch's theory that the experience of horror proceeds from intellectual uncertainty (curiosity?)—feelings of confusion, induced by an author or a coincidence, about who, what, and where one is.[61] One wonders, however, whether Freud would have been quite so dismissive if, instead of the mixed materials he used as evidence, he were presented with a coherent story corpus—forty slashers, say—in which the themes of incest and separation were relentlessly played out by a female character, and further in which gender identity was repeatedly thematized as an issue in and of itself. For although the factors we have considered thus far—the conventions of the male gaze, the feminine constitution of abject terror, the value for the male viewer of emotional distance from the taboos in question, the special horror that may inhere, for the male audience, in phallic lack, the homoerotic deflection—go a long way in explaining why it is we have Pauline rather than Paul as our victim-hero, they do not finally account for our strong sense that gender is simply being played with, and that part of the thrill lies precisely in the resulting "intellectual uncertainty" of sexual identity.

The "play of pronoun function" that underlies and defines the cinefantastic is nowhere more richly manifested than in the slasher; if the genre has an aesthetic base, it is exactly that of a visual identity game. Consider, for example, the by now standard habit of letting us view the action in the first person long before revealing who or what the first person *is*. In the opening sequence of *Halloween*, "we" are belatedly revealed to ourselves, after committing a murder in the cinematic first person, as a 6-year-old boy. The surprise is often within gender, but it is also, in a striking number of cases, across gender. Again, *Friday the 13th*, in which "we" stalk and kill a number of teenagers over the course of an hour of screen time without even knowing who "we" are; we are invited, by conventional expectation and by glimpses of "our" own bodily parts—a heavily booted foot, a roughly gloved hand—to suppose that "we" are male, but "we" are revealed, at film's end, as a woman. If this is the most dramatic case of pulling out the gender rug, it is by no means the only one. In *Dressed to Kill*, we are led to believe, again by means of glimpses, that "we" are female—only to discover, in the denouement, that "we" are a male in drag. In *Psycho*, the dame we glimpse holding the knife with a "visible virility quite obscene in an old lady" is later revealed, after additional gender teasing, to be Norman in his mother's clothes.[62] *Psycho II* (1983) plays much the same game. *Cruising* (in which, not accidentally, transvestites play a prominent role) adjusts the terms along heterosexual/homosexual lines. The tease here is whether the originally straight detective assigned to the string of murders in a gay community does or does not succumb to his assumed homosexual identity; the camerawork leaves us increasingly uncertain as to his (our) sexual inclinations, not to speak of his (our) complicity in the crimes. Even at film's end we are not sure who "we" were during several of the first-person sequences.[63]

The gender-identity game, in short, is too patterned and too pervasive in the slasher film to be dismissed as supervenient. It would seem instead to be an integral element of the particular brand of bodily sensation in which the genre trades. Nor is it exclusive to horror. It is directly thematized in comic terms in the recent "gender benders" *Tootsie* ([1982], in which a man passes himself off as a woman) and *All of Me* ([1984], in which a woman is literally introjected into a man and affects his speech, movement, and thought). It is also directly thematized, in the form of bisexual and androgynous figures and relations, in such cult films as *Pink Flamingos* (1973) and *The Rocky Horror Picture Show* (1975). (Some version of it is indeed enacted every few minutes on MTV.) It is further thematized (predictably enough, given their bodily concerns) in such pornographic films as *Every Woman Has a Fantasy* (1984), in which a man, in order to gain access to a women's group in which sexual fantasies are discussed, dresses and presents himself as a woman. (The degree to which "male" pornography in general relies for its effect on cross-gender identification remains an open question; the proposition makes a certain sense of the obligatory lesbian sequences and the phenomenal success of *Behind the Green Door* [1972], to pick just two examples.)[64]

All of these films, and others like them, seem to be asking some version of the question: What would it be like to be, or to seem to be, if only temporarily, a woman? Taking exception to the reception of *Tootsie* as a feminist film, Elaine Showalter argues that the success of "Dorothy Michaels" (the Dustin Hoffman character), as far as both plot and audience are concerned, lies in the veiling of masculine power in feminine costume. *Tootsie's* cross-dressing, she writes,

> is a way of promoting the notion of masculine power while masking it. In psychoanalytic theory, the male transvestite is not a powerless man; according to the psychiatrist Robert Stoller, in *Sex and Gender,* he is a "phallic woman" who can tell himself that "he is, or with practice will become, a better woman than a biological female if he chooses to do so." When it is safe or necessary, the transvestite "gets great pleasure in revealing that he is a male-woman. . . . The pleasure in tricking the unsuspecting into thinking he is a woman, and then

revealing his maleness (e.g., by suddenly dropping his voice) is not so much erotic as it is proof that there is such a thing as a woman with a penis." Dorothy's effectiveness is the literal equivalent of speaking softly and carrying a big stick.[65]

By the same literalistic token, then, Stretch's success must lie in the fact that in the end, at least, she "speaks loudly" *even though* she carries no "stick." Just as "Dorothy's" voice slips serve to remind us that her character really is male, so the Final Girl's "tits and scream" serve more or less continuously to remind us that she really is female—even as, and despite the fact that, she in the end acquits herself "like a man."[66] Her chainsaw is thus what "Dorothy's" skirt is: a figuration of what she *does* and what she *seems,* as opposed to—and the films turn on the opposition—what she *is.* The idea that appearance and behavior do not necessarily indicate sex—indeed, can misindicate sex—is predicated on the understanding that sex is one thing and gender another; in practice, that sex is life, a less-than-interesting given, but that gender is theater. Whatever else it may be, Stretch's waving of the chainsaw is a moment of high drag. Its purpose is not to make us forget that she is a girl but to thrust that fact on us. The moment, it is probably fair to say, is also one that openly mocks the literary/cinematic conventions of symbolic representation.

It may be just this theatricalization of gender that makes possible the willingness of the male viewer to submit himself to a brand of spectator experience that Hitchcock designated as "feminine" in 1960 and that has become only more so since then. In classic horror, the "feminization" of the audience is intermittent and ceases early. Our relationship with Marion's body in *Psycho* halts abruptly at the moment of its greatest intensity (slashing, ripping, tearing). The considerable remainder of the film distributes our bruised sympathies among several lesser figures, male and female, in such a way and at such length as to ameliorate the Marion experience and leave us, in the end, more or less recuperated in our (presumed) masculinity. Like Marion, the Final Girl is the designated victim, the incorporation of the audience, the slashing, ripping, and tearing of whose body will cause us to flinch and scream out in our seats. But unlike Marion, she does not die. If *Psycho,* like other classic horror films, solves the femininity problem by obliterating the female and replacing her with representatives of the masculine order (mostly but not inevitably males), the modern slasher solves it by regendering the woman. We are, as an audience, in the end "masculinized" by and through the very figure by and through whom we were earlier "feminized." The same body does for both, and that body is female.

The last point is the crucial one: the same female body does for both. The Final Girl (1) undergoes agonizing trials and (2) virtually or actually destroys the antagonist and saves herself. By the lights of folk tradition, she is not a heroine, for whom phase 1 consists in being saved by someone else, but a hero, who rises to the occasion and defeats the adversary with his own wit and hands. Phase 1 of the story sits well on the female; it is the heart of heroine stories in general (Red Riding Hood, Pauline), and in some figurative sense, in ways we have elaborated in some detail, it is gendered feminine even when played by a male. Odysseus's position, trapped in the cave of the Cyclops, is after all not so different from Pauline's position tied to the tracks or Sally's trapped in the dining room of the slaughterhouse family. The decisive moment, as far as the fixing of gender is concerned, lies in what happens next: those who save themselves are male, and those who are saved by others are female. No matter how "feminine" his experience in phase 1, the traditional hero, if he rises against his adversary and saves himself in phase 2, will be male.

What is remarkable about the slasher film is that it comes close to reversing the priorities. Presumably for the various functional or figurative reasons we have considered in this essay, phase 1 wants a female: on that point all slashers from *Psycho* on are agreed. Abject fear is still gendered feminine, and the taboo anxieties in which slashers trade are still explored more easily via Pauline than Paul. The slippage comes in phase 2. As if in mute deference to a cultural imperative, slasher films from the 1970s bring in a last-minute male, even when he is rendered supernumerary by the Final Girl's sturdy defense. By 1980, however, the male rescuer is either dismissably marginal or dispensed with altogether; not a few films have him rush to the rescue only to be hacked to bits, leaving the Final Girl to save herself after all. At the moment that the Final Girl becomes her own savior, she becomes a hero; and the moment that she becomes a hero is the moment that the male viewer gives up the last pretense of male identification. Abject terror may still be gendered feminine, but the willingness of one immensely popular current genre to rerepresent the hero as an anatomical female would seem to suggest that at least one of the traditional marks of heroism, triumphant self-rescue, is no longer strictly gendered masculine.

So too the cinematic apparatus. The classic split between "spectacle and narrative," which "supposes the man's role as the active one of forwarding the story, making things happen," is at least unsettled in the slasher film.[67] When the Final Girl (in films like *Hell Night, Texas Chainsaw, Part 2,* and even *Splatter University* [1985]) assumes the "active investigating gaze," she exactly reverses the look, making a spectacle of the killer and a spectator of herself. Again, it is through the killer's eyes (I-camera) that we saw the Final Girl at the beginning of the film, and through the Final Girl's eyes that we see the killer, often for the first time with any clarity, toward the end. The gaze becomes, at least for a while, female. More to the point, the female exercise of scopic control results not in her annihilation, in the manner of classic cinema, but in her triumph; indeed, her triumph *depends* on her assumption of the gaze. It is no surprise, in light of these developments, that the Final Girl should show signs of boyishness. Her symbolic phallicization, in the last scenes, may or may not proceed at root from the horror of lack on the part of audience and maker. But it certainly proceeds from the need to bring her in line with the epic laws of Western narrative tradition—the very unanimity of which bears witness to the historical importance, in popular culture, of the literal representation of heroism in male form—and it proceeds no less from the need to render the reallocated gaze intelligible to an audience conditioned by the dominant cinematic apparatus.

It is worth noting that the higher genres of horror have for the most part resisted such developments. The idea of a female who outsmarts, much less outfights—or outgazes—her assailant is unthinkable in the films of De Palma and Hitchcock. Although the slasher film's victims may be sexual teases, they are not in addition simple-minded, scheming, physically incompetent, and morally deficient in the manner of these filmmakers' female victims. And however revolting their special effects and sexualized their violence, few slasher murders approach the level of voluptuous sadism that attends the destruction of women in De Palma's films. For reasons on which we can only speculate, femininity is more conventionally elaborated and inexorably punished, and in an emphatically masculine environment, in the higher forms— the forms that are written up, and not by Joe Bob Briggs.

That the slasher film speaks deeply and obsessively to male anxieties and desires seems clear—if nothing else from the maleness of the majority audience. And yet these are texts in which the categories masculine and feminine, traditionally embodied in male and female, are collapsed into one and the same character—a character who is anatomically female and one whose point of view the spectator is unambiguously invited, by the usual set of literary-structural and cinematic conventions, to share. The willingness and even eagerness (so we judge from these films' enormous popularity) of the male viewer to throw in his emotional lot, if only temporarily, with not only a woman but a woman in fear and pain, at least in the first instance, would seem to suggest that he has a vicarious stake in that fear and pain. If the act of horror spectatorship is itself registered as a "feminine" experience— that the shock effects induce bodily sensations in the viewer answering the fear and pain of the screen victim—the charge of masochism is underlined. This is not to say that the male viewer does not also have a stake in the sadistic side; narrative structure, cinematic procedures, and audience response all indicate that he shifts back and forth with ease. It is only to suggest that in the Final Girl sequence his empathy with what the films define as the female posture is fully engaged, and further, because this sequence is inevitably the central one in any given film, that the viewing experience hinges on the emotional assumption of the feminine posture. Kaja Silverman takes it a step farther: "I will hazard the generalization that it is always the victim—the figure who occupies the passive position—who is really the focus of attention, and whose subjugation the subject (whether male or female) experiences as a pleasurable repetition from his/her own story," she writes. "Indeed, I would go so far as to say that the fascination of the sadistic point of view is merely that it provides the best vantage point from which to watch the masochistic story unfold."[68]

The slasher is hardly the first genre in the literary and visual arts to invite identification with the female; one cannot help wondering more generally whether the historical maintenance of images of women in fear and pain does not have more to do with male vicarism than is commonly acknowledged. What distinguishes the slasher, however, is the absence or untenability of alternative perspectives and hence the exposed quality of the invitation. As a survey of the tradition shows, this has not always been the case. The stages of the Final Girl's evolution— her piecemeal absorption of functions previously represented in males— can be located in the years following 1978. The fact that the typical patrons of these films are the sons of marriages contracted in the 1960s or even early 1970s leads us to speculate that the dire claims of that era— that the women's movement, the entry of women into the workplace, and the rise of divorce and woman-headed families would yield massive gender confusion in the next generation—were not entirely wrong. We may prefer, in the 1980s, to speak of the cult of androgyny, but the point is roughly the same. The fact that we have in the killer a feminine male and in the main character a masculine female—parent and Everyteen, respectively—would seem, especially in the latter case, to suggest a

loosening of the categories, or at least of the equation sex = gender. It is
not that these films show us gender and sex in free variation; it is that
they fix on the irregular combinations, of which the combination masculine female repeatedly prevails over the combination feminine male.
The fact that masculine males (boyfriends, fathers, would-be rescuers)
are regularly dismissed through ridicule or death or both would seem
to suggest that it is not masculinity per se that is being privileged, but
masculinity in conjunction with a female body—indeed, as the term
"victim-hero" contemplates, masculinity in conjunction with femininity. For if "masculine" describes the Final Girl some of the time and
in some of her more theatrical moments, it does not do justice to the
sense of her character as a whole. She alternates between registers from
the outset; before her final struggle she endures the deepest throes of
"femininity"; and even during that final struggle she is now weak and
now strong, now flees the killer and now charges him, now stabs and is
stabbed, now cries out in fear and now shouts in anger. She is a physical female and a characterological androgyne: like her name, not masculine but either/or, both, ambiguous.[69]

Robin Wood speaks of the sense that horror, for him the by-
product of cultural crisis and disintegration, is "currently the most
important of all American [film] genres and perhaps the most progressive, even in its overt nihilism."[70] Likewise Vale and Juno say of the
"incredibly strange films," mostly low-budget horror, that their volume surveys: "They often present unpopular—even radical—views
addressing the social, political, racial, or sexual inequities, hypocrisy in
religion or government."[71] And Tania Modleski rests her case against
the standard critique of mass culture (stemming from the Frankfurt
School) squarely on the evidence of the slasher, which does *not* propose
a spurious harmony; does not promote the "specious good" (but indeed
often exposes and attacks it); does *not* ply the mechanisms of identification, narrative continuity, and closure to provide the sort of narrative
pleasure constitutive of the dominant ideology.[72] One is deeply reluctant to make progressive claims for a body of cinema as spectacularly
nasty toward women as the slasher film is, but the fact is that the
slasher does, in its own perverse way and for better or worse, constitute
a visible adjustment in the terms of gender representation. That it is an
adjustment largely on the male side, appearing at the farthest possible
remove from the quarters of theory and showing signs of trickling
upward, is of no small interest.

NOTES

I owe a special debt of gratitude to James Cunniff and Lynn Hunt for criticism and encouragement. Particular thanks to James (not Lynn) for sitting with me through not a few of these movies.

1. Morris Dickstein, "The Aesthetics of Fright," *American Film* 5, no. 10 (September 1980): 34.

2. "Will Rogers never met a man he didn't like, and I can truly say the same about the cinema," Harvey R. Greenberg says in his paean to horror, *The Movies on Your Mind* (New York: Dutton/Saturday Review Press, 1975); yet his claim does not extend to the "plethora of execrable imitations [of *Psycho*] that debased cinema" (p. 137).

3. William Schoell, *Stay Out of the Shower: Twenty-Five Years of Shocker Films Beginning with Psycho* (New York: Dembner, 1985).

4. "Joe Bob Briggs" was evidently invented as a solution to the *Dallas Time Herald*'s problem of "how to cover trashy movies." See Calvin Trillin's "American Chronicles: The Life and Times of Joe Bob Briggs, So Far," *New Yorker*, December 22, 1986, pp. 73–88.

5. Lew Brighton, "Saturn in Retrograde; or, The Texas Jump Cut," *Film Journal* 2, no. 4 (1975): 25.

6. Stephen Koch, "Fashions in Pornography: Murder as Cinematic Chic," *Harper's*, November 1976, pp. 108–9.

7. Robin Wood, "Return of the Repressed," *Film Comment* 14, no. 4 (July–August 1978): 30.

8. Robin Wood, "Beauty Bests the Beast," *American Film* 8, no. 10 (September 1983): 63.

9. Dickstein, "Aesthetics of Fright," p. 34.

10. Sigmund Freud, "The Uncanny," in *Standard Edition of the Complete Psychological Works of Sigmund Freud*, ed. and trans. James Strachey (London: Hogarth Press, 1964), 17:244.

11. Steven Marcus, *The Other Victorians: A Study of Sexuality and Pornography in Mid-Nineteenth-Century England* (New York: Basic Books, 1964), p. 278.

12. William Castle, *Step Right Up! I'm Gonna Scare the Pants Off America* (New York: Pharos Books, 1992), p. 262.

13. Given the number of permutations, it is no surprise that new strategies keep emerging. Only a few years ago, a director hit upon the idea of rendering the point of view of an infant through the use of an I-camera at floor level with a double-vision image (Larry Cohen, *It's Alive*). Nearly a century after technology provided a radically different means of telling a story, filmmakers are still uncovering the possibilities.

14. Mick Martin and Marsha Porter, *Video Movie Guide, 1987* (New York: Ballantine, 1987), p. 690. Wood, "Beauty," p. 65, notes that the first-person camera also serves to preserve the secret of the killer's identity for a final surprise—crucial to many films—but adds: "The sense of indeterminate, unidentified, possibly supernatural or superhuman Menace feeds the spectator's fantasy of power, facilitating a direct spectator-camera identification by keeping the intermediary character, while signified to be present, as vaguely defined as possible." Brian De Palma's *Blow Out* opens with a parody of just this cinematic habit.

15. On this widely discussed topic, see Kaja Silverman, *The Subject of Semiotics* (New York: Oxford University Press, 1983), pp. 194–236; and Lesley Stern, "Point of View: The Blind Spot," *Film Reader*, no. 4 (1979): 214–36.

16. In this essay I have used the term *identification* vaguely and generally to refer to both primary and secondary processes. See Mary Ann Doane, "Misrecognition and

Identity," *Cine-Tracts,* no. 11 (1980): 25–32; and Christian Metz, "The Imaginary Signi-fier," *The Imaginary Signifier: Psychoanalysis and the Cinema* (Bloomington: Indiana University Press, 1982).

17. Mark Nash, "*Vampyr* and the Fantastic," *Screen* 17, no. 3 (Autumn 1976): 37. Nash coins the term *cinefantastic* to refer to this play.

18. Rosemary Jackson, *Fantasy: The Literature of Subversion* (London and New York: Methuen, 1981), p. 31.

19. As Dickstein puts it, "The 'art' of horror film is a ludicrous notion since horror, even at its most commercially exploitative, is genuinely subculture like the wild child that can never be tamed, or the half-human mutant who appeals to our secret fascination with deformity and the grotesque." "Aesthetics," p. 34.

20. James B. Twitchell, *Dreadful Pleasures: An Anatomy of Modern Horror* (New York: Oxford University Press, 1985), p. 84.

21. Donald Spoto, *The Dark Side of Genius: The Life of Alfred Hitchcock* (Boston and Toronto: Little, Brown, 1983), p. 421.

22. Wood, "Return of the Repressed," p. 26. In Wes Craven's *A Nightmare on Elm Street* (1985), it is the nightmare itself, shared by the teenagers who live on Elm Street, that is fatal. One by one they are killed by the murderer of their collective dream. The one girl who survives does so by first refusing to sleep and then, at the same time that she acknowledges her parents' inadequacies, by conquering the feelings that prompt the deadly nightmare. See, on the topic of dream/horror, Dennis L. White, "The Poetics of Horror," *Cinema Journal* 10, no. 2 (Spring 1971): 1–18. Reprinted in *Film Genre: Theory and Criticism,* ed. Barry K. Grant (Metuchen, N.J.: Scarecrow Press, 1977), pp. 124–44.

23. It is not just the profit margin that fuels the production of low horror. It is also the fact that, thanks to the irrelevance of production values, the initial stake is within the means of a small group of investors. Low horror is thus for all practical purposes the only way an independent filmmaker can break into the market. Add to this the film-maker's unusual degree of control over the product, and one begins to understand why it is that low horror engages the talents of such people as Stephanie Rothman, George Romero, Wes Craven, and Larry Cohen. As V. Vale and Andrea Juno put it, "The value of low-budget films is: they can be transcendent expressions of a single person's individual vision and quirky originality. When a corporation decides to invest $20 million in a film, a chain of command regulates each step, and no person is allowed free rein. Meetings with lawyers, accountants, and corporate boards are what films in Hollywood are all about." *Incredibly Strange Films,* ed. V. Vale and Andrea Juno (San Francisco: ReSearch #10, 1986), p. 5.

24. Despite the film industry's interest in demographics, there is no in-depth study of the composition of the slasher-film audience. Twitchell, *Dreadful Pleasures,* pp. 69–72 and 306–7, relies on personal observation and the report of critics, which are remarkably consistent over time and from place to place; my own observations concur. The audience is mostly between the ages of 12 and 20, and disproportionately male. Some critics remark on a contingent of older men who sit separately and who, in Twitchell's view, are there "not to be frightened, but to participate" specifically in the "stab-at-female" episodes. Roger Ebert and Gene Siskel corroborate the observation.

25. The development of the human-sausage theme is typical of the back-and-forth borrowing in low horror. *The Texas Chainsaw Massacre* hints at it; *Motel Hell* turns it into an industry ("Farmer Vincent's Smoked Meats: This is it!" proclaims a local bill-board); and *The Texas Chainsaw Massacre, Part 2* expands it to a statewide chili-tasting contest.

26. The release of sexuality in the horror film is always presented as perverted, mon-strous, and excessive, both the perversion and the excess being the logical outcome of repressing. Nowhere is this carried further than in *The Texas Chainsaw Massacre.* Here

sexuality is totally perverted from its functions, into sadism, violence, and cannibalism. It is striking that there is no suggestion anywhere that Sally is the object of an overtly sexual threat; she is to be tormented, killed, dismembered, and eaten, but not raped." Wood, "Return of the Repressed," p. 31.

27. With some exceptions—for example, the speargun used in the sixth killing in *Friday the 13th, Part III.*

28. Stuart Kaminsky, *American Film Genres: Approaches to a Critical Theory of Popular Film* (Dayton, Ohio: Pflaum, 1974), p. 107.

29. The shower sequence in *Psycho* is probably the most echoed scene in all of film history. The bathtub scene in *I Spit on Your Grave* (not properly speaking a slasher, though with a number of generic affinities) is to my knowledge the only effort to reverse the terms.

30. Schoell, *Stay Out of the Shower*, p. 35. It may be argued that *Blood Feast* (1963), in which a lame Egyptian caterer slaughters one woman after another for their body parts (all in the service of Ishtar), provides the serial-murder model.

31. This theme too is spoofed in *Motel Hell.* Farmer Vincent's victims are two hookers, a kinky couple looking for same (he puts them in room 1 of the motel), and Terry and her boyfriend Bo, out for kicks on a motorcycle. When Terry (allowed to survive) wonders aloud why someone would try to kill them, Farmer Vincent answers her by asking pointedly whether they were married. "No," she says, in a tone of resignation, as if accepting the logic.

32. "Scenes in which women whimper helplessly and do nothing to defend themselves are ridiculed by the audience, who find it hard to believe that anyone—male or female—would simply allow someone to kill them with nary a protest." Schoell, *Stay Out of the Shower*, pp. 55–56.

33. *Splatter University* (1984) is a disturbing exception. Professor Julie Parker is clearly established as a Final Girl from the outset and then killed just after the beginning of what we are led to believe will be the Final Girl sequence (she kicks the killer, a psychotic priest-scholar who keeps his knife sheathed in a crucifix, in the groin, runs for the elevator—and then is trapped and stabbed to death). So meticulously are the conventions observed, and then so grossly violated, that we can only assume sadistic intentionality. This is a film in which (with the exception of an asylum orderly in the preface) only females are killed and in highly sexual circumstances.

34. This film is complicated by the fact that the action is envisaged as a living dream. Nancy finally kills the killer by killing her part of the collective nightmare. See note 22 above.

35. Spoto, *Dark Side of Genius*, p. 454. See also William Rothman, Hitchcock: The Murderous Gaze (Cambridge, Mass.: Harvard University Press, 1982), pp. 246–341.

36. Edgar Allan Poe, "The Philosophy of Composition," in *Selected Prose, Poetry and Eureka* (San Francisco: Rhinehart Press, 1950), p. 425.

37. Quoted in Schoell, *Stay Out of the Shower*, p. 56.

38. Quoted in ibid., p. 41.

39. Spoto, *Dark Side of Genius*, p. 483.

40. Silvia Bovenschen, "Is There a Feminine Aesthetic?" *New German Critique* 10 (Winter 1977): 114. See also Doane, "Misrecognition and Identity."

41. E. Ann Kaplan, *Women and Film: Both Sides of the Camera* (New York and London: Methuen, 1983), p. 15. The discussion of the gendered "gaze" is lively and extensive. See, above all, Laura Mulvey, "Visual Pleasure and Narrative Cinema," *Screen* 16, no. 3 (Autumn 1975): 6–18; also see Christine Gledhill, "Recent Developments in Feminist Criticism," *Quarterly Review of Film Studies* 3, no. 4 (Fall 1978): 458–93.

42. Wood, "Beauty Bests the Beast," p. 64.

43. The locus classicus in this connection is the view-from-the-coffin shot in Carl

Dreyer's *Vampyr* (1932), in which the I-camera sees through the eyes of a dead man. See Nash, "*Vampyr* and the Fantastic," esp. pp. 32–33. The 1986 remake of *The Little Shop of Horrors* (originally a low-budget horror film, made the same year as *Psycho* in two days) lets us see the dentist from the proximate point of view of the patient's tonsils.

44. Two points in this paragraph deserve emending. One is the suggestion that rape is common in these films; it is in fact virtually absent, by definition (see note 26 above). The other is the characterization of the Final Girl as "sexy." She may be attractive (although typically less so than her friends), but she is with few exceptions sexually inactive. For a detailed analysis of point-of-view manipulation, together with a psychoanalytic interpretation of the dynamic, see Steve Neale, "*Halloween*: Suspense, Aggression, and the Look," *Framework* 14 (1981): 25–29; reprinted in *Planks of Reason: Essays on the Horror Film,* ed. Barry Keith Grant (Metuchen, N.J.: Scarecrow Press, 1984), pp. 331–45.

45. Wood is struck by the willingness of the teenage audience to identify "against" itself, with the forces of the enemy of youth: "Watching [*The Texas Chainsaw Massacre*] recently with a large, half-stoned youth audience, who cheered and applauded every one of Leatherface's outrages against their representatives on the screen, was a terrifying experience" ("Return of the Repressed," p. 32).

46. "I really appreciate the way audiences respond," Gail Anne Hurd, producer of *Aliens,* is reported to have said in the *San Francisco Examiner Datebook,* August 10, 1986, p. 19. "They buy it. We don't get people, even rednecks, leaving the theatre saying, 'That was stupid. No woman would do that.' You don't have to be a liberal ERA supporter to root for Ripley." *Time,* July 28, 1986, p. 56, suggests that Ripley's maternal impulses (she squares off against the worst aliens of all in her quest to save a little girl) give the audience "a much stronger rooting interest in Ripley, and that gives the picture resonances unusual in a popcorn epic."

47. "When she [the mother] referred to the infant as a male, I just went along with it. Wonder how that child turned out—male, female, or something else entirely?" The birth is understood to be parthenogenetic, and the bisexual child, literally equipped with both sets of genitals, is figured as the reborn Christ.

48. Linda Williams, "When the Woman Looks," in *Re-Vision: Essays in Feminist Film Criticism,* ed. Mary Ann Doane, Patricia Mellencamp, and Linda Williams (Frederick, Md.: University Publications of America/American Film Institute, 1984), p. 90. Williams's emphasis on the phallic leads her to dismiss slasher killers as a "non-specific male killing force" and hence a degeneration in the tradition. "In these films the recognition and affinity between woman and monster of classic horror film gives way to pure identity: she *is* the monster, her mutilated body is the only visible horror" (p. 96). This analysis does justice neither to the obvious bisexuality of slasher killers, nor to the new strength of the female victim. The slasher film may not, in balance, be more subversive than traditional horror, but it is certainly not less so.

49. Freud, "The Uncanny," p. 245. See also Neale, "*Halloween*," esp. pp. 28–29.

50. "The woman's exercise of an active investigating gaze can only be simultaneous with her own victimization. The place of her specularization is transformed into the locus of a process of seeing designed to unveil an aggression against itself." Mary Ann Doane, "The Woman's Film: Possession and Address," in *Re-Vision,* p. 72.

51. John Carpenter, interviewed by Todd McCarthy, "Trick or Treat," *Film Comment* 16, no. 1 (January–February 1980): 23–24.

52. This is not so in traditional film or in heterosexual pornography, in any case. Gay male pornography films female bodies.

53. Compare the visual treatment of the (male) rape in *Deliverance* (1972) with the (female) rapes in Hitchcock's *Frenzy* (1972), Craven's *Last House on the Left* (1972), or Bergman's *The Virgin Spring* (1959). The latter films study the victims' faces at length

and in close-up during the act; the former looks at the act intermittently and in longshot, focusing less on the actual victim than on the victim's friend who must look on.

54. Marcus, *The Other Victorians*, pp. 260–61. Marcus distinguishes two phases in the development of flagellation literature: one in which the figure being beaten is a boy, and a second in which the figure is a girl. The very shift indicates, at some level, the irrelevance of apparent sex. "The sexual identity of the figure being beaten is remarkably labile. Sometimes he is represented as a boy, sometimes as a girl, sometimes as a combination of the two—a boy dressed as a girl, or the reverse." The girls often have sexually ambiguous names as well. The beater is a female but, in Marcus's reading, a phallic one—muscular, possessed of body hair—representing the father.

55. Ibid., pp. 125–27.

56. "Suspense is like a woman. The more left to the imagination, the more the excitement. . . . The perfect 'woman of mystery' is one who is blonde, subtle, and Nordic. . . . Movie titles, like women, should be easy to remember without being familiar, intriguing but never obvious, warm yet refreshing, suggest action, not impassiveness, and finally give a clue without revealing the plot. Although I do not profess to be an authority on women, I fear that the perfect title, like the perfect woman, is difficult to find." Quoted in Spoto, *Dark Side of Genius*, p. 431.

57. This would seem to be the point of the final sequence of De Palma's *Blow Out*, in which we see the boyfriend of the victim-hero stab the killer to death but later hear the television announce that the woman herself vanquished the killer. The frame plot of the film has to do with the making of a slasher film (*Co-Ed Frenzy*), and it seems clear that De Palma means his ending to stand as a comment on the Final Girl formula of the genre. De Palma's (and indirectly Hitchcock's) insistence that only men can kill men, or protect women from men, deserves a separate essay.

58. The term is Judith Fetterly's. See her *The Resisting Reader, A Feminist Approach to American Fiction* (Bloomington: Indiana University Press, 1978).

59. On the possible variety of responses to a single film, see Norman N. Holland, "I-ing Film," *Critical Inquiry* 12 (Summer 1986): 654–71.

60. Marcus, *The Other Victorians*, p. 127. Marcus contents himself with noting that the scene demonstrates a "confusion of sexual identity." In the literature of flagellation, he adds, "this confused identity is also present, but it is concealed and unacknowledged." But it is precisely the femaleness of the beaten figures that does acknowledge it.

61. Freud, "The Uncanny," esp. pp. 219–21 and 226–27.

62. Paymond Durgnat, *Films and Feelings* (London: Faber and Faber, 1967), p. 216.

63. Not a few critics have argued that the ambiguity is the unintentional result of bad filmmaking.

64. So argues Susan Barrowclough: the "male spectator takes the part not of the male but of the female. Contrary to the assumption that the male uses pornography to confirm and celebrate his gender's sexual activity and dominance, is the possibility of his pleasure in identifying with a 'feminine' passivity or subordination." "Not a Love Story," *Screen* 23, no. 5 (November–December 1982): 35–36. Alan Soble seconds the proposal in his *Pornography: Marxism, Feminism, and the Future of Sexuality* (New Haven, Conn.: Yale University Press, 1986), p. 93. Porn/sexploitation filmmaker Joe Sarno: "My point of view is more or less always from the woman's point of view; the fairy tales that my films are based on are from the woman's point of view; I stress the efficacy of women for themselves. In general, I focus on the female orgasm as much as I can." Quoted in Vale and Juno, eds., *Incredibly Strange Films*, p. 94. "Male identification with women," Kaja Silverman writes, "has not received the same amount of critical attention [as sublimation into professional 'showing off' and reversal into scopophilia], although it would seem the most potentially destabilizing, at least as far as gender is concerned." See her discussion of the "Great Male Renunciation" in "Fragments of a Fashionable Discourse," in

Studies in Entertainment: Critical Approaches to Mass Culture, ed. Tania Modleski (Bloomington: Indiana University Press, 1986), p. 141.

65. Elaine Showalter, "Critical Cross Dressing: Male Feminists and the Woman of the Year," *Raritan* 3 (Fall 1983): 138.

66. Whatever its other functions, the scene that reveals the Final Girl in a degree of undress serves to underscore her femaleness. One reviewer of *Aliens* remarks that she couldn't help wondering why in the last scene, just as in *Alien*, "we have Ripley wandering around clad only in her underwear. A little reminder of her gender, lest we lose sight of it behind all that firepower?" Christine Schoefer, *East Bay Express*, September 5, 1986, p. 37.

67. Mulvey, "Visual Pleasure and Narrative Cinema," p. 12.

68. Kaja Silverman, "Masochism and Subjectivity," *Framework* 12 (1979): 5. Needless to say, this is not the explanation for the girl hero offered by the industry. *Time*, July 28, 1986, p. 44, on *Aliens*: "As director Cameron says, the endless 'remulching' of the masculine hero by the 'male-dominated industry' is, if nothing else, commercially shortsighted. 'They choose to ignore that 50% of the audience is female. And I've been told that it has been proved demographically that 80% of the time it's women who decide which film to see.'" It is of course not Cameron who established the female hero of the series but Ridley Scott (in *Alien*), and it is fair to assume, from his careful manipulation of the formula, that Scott got her from the slasher film, where she has flourished for some time among audiences that are heavily male. Cameron's analysis is thus both self-serving and beside the point.

69. If this analysis is correct, we may expect horror films of the future to feature Final Boys as well as Final Girls. Two recent figures may be incipient examples: Jesse, the pretty boy in *A Nightmare on Elm Street, Part 2: Freddy's Revenge* (1985), and Ashley, the character who dies last in *The Evil Dead* (1983). Neither quite plays the role, but their names, and in the case of Jesse the characterization, seem to play on the tradition.

70. For the opposite view (based on classic horror in both literary and cinematic manifestations), see Franco Moretti, "The Dialectic of Fear," *New Left Review*, no. 136 (1982): 67–85.

71. Vale and Juno, eds., *Incredibly Strange Films*, p. 5.

72. Tania Modleski, "The Terror of Pleasures: The Contemporary Horror Film and Postmodern Theory," in *Studies in Entertainment*, pp. 155–66. (Like Modleski, I stress that my comments are based on many slashers, not all of them.) This important essay (and volume) appeared too late for me to take it into full account here.

Stephen Prince

The Aesthetic of Slow-Motion Violence in the Films of Sam Peckinpah

Violence assumes a myriad of forms in contemporary cinema, but the aesthetic of violence has evolved to emphasize a cluster of predominant and recurring characteristics. In scenes involving gunplay, editors assemble footage filmed with multiple cameras into complex montages, intercutting normal-speed footage with slow-motion imagery. This style—multicamera montage with slow motion—has become the predominant aesthetic form for rendering gun battles in modern cinema. In their work on *The Wild Bunch* (1969), director Sam Peckinpah and editor Lou Lombardo gave this stylistic the emphasis and elaboration that transformed it into the essential template that it has now become, and Peckinpah has remained the most inventive and influential director to use this aesthetic. Accordingly, after examining the roots of this aesthetic, I examine Peckinpah's elaboration and transformation of it, his objectives and the controversies his work has provoked, and the implications of that work for later filmmakers.

Peckinpah used the montage aesthetic to break with realism in order to substitute a *stylized* rendition of violence. This point is most important, given the common critical (and wrongheaded) view that Peckinpah's signal contribution in the late 1960s was to bring to American cinema a more realistic depiction of violence whereby the bloodless deaths portrayed in previous decades of film gave way to a more forthright, and truer, presentation of gore. This view has tended to obscure the important point that Peckinpah aimed to stylize his materials and that this stylization proceeded from his conviction that it was the only way to wake people up to violence in a culture—late 1960s America—whose convulsions, he believed, had anesthetized them to bloody death. Peckinpah felt that people had become inured to violence through the medium of television, which domesticated the violence of the Vietnam War and, by sandwiching it between commercials, insinuated it into the daily routines of consumer life. In a culture and during a period so heavily saturated with killing, people had become oddly desensitized, he believed, and he felt that by heightening violence through the artifice of style he could break the cycle of consumption in which the era's disturbing social violence was embedded. In this regard, he was a filmmaker with a didactic social agenda, and he aimed to place camera style at the service of that agenda:

> We watch our wars and see men die, really die, every day on television, but it doesn't seem real. We don't believe those are real people dying on that screen. We've been anesthetized by the media. What I do is show people what it's really like—not by showing it as it is so much as by heightening it, stylizing it. . . . The only way I can do that is by not letting them gloss over the looks of it, as if it were the seven o'clock news from the DMZ. When people complain about the way I handle violence, what they're really saying is, "Please don't show me; I don't want to know; and get me another beer out of the icebox."[1]

The montage aesthetic served these didactic intentions because it was a decisive break with previous screen traditions of representing violence and with the unremarkable visual presence of daily TV violence. Peckinpah insisted that his visual approach was a reaction against the existing movie traditions, which he considered to be misleading and grossly out of step with the times. He believed that "violence in motion pictures is usually treated like fun and games."[2] In a letter to Paul Staniford, a lawyer and friend of the Peckinpah family (and whose name Peckinpah gave to a character in *Ride the High Country*), Peckinpah declared, "I personally feel it's time Hollywood quit glamorizing violence and let people see how brutalizing and horrible it really is. This is what I tried to do [in *The Wild Bunch*]."[3] By breaking the established representational conventions, Peckinpah hoped to convey the horror of violence to viewers he believed had been rendered complacent by decades of painless, bloodless movie killings. In late 1960s America, the traumatic impact of real social violence was misaligned with the tradition of sanitized movie violence.

For Peckinpah, conventional movie violence and television news performed a narcotizing function, insulating people from the

Figure 30. *Sam Peckinpah, the modern poet of screen violence, popularized the essential film style for depicting gun violence.*

events around them. His belief in this narcotizing function was consistent with the radical critique of popular culture in that period (as represented in the writings of Susan Sontag and Herbert Marcuse).[4] By using graphic imagery of bloodletting and the montage aesthetic, Peckinpah aimed to bring the era's violence inside the movie theater, which would no longer function as a place of refuge by shielding viewers from horrific images. His work would place the filmic representation of violence into proper synchronicity with the era, whose convulsions engulfed the sensibilities of filmmaker and audience alike. His object in doing this was to create a socially beneficial effect. "To negate violence it must be shown for what it is," he argued, "a horrifying, brutalizing, destructive, ingrained part of humanity."[5] If the narcotizing functions of the media were broken, Peckinpah believed, people would see violence for what it is and thereby stand a chance of gaining more control over it and its destructive effects on a nation in turmoil. After receiving a letter from a viewer critical of *The Wild Bunch*, Peckinpah wrote back and asked that the viewer consider that the graphic screen carnage had these larger objectives. "I am sorry you did not enjoy *The Wild Bunch*. Perhaps some of its vulgarity and violence will remain with the people who will see it and they will understand better the nature of this continuing plague that infects our country."[6]

With this description of Peckinpah's objectives in mind, we should now examine the origins of the aesthetic and the distinctive structure of the montage editing in his films, its operation and effects. What are the characteristic manipulations of time and space that this aesthetic makes possible? And what are their effects on the viewer? Does the montage aesthetic enable a filmmaker to develop a critical perspective on the represented violence, or does it tend, instead, toward spectacle and the incitement of excitatory responses?

Antecedents of Peckinpah's Montage Style

The essential influences on his montage aesthetic are easily identified. The most important influence is the work of Akira Kurosawa because it was Kurosawa who first showed filmmakers how to intercut slow-motion and normal-speed footage in scenes of violence. As an initial transposition of Kurosawa's work and the immediate stimulus for *The Wild Bunch*, there is Arthur Penn's demonstration of slow-motion and multicamera filming in *Bonnie and Clyde*. In a distant context, of course, there is the montage editing of Sergei Eisenstein. (Other precedents, more prosaic, perhaps, were also important. While working in the early 1950s as a stagehand at KLAC-TV in Los Angeles, Peckinpah watched an experimental film made by another station employee. It included a slow-motion shot of a falling lightbulb that intrigued Peckinpah. Also, prior to cutting *The Wild Bunch*, Lou Lombardo showed Peckinpah an episode of the TV show "Felony Squad" that he had edited that included some slow-motion work during a gunfight.)[7]

Kurosawa, whose *Rashomon* (1950) Peckinpah always cited as

a favorite film, doubtless because its theme of the relativity of truth deeply appealed to his sense of irony, exerted a decisive stylistic influence on Peckinpah's work in several ways. Beginning with *Seven Samurai* (1954), Kurosawa customarily used from three to five cameras running simultaneously to film his scenes. This approach gave him much better coverage of that film's complexly choreographed fight scenes and also helped to elicit better performances from the actors by extending the length of each take. Peckinpah obviously appreciated the strategic advantages that multicamera filming afforded the shooting of action scenes. For the scene in *Bring Me the Head of Alfredo Garcia*, where the professional killers Quill and Sappensly massacre a Mexican family, Peckinpah used five cameras, two of which were running at high speed to produce slow motion.[8] (Slow motion is produced by filming at very high speeds—this captures the action on a much greater number of frames that, when projected at the industry standard of twenty-four frames per second, will appear as slow motion.) On *Junior Bonner*, for the critical sequence in which the bulldozers wreck Ace's house, Peckinpah employed four cameras: two high-speed cameras with zoom lenses at opposite angles on the house, an Arriflex wide angle for a long-shot on the front of the house, and an Arriflex telephoto for a low angle on the right of the house.[9] Covering the action simultaneously from so many angles and with different camera speeds amplifies the material available for montage editing, an obvious strategic advantage given Peckinpah's desires to transform the normative conventions of American cinema.

Kurosawa's multicameras, though, described a fixed and unique geometry of space. They were often set at right angles to one another so that the cuts shift the viewer's axis of vision by 90 degrees. While space in Kurosawa's cinema is extremely angular, the disjunctiveness of his cutting is softened somewhat by the recurrent regularities of these 90-degree perspective realignments. The angularity of Peckinpah's cutting exhibits none of the rectilinear "normality" of Kurosawa's 90-degree-angle shifts. Peckinpah's angularity is totally acute or oblique, always off-center, and, as a result, it imposes a much higher degree of fragmentation upon the space that it carves up. Peckinpah learned from Kurosawa's disjunctive editing of space and carried its implications much further, as the cutting throughout *Straw Dogs* clearly demonstrates.

Kurosawa's cinema also taught Peckinpah about the perspective-distorting effects of telephoto lenses, a signature Kurosawa element that became a signature Peckinpah element, because the telephoto lens works extremely well in conjunction with multicamera filming. By equipping multicameras with long-focal-length lenses, the cameras can be positioned more easily about the periphery of the set. Since the focal length of the lenses will produce a narrow field of view that can be used to prevent the cameras from seeing each other, telephoto lenses facilitate the blocking of multicamera positions. Peckinpah quickly grasped the implications of this advantage. *Ride the High Country*, a nonmontage-based film, does not conspicuously utilize telephoto lenses, while *The Wild Bunch*, a montage and multicamera film, clearly does, as do many of his later films.

In addition to the multicamera filming, disjunctively angular cutting, and reliance on telephoto lenses that Peckinpah found in Kurosawa's work, the most explicit area of influence from Kurosawa to Peckinpah is, of course, Kurosawa's exploration of slow motion within scenes of violent death. (Kurosawa's use of slow motion was also an important influence on Walon Green in his thinking about the script for *The Wild Bunch*, although he did not write out these ideas. He told an interviewer, "The violence in slow motion is very expressly in the script. I put the slow motion in because when I wrote it, I had just seen *The Seven Samurai*, which had the first use of slow motion in an action scene that I'd ever seen." Peckinpah scholar Paul Seydor points out that Green told him this claim was an error: that he did not, in fact, write slow motion into the script, but was thinking about it while working on the script because of the Kurosawa film, which had tremendously impressed him.)[10]

This interest appeared as early as Kurosawa's first film, *Sanshiro Sugata* (1943), but it was *Seven Samurai* (1954), widely seen and admired in the West, with its all-male band of heroes, adventure narrative, and martial values, that explicitly demonstrated the stylistic patterning that the intercutting of footage shot at different camera speeds could bring to the dramatic and temporal rhythms of a scene. In this respect, *Seven Samurai* furnished the stylistic template utilized and popularized by Peckinpah and by Arthur Penn and used by every action scene choreographer ever since. Kurosawa's work occasioned Peckinpah's famous remark, following completion of *Ride the High Country*, "I'd like to be able to make a Western like Kurosawa makes Westerns."[11] Weddle's biography claims that Kurosawa's use of slow motion was primitive compared to the complexities introduced by Peckinpah. "Editorially it was static. The weaving of slow motion into the very fabric of a sequence . . . had still to be achieved."[12] While it is true that Peckinpah used slow motion far more extensively than Kurosawa (and that he began using it well before *The Wild Bunch*, as Weddle and Seydor have pointed out), who seemed to have only an occasional interest in the device, the essentials of Peckinpah's usage are clearly already contained in *Seven Samurai*.

Contrary to Weddle's claims, Kurosawa does cut in and out of the slow-motion footage in a dynamic manner. During the scene where the leader of the samurai, Kambei (Takashi Shimura), rescues a kidnapped child from a crazed thief and kills the thief with a short sword, Kurosawa dynamically intercuts footage filmed at normal speed with slow-motion footage so that the rhythms of the scene oscillate between these two different temporal modes. The mortally wounded thief crashes through the hut's doorway to the village square outside, where amazed onlookers witness his dying. Kurosawa intercuts three slow-motion shots of the thief crashing through the door, running a few steps forward, and rising up on tiptoe with three normal-speed shots of the onlookers' reactions. Since movement also occurs in these shots, the scene builds an internal tension between these differing rhythms. After

Figure 31. In Seven Samurai, *Kurosawa intercuts slow-motion shots of the dying thief (foreground) with normal-speed shots of onlookers. This scene provided the essential template for modern movie violence, showing other filmmakers how to integrate footage shot at differing camera speeds to aestheticize violence.*

these six shots, Kurosawa shows the thief fall to the ground in slow motion but without the sound of an impact. This sound has been withdrawn from the scene, setting up a dynamic visual–acoustic conflict that accompanies the temporal conflicts.

But the visual–acoustic conflicts in the film are more subtle still and hold yet greater relevance for Peckinpah's work and for the slow-motion aesthetic. During the scene's slow-motion shots, Kurosawa includes amplified sound effects—the baby's cry, the mother's scream, howling wind—which involve no temporal distortion. Amplified, but temporally unmodified, sound accompanies the slow-motion images, and this disjunction emphasizes the heightened artifice of these images, their uniquely expressive power. What we have yet to appreciate is not only how fundamentally Kurosawa's brief exploration of slow-motion effects influenced Peckinpah's work, but also how Kurosawa had already made the essential discovery that a temporal nonsynchrony of image and sound accentuates the contrast of footage shot at differing camera speeds. The normal-speed sound emphasizes the otherness of the slow-motion image. This visual–acoustic principle is basic to the expressive power of such sequences.

Following Kurosawa, Peckinpah manipulates sound during the slow-motion shots by amplifying selected effects. The cries of the baby and mother and the howling wind are selectively amplified during the slow-motion shots in *Seven Samurai* to accentuate the temporal mismatch between the audiovisual tracks. In the opening shoot-out in *The Wild Bunch*, when an outlaw crashes his horse through a glass window in slow motion, the sound of shattering glass heard at normal tempo is mixed above the general battle sounds to accentuate the temporal mismatches, and when Dutch (Ernest Borgnine) falls off his horse into a wooden structure in slow motion, the amplified crunch of wood is the dominant sound. In Peckinpah's work, the slow-motion image is carefully contrasted with amplified sound effects to create an intermodal, cross-sensory montage, and, as we have established, the expressive power of these combinations had been explicitly demonstrated by Kurosawa.

Kurosawa's disjunctive editing and audiovisual combinations are indebted to the montage tradition exemplified by Eisenstein and so, too, therefore, is Peckinpah's work. Care needs to be exercised in extending these comparisons, however. Eisenstein's montage principles belong to a rich and specific ideological and social context that informed his filmmaking, a context that does not translate to either

Kurosawa or Peckinpah, who both employed a much more limited use of montage. The Odessa Steps massacre in *Potemkin*, for example, features a complex orchestration of graphic, volumetric, kinetic, and temporal elements in a design whose intricacy surpasses the narrower range of manipulations Peckinpah carried out in his montages. This is why Eisenstein looms as a more distant and general example for Peckinpah's cinema rather than as a direct and immediate influence. Despite this caveat, it is worth noting that Peckinpah's artistic relationship with Kurosawa and Eisenstein achieved a degree of self-consciousness during the production of Peckinpah's films. On *Cross of Iron*, production designer Ted Haworth told Peckinpah that a particular effect would be "Kurosawa Peckinpah at his best."[13] Discussing with Peckinpah the story structure as scripted for *The Wild Bunch*, producer Phil Feldman noted that an improperly placed scene with the bounty hunters "would interrupt your Eisenstein structure."[14]

While Kurosawa's work had impressed Peckinpah, it was Arthur Penn's demonstration in *Bonnie and Clyde* of Kurosawa-style montage that fired Peckinpah with the determination to outdo the level of bloodshed—and its aesthetic rendering—that Penn had achieved. Penn's work is historically important in this context because of its timing—*Bonnie and Clyde* appeared two years before *The Wild Bunch*. Furthermore, as with Peckinpah, Penn was a stylistic disciple of Kurosawa, whose editing in *Seven Samurai* had furnished the essential template. Penn graciously acknowledged Kurosawa's importance for the multispeed montage that caps *Bonnie and Clyde*. Discussing his conceptualization of that scene, he remarked, "Having seen enough Kurosawa by that point, I knew how to do it."[15] Throughout his career, Penn remained a vivid stylist of violence, but he never again filmed anything like the slow-motion, multicamera carnage that caps *Bonnie and Clyde*. Thus, although that is a seminal film, Penn remains an intermediary figure—not a primary one—in the history of modern screen violence, standing between Kurosawa (as the stylistic mentor) and Peckinpah (as the filmmaker who became the exponent of slow-motion violence). In this regard, it is important to understand the contribution of *Bonnie and Clyde* to Peckinpah's work, but equally important to recognize that, while Penn moved on to make films on other topics, Peckinpah remained preoccupied by the issue of violence in human life and as a subject for film.

Peckinpah claimed to have seen *Bonnie and Clyde* only after finishing *The Wild Bunch* and claimed ownership of Penn's slow-motion work, remarking "they did all my shtick."[16] Despite this claim, however, wardrobe supervisor Gordon Dawson recollected that Peckinpah wanted to surpass *Bonnie and Clyde*'s violence and stylistics while in production on *The Wild Bunch*. Furthermore, in a letter of March 19, 1968, Warner Bros. confirmed with the film's production manager that a print of *Bonnie and Clyde* would be shipped to Peckinpah's Mexico location for a screening the next weekend (March 23–24). This was immediately prior to the start of principal photography on the 25th. Peckinpah was studying Penn's film and wanted to see it before commencing work on his own. He knew exactly what he was doing on *The Wild Bunch* and how it related to Penn's achievements in *Bonnie and Clyde*.[17]

If Peckinpah did not discover anything new about intercutting slow-motion shots into a montage sequence, he undeniably extended and built upon the principles informing Kurosawa's editing of multi-camera footage. Like Penn's use of slow motion within the bloody montage that concludes *Bonnie and Clyde*, which Penn said conveyed "both the spastic and the balletic" qualities of the gangsters' death agonies,[18] Peckinpah's editing emphasized the brutality of physical violence while also giving it a graceful beauty. This contradiction between the aesthetic beauty of the visual spectacle and the emotional and physical pain that Peckinpah also dramatized as part of his screen violence is a complex and important one, and Peckinpah used slow motion and montage to stylize screen violence in ways that far surpassed what Penn had done in *Bonnie and Clyde*. An comparison with Penn's films can help illuminate why Peckinpah's slow-motion inserts are more striking and achieve a more heightened stylistic intensity than do Penn's.

Penn began to explore slow motion in *The Left-Handed Gun* (1958), about the legend of Billy the Kid, during the scene where Billy (Paul Newman) kills Deputy Ollinger (Denver Pyle), a scene that Peckinpah closely re-creates in *Pat Garrett and Billy the Kid*. It is important to note here that Penn's film contains numerous images and bits of business that Peckinpah borrowed for his own film, including the Christ-pose Billy adopts when Garrett arrests him following the Stinking Springs shoot-out. Both films also reference the fascinated reaction of children to violent death, a major Peckinpah preoccupation. In Penn's film, a little girl runs out and laughs at the dead Ollinger, who has been blown out of his boot, while Peckinpah's film shows kids playing and laughing on the gallows that has been erected for Billy. And, again, much of this can be traced back to Kurosawa, who in *Seven*

Samurai had shown children playing and climbing on the fortress walls built to protect the village from the bandits and across which much killing would occur.

When Billy shoots Ollinger, Penn cuts from a slow-motion shot of Ollinger waving his arms and starting to fall backward to a fast-motion shot of his body hitting the ground. The transition from slow to fast motion is abrupt, and as a stylistic design it is clearly an experimental effort. "I was just playing with the medium," says Penn.[19] The experimentation doesn't work very well because the action rendered in slow motion—Ollinger flailing his arms—is not effectively suited for the temporal manipulation. It is neither balletic nor spastic. By contrast, in *Bonnie and Clyde,* Penn more shrewdly incorporates slow motion by intercutting it at multiple points with the jerky convulsing of the gangsters as they are riddled with bullets. By alternating between slow and apparently accelerated tempos (the apparent acceleration produced at normal film speed by virtue of the Texas Rangers' fast rate of fire), Penn successfully brings out the balletic and spastic qualities of the scene. Furthermore, Penn switches to slow motion at a more judicious moment than in *The Left-Handed Gun.* After a quick series of glances between Bonnie and Clyde that conveys their awareness of what is about to happen, Clyde runs toward Bonnie, at which point they are raked with machine-gun fire. As Clyde starts to fall, Penn switches to slow motion for the first time so that the arc of Clyde's dying fall is poetically extended.

The imagery is extremely vivid, and it discloses a fundamental principle that Peckinpah would observe in his own films: slow motion is especially powerful when it correlates with a character's loss of physical volition. Clyde's dying arc; the trajectories of falling, dying men shot from the rooftops of San Rafael or the army personnel blasted off the flatcars of the train in *The Wild Bunch;* the Gorch brothers dead on their feet but kept up convulsively by the impact of bullets fired by Mapache's men; Holly's mortal fall, blasted backward across the saloon by the force of Pat Garrett's shot; Lt. Triebig's grotesque writhing under Steiner's machine gun fire in *Cross of Iron*—all of these slow-motion images derive their poetic force from the metaphysical paradox of the body's continued animate reactions during a moment of diminished or extinguished consciousness. Slow motion intensifies this paradox by prolonging it. It is not just the moment of violent death which is extended, but the mysteries inherent in that twilit zone between consciousness and autonomic impulse, that awful moment when a personality ceases

to inhabit a body that is still in motion. Peckinpah, and Penn, intensified the trauma of violent death by visualizing this loss of human volition in a tangle of rioting flesh and nerve. To achieve maximum
intensity on this point, it was necessary to employ extremely fast camera speeds, for only by slowing down the action could the metaphysical
poetry of these scenes be elicited. This is why the slow-motion insert in
The Left-Handed Gun does not work very well. The slow speed is not
slow enough, and Ollinger has not yet lost control of his body.

As we can now see, ample precedent existed in the films of Kurosawa and Penn for the stylistic inflections that Peckinpah would
explore. However, with characteristic solipsism, Peckinpah claimed to
have gained insight into the cinematic usage of slow motion through
personal experience. He got into the habit of telling interviewers that
during his military service in China in 1945 he realized how slow
motion might apply to such scenes after seeing a Chinese passenger shot
while riding on a train. Peckinpah called it one of the longest split seconds of his life.[20] On other occasions when he told the story of learning
about slow motion, it was he who had been shot: "I was shot once and
I remembered falling down and it was so long . . . I noticed that time
slowed down and so I started making pictures where I slowed down
time, because that's the way it is."[21] We should be very skeptical of these
claims, because they sound like retrospective attempts to justify a stylistic inflection in the face of hostile critical reception (criticism that
Peckinpah's slow motion was self-indulgent) by attributing to the style
an empirical and phenomenological foundation in personal experience.

If, as he claims, Peckinpah's slow motion has its basis in real
perceptual experience, then—and this is the implied message to his
critics—he is no exploiter and glorifier of screen violence but merely an
observer of the psychological reality of living through a violent experience. But, phenomenologically, there seems no necessity for equating
the vividness of a brief traumatic episode with a subjective sense of
extended duration. This may occur, and perhaps it did for Peckinpah,
but it does not seem to be a necessity. It seems more likely that Peckinpah was struck by the stylistic manipulations of Kurosawa and Penn,
began trying them himself, and subsequently projected his World War
II memory onto the results. Through their montage structures, Peckinpah's films effect a formal transformation of violence, not an imitation of its psychological contours. These montages may incorporate
psychological dimensions of meaning, but they function as aesthetic
translations of the idea of violence, not as mimetic constructions that
seek to imitate faithfully the contours of an experience. The complex-

ity of these formal transformations constitutes one of Peckinpah's claims to being a great filmmaker, not his dubious assertions about the psychological basis of his slow-motion editing.

Slow-Motion Inserts

Peckinpah's aesthetic transformation of violence through montage led him toward three principal types of montage construction: the relatively simple, slow-motion insert crosscut into the body of a normal-tempo sequence; the synthetic superimposition of multiple lines of action with radical time-space distortions in a montage set-piece; and montages approaching Eisenstein's notion of intellectual editing, wherein the viewer is moved to cognitively grasp psychological or social truths. I examine here the first two categories of montage. Peckinpah used the third category—the psychological and poetic montages—to probe and visualize the subjective responses of characters to emotional and physical trauma. In this regard, he did not use it primarily to stylize gun violence, and since it falls outside the strict focus of this essay, I omit it from discussion here. (Readers interested in this category of montage should consult my extended discussion in *Savage Cinema*.)[22]

Slow-motion inserts crosscut into the body of a normal-tempo sequence may be found in all of Peckinpah's post-*Dundee* films. Even *The Ballad of Cable Hogue,* distinguished by its use of fast-motion footage and general absence of montage-based violence, opens with a Mexican beaded lizard (subbing for an iguana) exploding from gunfire in a slow-motion shot (followed by a three-frame 'subliminal' flash) that is inserted (but not crosscut) into the body of an otherwise normal-tempo sequence. It is easy enough to locate similar moments in the other films. As previously noted, Holly's backward lurch in *Pat Garrett and Billy the Kid,* after Garrett shoots him, describes a beautiful, slow-motion arc across the saloon floor and is cut into this scene, which is otherwise free of such temporal distortions. *The Wild Bunch*'s train heist is edited, for the most part, without temporal distortions, but when Pike throws the engineer and a crewman off the locomotive, the editing crosscuts their falling bodies, in slow motion, with the dying falls of the two soldiers Lyle Gorch shoots off the front of the train. In *Straw Dogs,* when the thuggish Tom Hedden (Peter Vaughan) blasts Major Scott (T. P. McKenna) with his shotgun, three shots crosscut with other action in the scene show Scott's misshapen body flying backward with slow-motion grace. In *The Killer Elite*, when professional killer George Hansen (Robert Duvall) executes Vorodny (Helmut Dantine), three slow-motion close-ups of Dantine falling onto the couch are crosscut with normal-tempo close-ups of Hansen watching this action. In the next scene, when Hansen cripples his friend Mike Locken (James Caan) by shooting him in the elbow and knee, Locken convulses in normal time but rolls off the stool onto the floor in slow motion.

I could continue to multiply examples, but the essential point should be clear. One of Peckinpah's basic montage structures involves the sudden intrusion of one or more slow-motion details inserted or crosscut into the body of a sequence whose temporal rhythms are otherwise normal. The perceptual shock of such intrusions comes from the sudden disruption of ordinary time through the influx of an alternate mode of time. In most cases, when squib-work is involved, the explosion of blood is not the main focus of the slow-motion insert. While the detonating squibs (electrical firing devices used to simulate bullet hits) were certainly shocking for audiences in 1969 when Peckinpah unleashed them, the bulk of the visual attention in the slow-motion inserts is devoted, as previously noted, to the body's loss of volitional control over its actions. The exploding squib behind Vorodny's head when Hansen shoots him is one of Peckinpah's most elaborate and graphically bloody, but it is only a few frames long, so that it appears as a flash cut despite occurring in slow motion. The aftereffects—Vorodny's slow fall onto the couch—take up much more screen time. Paul Seydor points out that Peckinpah purposely kept his slow-motion shots brief: "It is the build-up and the release that he wanted to capture, because perception and feeling, violence as psychological effect, are what chiefly interested him."[23]

While this is certainly true for such scenes as Vorodny's killing or, more remarkably, Garrett's killing of the Kid, the presence of extended, violent set-pieces in *The Wild Bunch, Straw Dogs, Bring Me the Head of Alfredo Garcia, Cross of Iron, The Killer Elite,* and *The Osterman Weekend* demonstrate that the act of violence, in itself, exerted tremendous fascination for Peckinpah. While I argue in *Savage Cinema* that Peckinpah's work is distinguished by the emotional and self-reflective frameworks it builds around the violence that it depicts, Peckinpah was also obsessive about this concern for violence and enthralled by the possibilities that cinema offers for visualizing it. His interests included the build-up and release of tension, the psychological effects of violent action, as well as the action and act of killing itself, only part of which is visualized in the squib-work.

The simplest of these cinematic possibilities lies in the momentary disruption of time by the brief, slow-motion insert placed to accentuate the lyrical appearance of the human body acted upon by violent physical forces that have extinguished its ability to respond in an intentional manner. It seems most probable that Peckinpah kept his slow-motion imagery brief not because he was interested exclusively in the psychological effects of violence, but rather because it worked best that way from a visual standpoint. Brevity accentuates the poetic effects of slow motion. Too much slow motion, or for too extended a period, would rob the scenes of their kinetic charge and their physical edge by making the action seem like it is occurring underwater or in a strange condition of weightlessness. By quickly (i.e., briefly) puncturing normal time and space with the slow- motion imagery, Peckinpah could stress the balletic beauty that, as a filmmaker, he discovered he could create within a maelstrom of death, and he could retain the sharp edge of physicality that was essential to his didactic intention.

This physicality is communicated by the normal-tempo images, not the slow-motion inserts, and by the sound effects that sensuously detail the thud of bullets into flesh, the violent exhalation of breath, shattering pottery, or crashing glass. When one of the outlaws is shot from his horse in the opening massacre of *The Wild Bunch*, we see rider and horse fall in beautiful slow motion. Because the pair's falls are so extended and the rate at which man and animal strike the ground is so gradual, the spill, as an image, lacks a strong physical dimension. But on the sound track as the horse goes down we hear a loud cracking sound like a bone breaking, and this gives the image a concreteness that the slow motion has removed from it. Peckinpah used the expressive poetry of slow motion to elicit balletic effects and to visualize that moment when death or grievous wounding robs or threatens to rob the body of its spirit or personality. He was striking a delicate balance between the slow-motion inserts and the normal-tempo continuum of the sequence proper. Too much slow motion would become ludicrous because it would bog down the violent outburst and remove all sense of its physical consequences. Slow motion, therefore, had to exist in a state of tension with the normal-tempo sound track and body proper of the sequence. Extended slow-motion imagery would not create this requisite tension. Slow motion had to constitute a brief interlude, disrupting the texture of the scene to offer a privileged glimpse at the metaphysical mysteries of violent death. Too long a glimpse and its effects would be vitiated.

Peckinpah rarely employed extended slow-motion imagery. In

the climax of *Straw Dogs,* when David Sumner (Dustin Hoffman) grapples with Charlie Venner following the shooting of Norman Scutt (both Venner and Scutt are members of the gang that has invaded the Sumners' house), Peckinpah presented their struggle in a lengthy series of slow-motion shots. It is an interesting usage, but it softens the hard edge the film's violence has heretofore had. The viewer feels that little harm can come to either David or Charlie while they slog slowly around as if underwater. Significantly, when David brings the mantrap down on Charlie's head, the film reverts to normal speed. Furthermore, because the slow-motion shots have lasted an uncommonly long time, the transition back out, to normal tempo, feels abrupt and harsh. The paradoxical thing about the brief slow-motion inserts that typify Peckinpah's work is that they mesh so well with the ordinary temporal continuum. When the insert is brief, the editor can slip into and out of the decelerated moment in a highly fluid manner. Despite the temporal disruption, strong continuity prevails, unlike the just-described scene from *Straw Dogs,* where the return to normal time occasions a perceptible loss of continuity.

Slow-motion images are not of themselves dynamic. Their tendency is toward inertia, a deceleration not only of represented time but of the internal rhythms and pacing of the sequence in which they appear. They become dynamic with reference to their surrounding context—the normal-tempo actions against which they play as stylistic opposites. By maximizing this opposition, Peckinpah and his editors could give the slow- motion inserts a dynamism which they do not in themselves possess. Intercutting slow motion with normal speed became an essential and highly effective way of achieving this. When two thugs in *Bring Me the Head of Alfredo Garcia* lose control of their station wagon, it skids off the road, churning up a huge spray of dirt. This is rendered in two slow-motion shots that are crosscut with the startled reactions of passengers on a passing bus. The decelerated action of the skid is slowed down so much that the resulting images seem robbed of nearly all movement, which heightens the dynamic contrast with the surrounding normal-tempo imagery. The viewer experiences a perceptual shock because of this radical misalignment between the alternate tempos. Intercutting the two accentuates the misalignment and the dynamic contrast and works against the tendency for slow motion to create inertia and a brake on the action.

Later in that film, when the protagonist, Bennie (Warren Oates), ambushes these thugs and shoots them, Peckinpah had his editors crosscut three slow-motion shots of one thug's dying fall with normal-tempo images of Bennie exchanging fire with the other. Peckinpah's most effective uses of slow motion almost always occurred with this kind of intercutting. As we have noted, when Weddle discusses Peckinpah's editing, he refers generally to his "weaving of slow motion into the very fabric of a sequence."[24] Although Weddle does not discuss how this occurs, we can now see that it occurs through a brief but sustained contrasting or crosscut series of shots that accentuate the different modes of time. The dynamic qualities of the technique lie in the accentuation of these differences. To achieve this accentuation, it is imperative that the represented actions—a skidding car, a shooting victim flung backward—be ones that explicitly occur with, and denote, speed or force. This, in conjunction with the crosscutting, sets up two types of opposition within the editing. The slow motion is set into a relation of striking opposition with the normal tempo of the surrounding imagery, and, internally, the slow-motion shots by themselves contradict the viewer's narrative understanding of the speed at which these events are actually occurring.

When Peckinpah's slow-motion inserts fail to observe either of these principles, and when there is an insufficient narrative context supporting the device, the dynamic force of the technique is diminished. Near the end of *Alfredo Garcia*, when Bennie guns down a pair of corrupt executives and their hired guns in the El Camino Real hotel suite, he steps in front of a mirror to drill his last opponent. Peckinpah showed this man flung backward against a table and chair and crashing to the floor in a single, rather extended slow-motion shot. Because this action is not crosscut with normal-tempo shots of Bennie's reactions or any other ongoing activity, and because it lasts too long, the deceleration of time here becomes what it rarely ever does in Peckinpah's films—a simple slowing down. It is nondynamic because it has minimal structural relationship with the surrounding material. A much better set of isolated slow-motion inserts occurs in *Straw Dogs* when Major Scott is shotgunned by Tom Hedden. The inserts acquire considerable force by virtue of the narrative context. Scott is the narrative's chief authority figure, and with him dead, the viewer knows that all hell is about to break loose as the gang of thugs converges on the Sumners' house.

Peckinpah incorporated the brief slow-motion interlude into his more complex montage sequences because the dynamic oscillation between normal and decelerated time demands a continuing perceptual reorientation from viewers. He apparently hoped the stylistic artifice would alternately immerse viewers in the spectacle on screen and then realign their perspective through the nonrealistic slow-motion insertions. These perceptual realignments he hoped would establish a new, less complacent, and passive relationship between viewers and the screen spectacle, would, as he put it, wake viewers up to what violence is really all about. This functional intent was in addition to the other uses to which he put slow motion, which we have just reviewed: to create a temporal dialectic across the body of a scene; to interrupt the concrete physicality of violence with more abstract contemplations of its balletic and metaphysical aspects; and to shuttle between these concrete and abstract dimensions in a way that would superimpose them on top of each other.

Extended Montage Set-Pieces

Before evaluating the extent to which his montage editing of different film speeds successfully establishes a new viewing position for film spectators, we need to explore how Peckinpah incorporated slow motion into more elaborate montages that work as extended violent set-pieces. These extended spectacles of death and destruction appear, of course, in *The Wild Bunch* and *Straw Dogs* and, to a lesser extent, in *Alfredo Garcia, The Killer Elite, Cross of Iron,* and *The Osterman Weekend.*

As we have seen, the editing of the opening and closing battles in *The Wild Bunch* has been compared to the Odessa Steps scene in Eisenstein's *Potemkin.*[25] Yet despite their more exhilarating quality, they lack the enormous structural variety and richness that characterize the Eisenstein sequence. Like that sequence, however, these scenes in *The Wild Bunch* take what exists in the narrative as linear, separate lines of action (e.g., each member of the Bunch separately trying to escape the ambush, the bounty hunters picking their targets, and the panicked reactions of the pedestrians caught in the cross fire) and integrate them as a synthesized collage of activity. The film's editor, Lou Lombardo, remarked that, following Peckinpah's advice, he

> intercut all the separate lines of action. I might start with this guy being hit, then cut to that guy being hit, cut to this guy falling, that guy still falling, then cut to somebody else over there getting hit, to a horse spinning over there, somebody going through a window there, and then back to the first guy just landing on the ground. I meshed it. I took every piece of action and intercut it with another.[26]

Indeed, the shot lists that survive among Peckinpah's papers, corresponding to the opening and closing shoot-outs in San Rafael and Agua Verde, present a linear and chronological list of images.

As Lombardo's description indicates, and as a careful viewing of the film demonstrates, the basic device used to mesh the lines of action is crosscutting. However, instead of a simple cutting back and forth, the lines of action are interrupted for extended periods by cutaways to other things before they resume. In its elaborate patterns of crosscutting, Peckinpah's editing performs four distinct functions. It slows down, interrupts, parallels, and returns to ongoing lines of action. These functions collectively establish the collage-like structure of the montage set-pieces, and they are clearly illustrated by a scene within the San Rafael massacre that opens *The Wild Bunch,* one that Lombardo alludes to in his description of how he meshed the lines of action. The Bunch have just robbed the depot and are being fired upon by the rooftop snipers. They return fire, hitting two victims on the rooftop. An early, written visualization of this scene differs substantially from the final montage and describes mainly a linear progression of images with little intercutting.

23. Bounty hunter Shannon rises up to fire and is hit and wounded, starts to pitch forward over the parapit [*sic*].
24. Another bounty hunter (who?) grabs for him, exposes himself and is hit and killed, slumps back releasing Shannon who rolls down the roof and pitches to the street.
25. Burt sees the body fall beside him and jumps on his horse racing out firing steadily until he is caught in the bounty hunter fire, causing both he [*sic*] and his horse to plunge through the window of the dress shop.
26. Wild Bunch:—Pike stays in the street with Dutch as the others die or mount and ride out.
27. Then following, Frank who has been wounded while mounting, is shot while riding out and goes into a drag still clutching the bags of silver from the pay station.
28. As Frank is dragged down the street, the horse is shot down.[27]

The editing in the finished film parallels the falls of both rooftop victims by crosscutting between them, but it also interrupts these lines of action by cutting away to other, ongoing lines of action before returning to the two victims. As victim one ('Shannon' in the early shot continuity) topples forward, off the roof, the first cutaway occurs to a shot

Figures 32 & 33. Peckinpah uses slow motion and montage editing to mesh together multiple lines of action in the violent gun battles that open and close The Wild Bunch, *as in this intercutting of the trajectories of two victims shot off the rooftops of the town of Starbuck.*

of Pike running out of the depot office. The next shot returns to a continuation of the previous action as victim one falls below the bottom of the frame line. The next three shots are all cutaways. Angel, another of the Bunch, dashes out of the depot office, returning fire as he runs. A low-angle longshot of the rooftop snipers is followed by a high-angle longshot of several of the Bunch shooting toward the snipers from inside the depot. After these three cutaways, the montage returns to victim one, and slow motion is introduced to retard the rate of his fall. The composition is very dramatic. The victim arcs against the blue sky, the slow motion suspending him weightlessly in space.

The next three shots are more cutaways, but they also introduce the fate of the second rooftop victim. In the first cutaway, a medium shot shows the Bunch firing from inside the depot. Then, in the next shot, the second rooftop victim is struck and falls forward, toward the camera. Next, a medium shot shows Angel running from the depot, firing, continuing an action introduced six shots previously. The next shot, in slow motion, returns to the first victim, continuing his lethargic descent to earth. Next, the montage cuts to the second victim still toppling forward, but not off the roof. His fall will be broken by the rooftop ledge. A medium close-up shows Deke Thornton firing from the roof. Then, in the next two shots, both victims land simultaneously, in a matched cut, victim one in the street and victim two on the rooftop ledge.

The editing reconfigures, stylistically transforms, the deaths of the two rooftop victims. The action cuts away from victim one's fall four times, initially for one shot, then for three shots, again for three shots, and finally for two shots. Two cutaways interrupt the fall of the second victim, for two shots each time. The cutaways and the use of slow motion impose a marked distortion upon the time and space of the represented action. The editing creates a false parallel between the two victims. Victim one falls off the roof in slow motion, and victim two, hit later in the sequence, falls at normal speed, yet they strike ledge and street at precisely the same moment, as the matched cut that closes off these events indicates. The editing imposes a false parallel between normal time and decelerated time. The simultaneous impact of the two victims represents an impossible time-space relationship within the sequence, yet Peckinpah and Lombardo convincingly intercut normal speed and slow motion to extend this discontinuity.

This is certainly what Peckinpah meant when he rejected allegations that his work represented a greater realism, stressing instead that it stylized violence, heightened it through artistic transformation. The elaborate montages of *The Wild Bunch* effect such an artistic transformation of space, time, and perception by rendering space and time as totally plastic and unstable entities. Time slows, stretches, folds around on itself and becomes the fourth dimension of a spatial field in which the ordinary laws of physics do not apply. When the outlaw trying to flee the rooftop sniper ("Burt" in the early visualization) crashes his horse through a storefront window, three slow-motion shots of this action are intercut with three normal-speed shots of another rider crashing to the street after his horse is shot out from under him. The cutting creates a false spatial parallel. The amount of space traversed by each rider who takes a spill is roughly the same—from saddle to ground—but the different rates of time indicate different spaces, since time and space alike are part of a four-dimensional continuum. By intercutting the falls of these riders in slow motion and normal speed, Peckinpah and Lombardo reconfigured space as well as time. The slow motion implies an alternate spatial field in which the reconstituted dynamics play out.

Peckinpah and Lombardo also employed the pattern of inter-rupting ongoing lines of action with cutaways to other events in a way that is analogous with their use of slow motion—to extend the dura-tion of the represented events and retard their completion. In the con-cluding shoot-out at Mapache's headquarters, the film's crowning montage set-piece, Pike bursts into a room where a woman stands, shoots into a mirrored door to kill a soldier hiding there, and is then shot by the woman on whom he had turned his back. This simple series of events is broken up and extended with a very long set of cutaways. After Pike shoots the soldier, the action cuts away from him for seven-teen shots, which show, primarily, Dutch using a woman as a shield as he exchanges gunfire with Mapache's men. Then, returning to Pike, a single close-up shows him glancing outside the woman's room. A sec-ond lengthy cutaway, twenty-eight shots long, shows Lyle Gorch behind the machine gun, howling like a demon. Then the action returns to Pike, still in the room, at which point he is shot. The elaborate cut-aways extend the duration of the action and thereby expand time.

As this description indicates, Peckinpah and Lombardo did not employ slow motion in any simple capacity. The slow-motion inserts are placed within a complex montage that crosscuts multiple lines of action so that the slow motion functions in concert with the extended cutaways to reconfigure time. Furthermore, the temporal manipula-tions include not just deceleration but also parallelism, disruption, and resumption. The resulting stylistic transcends a naturalistic presenta-tion of violence, and it is notable that critics have discussed Peckin-pah's work as if its use of bloody squibs and slow motion was more realistic than previous generations of Hollywood gunfights. It certainly is bloodier, but Peckinpah's is far from a realist's aesthetic. Peckinpah's montage set-pieces in *The Wild Bunch* work primarily on the level of form rather than by their representational content. They work as exquisitely crafted artifacts that emphasize physical spectacle. Their design foregrounds the hyperkinetic spectacle so that it becomes a detachable part of the film. Although, within the narrative, complex issues of character and theme lead up to and into the film's climactic slaughter at Mapache's headquarters, in terms of its montage design this scene is complete, self-contained, and utterly sufficient unto itself. For the filmmakers involved, the scene must have been a lot of fun to craft and edit. Herein lies a significant problem for the didactic uses to which Peckinpah wanted to put his screen violence. This problem has persisted, and it affects the work of virtually all filmmakers who have chosen to stylize graphic violence by using this aesthetic approach.

Peckinpah himself noted that audience reactions were at variance with the responses he intended viewers to have. Writing to Paul Staniford, who had condemned the brutality of *The Wild Bunch*, Peckinpah observed that "better than 50% of the people who saw the picture felt as you did. However, better than 30% of the people thought it was an outstanding and much needed statement against violence."[28] Elsewhere, he admitted, "unfortunately most people come to see it [violence] because they dig it, which is a study of human nature, and which makes me a little sick."[29]

As Peckinpah recognized, viewer reactions to *The Wild Bunch* included outrage and shock over the scale and explicitness of the violence but also excitement and exhilaration. By aestheticizing it, Peckinpah's montages made violence pleasurable and beautiful and turned it into an exciting spectacle. The very stylization that Peckinpah thought would wake people up to the horror of violence instead excited and gratified many. This pleasure is an inevitable result of the aestheticizing functions of Peckinpah's montage editing and its balletic incorporation of slow motion, and it is a virtually inescapable effect of the montage aesthetic that characterizes the work of all filmmakers who have employed it. The director occasionally acknowledged his own culpability in eliciting a dualistic response. "In *The Wild Bunch* I wanted to show that violence could be at the same time repulsive and fascinating."[30]

Many critics noted these contradictions in 1969 when *The Wild Bunch* was released. The reviewer for *The Nation* confessed his own complicity in sharing the audience's gleeful reaction to all the carnage. "At all this the audience laughed (and so did I), not with merriment, exactly, but in tribute to such virtuosity of gore."[31] The reviewer for *The Christian Century* noted that "even while gasping at Peckinpah's bloodbath, the people seated near me in the theater continued to cram their mouths with popcorn."[32]

Several perceptive reviewers pointed to the contradiction between Peckinpah's stated aims and his montage style: the style is so ritualistically elaborated in the opening and closing scenes of *The Wild Bunch* that it turns violence into a pleasurable spectacle. Furthermore, the excessive elaboration of these montages indicates that the filmmaker took an overwhelming interest and delight in the mechanics of crafting them. Arthur Knight in *Saturday Review* pointed out that the stylistics of the film tend to displace the intended moral commentary. "But when the movies attempt to show violent killing in detail, the mind turns against the fact of death and toward the mechanics that produced it. And, curiously, one comes away convinced that the director was also more concerned with the mechanics than with the fact."[33] Joseph Morgenstern in *Newsweek* stressed the apparent falsity of Peckinpah's premise that the repetition of stylized violence could become an artistic device commenting on itself.[34] These reviewers are wrong in their dismissal of Peckinpah's moral involvement with his material and in their objections that the film is without ethical content. But they are dead right in arguing that the tendency of Peckinpah's montage set-pieces in *The Wild Bunch* is to spectacularize violence in ways that will incite the aggressive fantasies of many viewers. Recalling his first encounter with *The Wild Bunch* when he was a teenager, screenwriter Charles Higson stressed that the film's violence stimulated an "orgiastic" release of energy in him. "Once the film was over, I was exhausted and in a state of high nervous excitement. I wanted to go out in a blaze of glory. I wanted a Gatling gun. I wanted to be pierced by a hundred bullets."[35]

Peckinpah did not overtly intend to elicit this kind of reaction in his viewers, any more than Martin Scorsese wanted to arouse vigilante responses in viewers of his bloody *Taxi Driver* (1976), but both filmmakers crafted sequences that have done so. If we ask why, the answer lies in the way that Peckinpah, and Scorsese, too, was seduced by the artistic excitement of putting those violent montages together, of manipulating time and space with images of bodies flying this way and that. The sheer pleasure of crafting these montage scenes would have been exhilarating for Peckinpah. That pleasure is plainly evident in the the San Rafael massacre and the flamboyant Agua Verde shoot-out, violent set-pieces that open and close the film. Through their dynamic energies, these montages convey the excitement and thrill of a filmmaker no longer in moral control of his material to the viewer, who reacts accordingly. Discussing *Taxi Driver*, which climaxes with an astoundingly bloody shoot-out, Scorsese exhibits confusion about his intellectual intent and the seductive excitement he derives from crafting screen violence. The audience, he says, was

> reacting very strongly to the shoot-out sequence in *Taxi Driver*. And I was disturbed by that. It wasn't done with that intent. You can't stop people from taking it that way. What can you do? And you can't stop people from getting an exhilaration from violence, because that's

human, very much the same way as you get an exhilaration from the violence in *The Wild Bunch*. But the exhilaration of the violence at the end of *The Wild Bunch* and the violence that's in *Taxi Driver*—because it's shot a certain way, and I know how it's shot, because I shot it and I designed it—is also in the creation of that scene in the editing, in the camera moves, in the use of music, and the use of sound effects, and in the movement within the frame of the characters. . . . And that's where the exhilaration comes in.[36]

As did Peckinpah, Scorsese wanted to disassociate himself from the aggressive reactions of his viewers, but, like Peckinpah, he was keenly responsive to the physical and artistic pleasures of crafting screen violence. This contradiction accounts for the filmmakers' dismay at the responses of viewers to the scenes that they had so lovingly crafted and choreographed. Neither Scorsese nor Peckinpah wished to evoke violent fantasies in their viewers. When asked if that was their intention, both passionately denied it. But they could not disengage themselves, as artists, from the sensuous gratifications of assembling spectacularized violence. While one should not doubt the sincerity of their belief in their own stated intentions, one may still be amazed at their blindness to their own artistic complicity in stimulating the aggressive reactions of their viewers.

Recognizing this contradiction between Peckinpah's laudable moral intention of shocking his viewers into confronting the horror of violence and his own fascination with the montage spectacle in *The Wild Bunch* brings us to an important point. If the montage-based representation of violence were Peckinpah's only artistic contribution to late 1960s cinema and to the dilemmas of social violence wracking American society in those years, he should be condemned as an aesthete of violence, an inciter to aggression, a director whose films reinforced and added to the violence of those years. If the montage aesthetic were the only frame of analysis deployed on the issue of violence in Peckinpah's films, then he would be everything his detractors have claimed him to be: a glamorizer and glorifier of violence. But this was not the only frame through which he approached the violence issue, as I have discussed elsewhere.[37] To the extent, though, that the montage aesthetic has become the enduring template for filmic presentations of graphic violence, cinema has turned death into a mechanized spectacle. The style has taken filmmakers down a gigantic artistic dead end. The montage aesthetic choreographs the outward manifestations of violence, not its inwardly spiritual and emotional components and consequences. These elude the template. Thus this aesthetic, when it becomes the chief means for representing violent death, as it all too often has been, is an insufficient means for probing the meaning and consequences of violence, should those be a filmmaker's intentions. The montage aesthetic conveys a filmmaker's delight to the audience, who is encouraged to respond in kind. The aesthetic evokes vigilante responses. Thus does death become pleasurable and its protracted physical agonies become emptied of human meaning.

NOTES

1. "Playboy Interview: Sam Peckinpah," *Playboy* 19, no. 8 (August 1972), p. 68.

2. Sam Peckinpah Collection, Margaret Herrick Library, *Wild Bunch*—response letters, statement on violence, folder no. 92.

3. SPC, *Wild Bunch*—response letters, May 13, 1969, folder no. 92.

4. See Stephen Prince, *Savage Cinema: Sam Peckinpah and the Rise of Ultraviolent Movies* (Austin: University of Texas Press, 1998), pp. 27–45.

5. SPC, *Wild Bunch*—response letters, statement on violence, folder no. 92.

6. SPC, *Wild Bunch*—response letters, September 3, 1969, folder no. 92.

7. David Weddle, *If They Move . . . Kill 'Em: The Life and Times of Sam Peckinpah* (New York: Grove Press, 1994), pp. 99, 333.

8. SPC, *Alfredo Garcia*—daily log, folder no. 45.

9. SPC, *Junior Bonner*—daily shots, folder no. 19.

10. Nat Segaloff, "Walon Green: Fate Will Get You," *Backstory 3: Interviews with Screenwriters of the 1960s* ed. Pat McGilligan (Berkeley: University of California Press, 1997), pp. 143, 135–56; and author's telephone conversation with Paul Seydor, July 22, 1997.

11. Ernest Callenbach, "A Conversation with Sam Peckinpah," *Film Quarterly* 17, no. 2 (Winter 1963–64), p. 10.

12. Weddle, p. 271.

13. SPC, *Cross of Iron*—script notes, letter of February 5, 1976, folder no. 26.

14. SPC, Feldman memos, October 29, 1967, folder no. 45.

15. Gary Crowdus and Richard Porton, "The Importance of a Singular, Guiding Vision," *Cineaste* 20, no. 2 (Spring 1993), p. 9.

16. Stephen Farber, "Peckinpah's Return," *Film Quarterly* 23, no. 1 (Fall 1969), p. 11.

17. SPC, *The Wild Bunch*—correspondence, letter of March 19, 1968, folder no. 43; and Weddle, p. 331.

18. Ibid.

19. Ibid., p. 5.

20. Garner Simmons, *Peckinpah: A Portrait in Montage* (Austin: University of Texas Press, 1982), p. 19.

21. Bryson, "Wild Bunch in New York," p. 28.

22. *Savage Cinema*, pp. 72–97.

23. Seydor, p. 20.

24. Weddle, p. 271.

25. See, for example, Weddle, p. 356.

26. Weddle, p. 355.

27. SPC, *Wild Bunch*—editing, folder no. 40.

28. SPC, *Wild Bunch*—response letters, May 13, 1969, folder no. 92.

29. John Bryson, "Wild Bunch in New York," *New York* (August 19, 1974), p. 28.

30. SPC, *De Devoir* interview, interviews, folder no. 96.

31. Review of *The Wild Bunch* in *The Nation*, vol. 209, July 14, 1969, p. 61.

32. Sherwood Ross, "Blood and Circuses," *The Christian Century* (August 20, 1969), p. 1095.

33. Arthur Knight, "Violence Flares Anew," *Saturday Review* (July 5, 1969), p. 21.

34. Joseph Morgenstern, "The Bloody Bunch," *Newsweek* (July 14, 1969), p. 85.

35. Charles Higson, "The Shock of the Old," *Sight and Sound* 5, no. 8 (August 1995), p. 36.

36. Anthony DeCurtis, "What the Streets Mean: An Interview with Martin Scorsese," in *Plays, Movies and Critics*, ed. Jody McAuliffe (Durham, N.C.: Duke University Press, 1993), p. 211.

37. Prince, *Savage Cinema.*

The Effects
of Ultraviolence

Leonard Berkowitz

Some Effects of Thoughts on Anti- and Prosocial Influences of Media Events: A Cognitive-Neoassociation Analysis

Well before the onset of the twentieth century, the French sociologist Gabriel Tarde discussed what he termed *suggesto-imitative* assaults. He noted how news of a sensational violent crime often seemed to prompt similar incidents elsewhere, and pointed to the aftereffects of the Jack the Ripper murders as an example. According to Tarde, the great national attention given these brutal crimes led to eight absolutely identical crimes in London as well as "a repetition of these same deeds outside of the capital (and abroad)" (Tarde, 1912). "Epidemics of crime," he concluded in a once famous phrase, "follow the line of the telegraph."

Regardless of how well known Tarde's principle was several generations ago, social scientists have only recently obtained systematic quantitative support for his thesis. Berkowitz and Macaulay (1971) reported a significant jump in violent, but not property, crimes above what would be expected from the prevailing trend after several spectacular murders in the early and mid-1960s, including those after President Kennedy's assassination. Phillips published much more impressive evidence in a series of studies of the consequences of widely publicized suicides. He found that when the media paid considerable attention to a famous person's suicide, there was an increase in the number of people who also took their lives. According to Phillips (1974)

From *Psychological Bulletin*, vol. 95, no. 3, 1984, pp. 410–427. Copyright © 1984 by the American Psychological Association. Reprinted with permission.

the more publicity given to the suicide story, the greater the apparent impact. In the same vein, he later demonstrated that the number of automobile accidents increased several days after a widely publicized suicide; many of the accidents were single-vehicle incidents (Phillips, 1979). Interestingly, in these single-vehicle cases, the driver tended to be more like the suicide victim than were any passengers in the car. Phillips (1980) then cast his empirical net even further and showed that news stories of suicide-murders were followed by an increase in non-commercial airplane crashes. There is evidence that even the portrayal of suicides in television soap operas led to an increase in the number of white Americans who end their own lives (Phillips, 1982).

The implications of this research seem fairly clear: real and fictional depictions by the media of violence—killings, shootings, or suicides—can prompt audience members to act aggressively toward others or themselves. The present essay also argues that some of the now familiar effects of violent scenes on television and movie screens are similar to those producing the suggesto-imitative assaults discussed by Tarde and documented in the research into the contagion of violence just mentioned. In addition to these negative consequences, the mass media can also promote prosocial behavior (Liebert, Sprafkin, & Davidson, 1982; Rushton, 1979). A comprehensive account of media effects should deal with both positive and negative influences.

In attempting such an analysis, this essay considers a number of psychological processes that can contribute to these anti- and prosocial effects. In particular, it focuses on the role of the audience's thoughts. I suggest that the ideas activated by the witnessed or reported event tend to evoke temporarily other, semantically related thoughts in the audience that, under some circumstances, justify conduct similar to that portrayed by the communication and even lead the viewers to anticipate the benefits they might derive from this behavior. These ideas also tend to evoke associated expresive-motor responses or perhaps even behavioral reactions that might intensify the viewer's existing behavioral tendencies.

Priming Effects and Associative Networks

Several years ago I suggested that conditioning notions could profitably be used to account for many of the media effects considered here

(Berkowitz, 1973, 1974). However, because of the overriding importance of the media communications' meaning for the audience and the processes of memory and recall, I now believe that the concepts of cognitive-neoassociationism (Anderson & Bower, 1973; Landman & Manis,1983) provide a better framework for the analysis of these phenomena. How people react to the message they read, hear, or see depends considerably on their interpretations of the message, the ideas they bring with them to the communication, and the thoughts that are activated by it. It is therefore advisable to study media effects in a way that gives explicit attention to these matters; we can find such a useful formulation in cognitive-neoassociationism.

Only a brief outline of this conceptual scheme is necessary. Nor need we be concerned with the intricacies of this reasoning and the controversies regarding a number of the details (cf. Klatzky, 1980; Landman & Manis, 1983; Wyer & Hartwick, 1980; Wyer & Srull, 1981, for a more complete discussion). What is important is that memory is regarded as a collection of networks, with each network consisting of units or nodes (representing substantive elements of thought, feelings, and so on) that are interconnected through associative pathways. The strength of these pathways is presumably a function of a variety of factors, including contiguity, similarity, and semantic relatedness.

Priming Effects and Spreading Activation

Along with other similar analyses, the present formulation adds the concept of spreading activation advanced by Collins and Loftus (1975) and others to these structural notions. This argument maintains that when a thought element is brought into focal awareness, the activation radiates out from this particular node along the associative pathways to other nodes. This process can lead to a priming effect. Although theorists are not in agreement as to why the priming takes place, they generally maintain that for some time after a concept has been activated, there is an increased likelihood that it and associated thought elements will come to mind again. It is as though some residual excitation has remained at the activated node for a while, making it easier for this and other related thoughts and feelings to be activated. Thus, the aggessive ideas suggested by a violent movie can prime other semantically related thoughts, heightening the chances that viewers will have other aggressive ideas in this period. All of this can happen automatically and without much thinking. Cognitive theorists now differentiate between automatic and controlled processing (e.g., Shiffrin & Schneider, 1977), and it is often suggested that the memory effects just mentioned take place passively and involuntarily. Controlled processing, in contrast, requires conscious attention to a much greater extent.

Several social-psychological investigations (Wyer & Hartwick, 1980; Wyer & Srull, 1981) of the impact of recently activated concepts on impression formation illustrate this important priming effect. In one the subjects first had to construct sentences, each time using three of the four words supplied to them. Some of these sets contained words that had aggressive connotations, whereas other sets had neutral words. At a specified interval after this initial priming phase (immediately after, one hour later, or a day later), the participants were required to indicate their impression of a target person on the basis of a brief description. As the researchers predicted, the more aggression-related words in the sentence construction task and the more recent this task, the more unfavorable the subjects' evaluations of the target person. The use of the aggression-related words apparently activated other aggression-related thoughts that colored the participants' judgments of the target for a time afterward. Bargh and Pietromonaco (1982) showed how this process can operate automatically and without awareness. In their experiment the subjects were unknowingly exposed to single words; some of the words were semantically related to hostility. The subjects then had to rate a target person on the basis of a description provided to them. Although the subjects had not been consciously aware of the priming words, the greater the proportion of hostility-related words presented to them, the more negative their judgment of the target person.

Links with Emotion Components

The present conception does not stop with the individual's thoughts and memories. Making use of recent theoretical developments in cognitive psychology, it holds that externally presented ideas can activate particular feelings and even specific action tendencies as well as certain kinds of thoughts and recollections. This formulation builds on the network analyses of emotion, advanced by Bower (1981), Clark and Isen (1982), Lang (1979), and Leventhal (1980), which postulate associative connections among thoughts, memories, and feelings. As an example, Bower (1981) posited a memory-emotion network in which feelings or emotion nodes are associatively (and, especially, semantically) related to particular concepts and propositions and also to the autonomic responses and expressive behaviors exhibited on these occasions. For Bowers and the other investigators cited, the activation of any of the components in a given emotion network tends to evoke the other units to which it is tied. Isen and her associates demonstrated such a connection when they showed that the experience of a positive mood tends to facilitate the recall of information having a positive meaning (cf. Clark & Isen, 1982).

An experiment by Vaughan and Lanzetta (1981) also provides supporting evidence. When their subjects watched a person receive electric shocks, those observers who were asked to grimace at the time of the shock exhibited other indications of emotion arousal relatively strongly. The expressive facial movements apparently helped to activate other components of the emotional state. Lang (1979) emphasized the role of psychophysiological reactions in his conception. He noted that the imagery thoughts are often accompanied by specific patterns of efferent outflow. Also consider Velten's (1968) mood-induction procedure. As the subjects read a series of effectively toned statements (either positive or negative), they recalled conceptually similar incidents in their past that had the same affective tone. Consequently, they tended to have expressive-motor reactions and feelings similar to those experienced in the past situations. The activated components summated and reverberated as the subjects read from one statement to the next, and they then consciously experienced (to some degree) the feelings associated with the statements they read.

Because of the links among thought elements, feelings, and expressive-motor reactions, externally activated ideas can prompt automatic (involuntary) actions or even some controlled behaviors that are semantically associated with them. Lang's (1979) theory of emotional imagery is consistent with this suggestion in that it postulates semantic connections between "the cognitive structure of the image" and "specific patterns of physiological and behavioral responding" (p. 506). There is also some support for my position in Greenwald's (1970) discussion of the ideo-motor mechanism in performance control. On reviewing the available evidence, he concluded, along with William James (1890), that the perceptual image or idea of an action can initiate the performance of this behavior. More recent research by Anderson (1983) also yielded findings in keeping with the present analysis. People who imagined themselves carrying a particular type of behavior later reported having a greater intention to engage in that action than did others who imagined someone else performing the behavior. The thought of themselves carrying out the action evidently activated a readiness to perform the behavior. Later a number of conditions will be considered that might influence the degree to which media-induced thoughts are translated into open action.

Applications to Research Findings

Priming Effects in Prosocial Influences

Experiments involving children and young adults indicate that people seeing a display of helpfulness or generosity are often inclined to be helpful or generous themselves (Hearold, 1979; Liebert et al., 1982; Rushton, 1979). It is not likely that the communication's influence comes about in these instances through the reduction of the audience's restraints. In addition, the media do not necessarily produce a persistent learning because their effects are often relatively short-lived (Liebert et al., 1982; Rushton, 1979). Rather, the viewers appear to have been spurred temporarily into action. The first step in such a process might involve a priming effect in which there is an activation of thoughts semantically related to the depicted occurrence.

Hornstein and his colleagues (Blackman & Hornstein, 1977; Holloway, Tucker, & Hornstein, 1977; Hornstein, LaKind, Frankel, & Manne, 1975) provided evidence of such a priming effect in a series of experiments concerned with the impact of good news. Supposedly while waiting for the experiment to begin, the subjects in these studies listened to a news program on the radio playing in the laboratory, and then engaged in bargaining with a peer. In general, those who heard a report of prosocial behavior were especially inclined to be cooperative in their bargaining, particularly if the radio story was of someone who had intentionally given help (Holloway et al., 1977).

Other findings indicate that the overheard story did more than convey the specific message that the listeners ought to be generous in their dealings with others. Ratings made at the end of the session showed that the participants' conceptions of human nature and their social world had been affected by the news report. After listening to the prosocial news, the subjects had a stronger expectation that their bargaining partner would be cooperative toward them and thought that there were more people who led clean, decent lives and who were basically honest. Putting their results together with comparable observations published by other investigators, Hornstein and his associates concluded that "people function as social actuaries, relying upon the information they receive from the mass media and other sources . . .to make generalized inferences about human nature" (Blackman & Hornstein, 1977, p. 303).

These findings can readily be interpreted from a cognitive perspective. First, note the generalized effects. In the Hornstein research, as in other experiments (e.g., Aderman & Berkowitz, 1970; Collins & Getz, 1976; Sprafkin, Liebert, & Poulos, 1975), the portrayed prosocial behavior was quite different from the acts the subjects could carry out, but yet there was a carryover. The subjects apparently were responding to semantically related concepts (e.g., helpfulness, generosity, cooperation) that had been activated in their minds by the priming communication; they were not simply and narrowly imitating the reported conduct. In several studies the activation spread some distance along the associated pathways to other prosocial concepts such as honesty (Blackman & Hornstein, 1977) or good work and rule obedience (Friedrich & Stein, 1973). The present formulation holds that the mass communication's influence stems largely from the activation of concepts and propositions semantically related to the portrayed event. Those who lack these semantically related ideas will not be affected in the same way. In keeping with this possibility, Silverman and Sprafkin (1980) found that prosocial scenes in the children's television program *Sesame Street* had little effect on the behavior of young children. Although other interpretations are possible, it may be that the children did not possess the concepts and propositions that could be related to the depicted incidents.

In line with our analysis of the evidence, the thought activation often was only temporary, and the communication's impact typically declined with the passage of time. Priming effects usually subside as the initiating stimulus recedes into the past. In addition, rather than merely bringing related ideas to mind, the depicted action affected the observers' estimates of the prevalence of prosocial behavior in their social world, as Hornstein noted. The availability heuristic can account for this finding. Readily recalling the vivid instance of altruism reported in the mass media, the participants automatically assumed this conduct was relatively frequent and likely.

Research on the Priming Effects of Television and Movie Violence

Introductory remarks. Because a good deal of this analysis relies on investigations of the results of observed aggression, a few introductory

comments about these studies are warranted. It is not necessary to sum-
marize the hundreds of investigations in this area because a number of
fine reviews now exist (e.g., Andison, 1977; Comstock, 1975; Comstock, Chaffee, Katzman, McCombs, & Roberts, 1978; Geen, 1976;
Goranson, 1970; Liebert, Sprafkin, & Davidson, 1982; Murray & Kippax, 1979; Palmer & Dorr, 1980). However, it should be noted that the
majority of researchers are agreed that the depiction of violence in the
media increases the chances that people in the audience will act aggressively themselves. Meta-analyses of the published studies support such
a conclusion (Andison, 1977; Hearold, 1979). There is controversy, however, concerning the magnitude of this effect (e.g., see Comstock, 1975;
Cook, Kendzierski, & Thomas, 1983), and no claim is made here as to
how important media depictions are relative to the other sources of
antisocial conduct. Furthermore, because the greatest dispute in this
research area deals with the results of frequent exposure to violent
scenes (see Eron, 1982; Eron, Huesmann, Lefkowitz, & Walder, 1972;
Milavsky, Kessler, Stipp, & Rubens, 1982), most of our attention will
be given to experiments in which the participants see only one or a few
aggressive movies. The consequences of a high level of television or
movie viewing will receive much less emphasis here, and findings from
studies bearing on this issue will be discussed only if they are pertinent
to a particular theoretical point.

Some shortcomings of traditional interpretations.   Before considering
the priming effects of violent communications, a few of the difficulties
in the traditional analyses of media aggression should be examined. In
my opinion the priming effect analysis overcomes these problems.

The most popular interpretations of the effects of media violence emphasize the observers' learning. The depicted (or reported)
action serves as an example, teaching people in the audience how to
behave, what type of conduct is appropriate in a given situation, and
especially whether this action is likely to bring the rewards they desire
(e.g., Bandura, 1965, 1971, 1973). I do not want to deny or even minimize the importance of this learning. Nevertheless, it is apparent that
media influences do not operate through observational learning only, if
this concept is understood to refer to a relatively long-lasting acquisition of new knowledge or the adoption of a novel form of behavior.
Some media effects are fairly transient (e.g., Buvinic & Berkowitz, 1976;
Doob & Climie, 1972; Mann, Berkowitz, Sidman, Starr, & West, 1974),
as if the observed event had activated reactions or thoughts only for a

relatively brief period. Phillips's previously mentioned studies of the impact of widely publicized suicide stories also obtained evidence of a time decay. In a recent investigation, for example, Bollen and Phillips (1982) noted that the publicity given to suicide stories on television evening news programs did not produce a heightened probability of other suicides more than ten days after the initial report. It is my contention that at least part of this time decay is due to the diminution in a priming effect that often occurs with the passage of time (cf. Wyer & Srull, 1981).

Furthermore, I believe that the often demonstrated generality of the media influence is troublesome for those observational learning interpretations that are couched in terms of imitation. Imitation generally implies that the reproduced action is physically similar to the portrayed behavior, but yet, most of the experiments in this area use aggression measures that are physically different from the depicted conduct (e.g., Parke, Berkowitz, Leyens, West, & Sebastian, 1977). Phillips (1983) reported a startling demonstration of such a generalization. Again making use of demographic data, Phillips found that widely publicized heavyweight championship prize fights between 1973 and 1978 were typically followed by an increase in homicides throughout the United States. Rather than explaining these findings in terms of imitation (or even modeling), it may be better to say that the observers responded to the meaning of the media event and exhibited behavior having the same general meaning. Further, the depicted occurrence should be considered as producing a priming effect that activates semantically related ideas and behavioral tendencies.

For many researchers the knowledge transmission interpretation of media influences maintains that these influences arise largely through a permission-giving (or disinhibitory) process. People in the audience are supposedly disposed to engage in some antisocial behavior but are reluctant to do so until the media tells them, directly or indirectly, that the behavior is permissible or even profitable. Wheeler's (1966) discussion of behavioral contagion essentially follows this reasoning, and other investigators have offered a similar analysis. Comstock and his associates (Comstock, 1980; Comstock et al., 1978) emphasized the disinhibitory consequences of media violence, maintaining that the portrayed action lessens the audience's restraints against such conduct.

I do not doubt that media events can lower observers' inhibitions by indicating that the behaviors they are tempted to carry out may benefit them (Bandura, 1965) or might be appropriate in the given situation.

Indeed, my colleagues and I have published a good number of experiments demonstrating a permission-giving phenomenon (e.g., Berkowitz & Geen, 1967; Berkowitz & Rawlings, 1963). My contention here is that the relatively short-lived aggression-enhancing influences are not due to a disinhibitory process only.

Priming Effects and Antisocial Influences

I have already implied that the contagion of violence reported by Tarde, Berkowitz and Macaulay, and Phillips might be partly due to priming effects generated by news stories of spectacular violent crimes. Indeed, the rise in homicide rates often following a war, in the victorious as well as defeated nations (Archer & Gartner, 1976), conceivably might also be affected by aggression-related ideas activated by media reports of the conflict and kept alive by other influences.

Activation of aggression-related ideas. Both direct and indirect evidence indicates that the observation of aggression evokes aggression-related thoughts and ideas in the viewers. In the latter category, Berkowitz, Parker, and West (cited in Berkowitz, 1973) offered information suggesting such a possibility. In their experiment, schoolchildren were asked to complete sentences by selecting one of two words supplied to them. The children were more likely to choose words having aggressive connotations if they had just read a war comic book rather than a neutral comic book. Exposure to the violent scenes in the former condition apparently had brought aggression-related ideas to mind so that words with aggressive meanings seemed more appropriate in constructing the sentences.

Turning to more direct evidence, the research by Wyer and Srull (1981) and Bargh and Pietromonaco (1982) already has been cited as a demonstration of how the priming effect can influence one's reaction to others. In these studies, presenting the participants with words having hostile connotations led them to make hostile evaluations of an ambiguous target person. Carver, Ganellen, Froming, and Chambers (1983) extended the research paradigm that Wyer and Srull and Bargh and Pietromonaco used and showed that people who had watched a brief film depicting a hostile interaction between a businessman and his secretary subsequently perceived more hostility in an ambiguous stimulus person. A study of the consequences of aggressive humor (Berkowitz, 1970) is conceptually similar to these investigations. In this experiment, young women who listened to a tape recording of a hostile comic routine were subsequently harsher in their ratings of a job applicant than were other women who heard a nonaggressive comic routine. This happened even when the subjects had not been provoked by the person they were judging.

In these instances the initial communication had evidently primed aggression-related ideas which then affected the subjects' interpretation of an ambiguous stimulus person. These activated ideas might also change at least temporarily the viewers' impression of the desirability of aggression. Other studies have shown that people seeing violent encounters are at times inclined to favor the use of violence in interpersonal conflict. Leifer and Roberts (1972) and Drabman and Thomas (1974) reported such an effect in experiments with schoolchildren, and Malamuth and Check (1981) found that movies portraying sexual violence against women increased the male viewer's belief that this type of violence was sometimes acceptable. Even the mere presence of weapons might also produce a heightened acceptance of violence at times. The participants in an experiment by Leyens and Parke (1975) who were shown slides of weapons were more willing to punish an available target severely than were the participants who had seen only neutral slides.

Conceptions of others: The cultivation thesis.   A number of students of the mass media have gone even further with the line of reasoning just introduced. George Gerbner and his associates (e.g., Gerbner, Gross, Morgan, & Signorielli, 1980; Gerbner, Gross, Signorielli, Morgan, & Jackson-Beeck, 1979) argued that television violence does more than produce a relatively transient acceptance of aggression. It may also cultivate a long-lasting conception of the social environment as wicked and dangerous. Television programs often portray a world of violence, danger, and evil. Consequently, it is maintained that those who watch television frequently develop a perception of social reality that is consistent with this usual depiction of life and society. In a word, the viewers supposedly acquire a paranoid conception of their environment. Evidence suggests that the Gerbner argument is valid in some respects but may be overstated. The best support for this position comes from research in which subjects are exposed to only a single communication. Thus, in an experiment by Thomas and Drabman (1977), children shown a television detective scene were subsequently inclined to believe that other children would prefer to act aggressively in their interpersonal encounters. Thinking this, the subjects would be apt to conclude that aggression is relatively frequent in their social world. The previously cited findings of Hornstein and his colleagues (e.g., Blackman & Hornstein, 1977) are also in accord with the Gerbner formulation, even though these studies involve the perception of prosocial behavior. Recall that in the Hornstein experiments, the subjects who heard a radio report of helpful behavior tended to guess that helpfulness was relatively prevalent in the world.

The research evidence is much less clear, however, when we turn to studies of people repeatedly exposed to scenes of violence. In the investigation by Gerbner and his associates (Gerbner, Gross, Signorielli, Morgan, & Jackson-Beek, 1979), adolescents who watched a great deal of television were especially likely to overestimate the amount of violence in society and believe that the social world was dangerous. However, several investigators have published opposing observations. Wober (1978) failed to obtain indications of a paranoid conception of life in a national sample of British television viewers, and Doob and MacDonald (1979) showed that the relationship between television viewing and fear of crime was eliminated in a Toronto, Ontario sample when the actual incidence of crime in the viewers' areas was controlled for statistically. Gerbner et al. (1980) produced further data from a national sample of adults and a statistical analysis indicating that heavy television viewing can lead to later perceptions of danger. Cook et al.'s (1983) position lies somewhere between that of Gerbner and his critics. Upon examining the published data, Cook et al. concluded that television viewing can influence general beliefs about the world, but suggested that this cultivation effect was extremely modest.

One way to reconcile the opposing contentions is to refer to two possibilities. The first possibility is that the priming effect is relatively short-lived. As noted earlier, media reports apparently activate semantically related thoughts for only a brief period. It is during this time that the viewers, guided by the availability heuristic, are apt to exaggerate the prevalence of antisocial behavior in the world. However, other influences may be necessary if the activated ideas are to be learned so that there is an abiding conception of the surrounding environment. These influences are not always present and television's portrait of social reality is not necessarily always accepted as true by the people in the audience.

The second possibility has to do with a difference between estimates of the prevalence of antisocial behavior and judgments of being personally in danger. Hawkins and Pingree (1980) suggested that a heavy diet of television increases the perceived frequency of antisocial behavior in the world, but does not necessarily create the belief that the viewers themselves are likely to be victimized. Some support for this suggestion can be found in path analyses conducted by Tyler (1980). Making use of samples of respondents in cities on the East and West Coasts, Tyler demonstrated that mass media reports of crimes affected respondents' estimates of the crime rate in their neighborhoods, but did not influence their sense of being personally vulnerable to crime. This latter perception was influenced, however, by their own or another's personal experience with crime.

All in all, theory and empirical research, and Gerbner's (Gerbner et al., 1979; Gerbner et al., 1980) cultivation thesis, propose that vivid portrayals of antisocial behavior on television and radio can lead, at least temporarily, to the belief that this kind of behavior is relatively frequent in the social environment. Nevertheless, additional factors apparently have to operate if these activated judgments are to be turned into a persistent perception of the world or are to affect the sense of being personally in danger.

Inciting an action tendency. The research reviewed to this point indicates that the media can activate particular thoughts and ideas. The question now is whether specific action tendencies are also incited. In my summary of the network analyses of emotion, I argued for such an effect when I suggested that activation can spread from the concepts and propositions that come to mind to feelings, expressive movements, and even action tendencies. Is there any evidence that media-activated thoughts can generate such behavioral inclinations?

The aggressive humor experiment mentioned before (Berkowitz, 1970) points to such a possibility. The hostile comic routine led the subjects to treat the job applicant harshly. Better evidence is provided in the second study conducted by Carver, Ganellen, Froming, and Chambers (1983). Making use of the Wyer and Srull (1981) scrambled sentence task, the investigators showed that male undergraduates who had been primed to have aggressive thoughts subsequently administered the most intense electric shocks to a fellow student whenever that person made a mistake. Their aggressive ideas apparently led to aggressive acts.

Other relevant findings were obtained in experiments on the effects of aggression-associated cues in the surrounding environment. This research is discussed in more detail later, and only one such study need be mentioned here. Josephson (1982) conducted an experiment in which deliberately frustrated schoolboys were shown an excerpt from a popular television program that was either violent or nonviolent in nature and then played a game of floor hockey in which they could exhibit naturalistic aggression against their opponents. The villains in the violent television program used walkie-talkie radios in the course of their misdeeds, so Josephson assumed that the presence of a walkie-talkie would serve as a retrieval cue: it would remind the subjects in the violent movie condition of the aggression they had seen and might also activate the thoughts and feelings that the film had evoked. Thus, the adult referees supervising the boys' game sometimes carried walkie-talkies. The researcher found that the children were most aggressive if they had previously watched the violent program and the referees carried the aggression-associated walkie-talkie radios. My proposal here is that this cue strengthened the activation generated by the aggressive movie.

An experiment by Worchel (1972) also suggests that violent scenes can incite aggressive inclinations. Young boys and girls were shown a brief fight scene or an interesting movie about boats or they were not shown any film. They then were told they could choose between engaging in a pie fight (an aggressive activity) or riding on a raft (nonaggressive activity). The children's choices of activities tended to be consistent with the movie they had seen, as if this film had evoked an appetite for that type of behavior. Another experimenter then entered the room and put pressure on the children to select one of the activities, the activity that was either consistent or inconsistent with the movie they had watched. In keeping with Worchel's expectation (based on reactance theory), when the subjects were again asked to state their preferences, they overwhelmingly reacted against the pressure if it had been inconsistent with the film. Both films had evidently generated a desire for a particular type of activity, and the subjects countered the opposing pressure with an even stronger insistence on this activity.

Disinhibition and indifference. The media-induced activation of aggression-related thoughts can account for other consequences of media depictions of violence. I have suggested so far that these thoughts can (1) influence the audience's interpretation of an ambiguous stimulus person, (2) heighten the estimated frequency of aggressive and other antisocial acts in the social world, (3) incite inclinations to aggressive behavior, and (4) strengthen the belief that aggression is desirable or

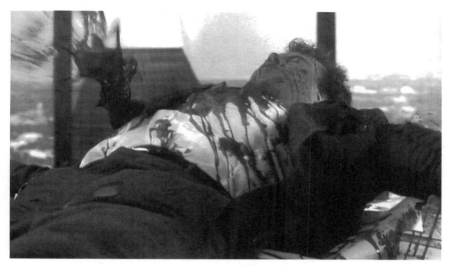

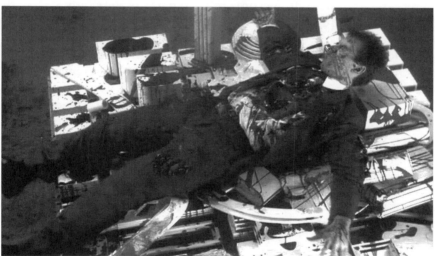

Figures 34 & 35. Director Paul Verhoeven (Robocop, Total Recall, Starship Troopers) has created some of the most extreme and outlandish violence in mainstream films. In Robocop, a police robot machine-guns a corporate executive, whose body explodes in a shower of blood and torn clothing. The MPAA threatened the film with an X rating unless Verhoeven trimmed its violence.

acceptable at times. All of these possible reactions, and especially the last one, can lead to a lowering of restraints against aggression and even lessen the observers' anxieties about aggression.

Some investigators have labeled this process a trivialization of aggression; violence becomes a small matter not worthy of special note as it becomes more acceptable. I have already mentioned one indication of this in the experiment by Malamuth and Check (1981), but much more direct evidence has been provided by Zillmann and Bryant (1982). In accord with Gerbner's cultivation thesis, the men and women in this experiment who were exposed to a massive amount of filmed sex scenes gave the highest estimate of the prevalence of unusual sexual practices in the general population, and they were also least likely to object to the open display of pornography. More important, when all of the subjects were asked to recommend a jail sentence for a convicted rapist, those men and women who had been exposed to a large number of unusual sex scenes favored the shortest terms of imprisonment. Rape had evidently become a more trivial matter for them. Can it be that the activation of sexual-aggressive ideas in these people and the resulting increased acceptance of such behavior also led to a diminution in sexual-aggressive concerns?

This conjectured reduction in aggression anxiety implies that observers will tend to become physiologically less aroused with repeated exposure to aggressive scenes. Thomas, Horton, Lippincott, and Drabman (1977) conducted two experiments—one involving schoolchildren and the other involving college students—in which subjects first saw either a fictional portrayal of violence or a nonaggressive movie and then watched a film clip showing realistic aggression. In both studies the viewers exhibited less emotionality (inferred from changes in skin resistance) in reaction to the realistic aggression if they had previously been exposed to the aggressive incident. Geen (1981) also reported that prior exposure to a violent scene reduced arousal to a later aggressive depiction. He suggested that the earlier observation of aggression was particularly likely to lessen the viewers' sensitivity to cues that normally restrain their aggression.

It is important to note that the lower arousal is presumably an indicant of a reduced concern about aggression and not a sign of a decreased inclination to aggression. Thomas (1982) produced some supporting evidence. In her experiment angry men exposed to a fifteen-minute aggressive television program subsequently tended to have a lower heart rate than their angered counterparts who were shown a neutral movie. Nevertheless, in spite of their lower arousal level, the former also tended to give their antagonist more electric shocks soon afterward. Apparently less anxious about aggression because of the aggression-approving ideas generated by the violent program, the former group became calm, but also punished their tormentor more severely.

Conditions Facilitating the Occurrence of Overt Aggression

There is a substantial gap between the media-activated ideas, feelings, and action tendencies and the open display of behavior. Other factors can intervene to affect the chances that people in the audience will be overtly assaultive themselves. It is important to consider these conditions.

Meaning of the Communication

Defining the witnessed action as aggression. The present essay repeatedly emphasizes the importance of the media's meaning for the audience. Aggression is in the mind of the beholder, and a movie will not activate aggression-associated thoughts unless the viewer regards what is seen as aggression. This term, of course, is used in a variety of ways in our everyday language, but most people seem to think of aggression as the deliberate injury of another. Berkowitz and Alioto (1973) assumed this was the common meaning of the term when they argued that contact sports are most likely to stimulate aggressive inclinations in the onlookers when they believe the players are trying to hurt each other. The angered university men in this study watched a film of either a prize fight or a football game and were induced to interpret the contest either as aggressive (the opponents supposedly were trying to injure each other) or as nonaggressive (the contestants were professionals unemotionally engaged in their business). When the subjects were given an opportunity to shock their tormentor at the end of the movie, those who had seen the encounter described as aggressive were most punitive. The viewers had to define what they saw as aggression if the event was to activate strong aggression-related ideas and responses in them.

Donnerstein and Berkowitz (1983) obtained findings consistent with this theory. The intensity of their male subjects' punishment of a woman who had provoked them earlier was significantly correlated with the rated aggressiveness of the movie they had seen before they could deliver the shocks. The observers' definition of the scene as aggressive had presumably activated aggression-related thoughts and other aggression-facilitating reactions in them which strengthened the punishment they gave to the provocateur.

Other aggressive ideas. Besides imparting an aggressive meaning to the witnessed event, when they watch this occurrence the observers might also have other aggressive thoughts that can intensify the activated aggressive inclinations. Turner and Berkowitz (1972) showed their provoked male subjects a movie of a prizefight and asked most of the subjects to think of themselves either as the winner or the referee. The others were asked simply to watch the film. Half of the people in each condition were led to have aggressive ideas as they viewed the scene by requiring them to think "hit" each time the victor landed a blow. The two experimental variations interacted to affect the number of shocks the subjects subsequently gave to their tormentor. In general, the men attacked this person most severely if they had imagined themselves as the winner and thought "hit" with each punch they saw.

The "imagine-self " finding in this experiment is reminiscent of the results reported more recently by Anderson (1983). The college students in this later study expressed the strongest intention to carry out a certain kind of behavior if they had previously imagined themselves engaging in that action.

The "hit" ideas conceivably might have served as aggression retrieval cues, especially for those who thought of themselves as the victor. As the subjects imagined themselves hitting their opponent, the word *hit* that they periodically uttered to themselves might have evoked memories of other occasions in which they had fought an antagonist. Thoughts, feelings, and expressive movements related to the aggression they exhibited might have been activated by these words so that their present aggression was intensified.

Turner (Turner & Layton, 1976) was the first to recognize how the words used in thoughts can function as aggression retrieval cues to affect subsequent behavior. On the basis of other research on the psychology of memory, he predicted that words having an aggressive meaning would be especially strong activators of aggressive inclinations to the degree that they could easily evoke images. These high-imagery aggression words presumably would better retrieve prior aggressive episodes from memory, and thus should activate other aggression-related thoughts and inclinations. To test this prediction, Turner and Layton (1976) required their male subjects to learn lists of words varying in aggression connotation (aggressive or neutral) and imagery value (high or low), and then gave them an opportunity to shock a partner. All of the subjects were physiologically aroused by exposure to white noise when they were delivering these shocks. In keeping with Turner's prediction, the aroused subjects were most punitive if they had been previously exposed to the high-imagery aggressive words.

Identification and imagination. Several students of mass communications (e.g., Dorr, 1981; Tannenbaum & Gaer, 1965) have sugested that the observers' identification with the media characters influences the extent to which they are affected by the witnessed occurrence. From the present perspective, onlookers who identify with the observed actors are vividly imagining themselves as these characters and are thinking of themselves as carrying out the actions they see. The viewers identifying with a movie aggressor should therefore be providing themselves with aggressive thoughts having a relatively high imagery value, and thus should be priming themselves aggressively. The previously cited experiment by Turner and Berkowitz (1972) supports this analysis, as does a later study by Leyens and Picus (1973). In this investigation the angry subjects who had been asked to imagine themselves as the victor of the filmed fight shown to them were later most aggressive toward the person who had insulted them. Their high degree of aggression was presumably because of their high level of aggression-related thoughts as they watched the movie.

Several field studies have also highlighted the importance of the media viewers' identification with the observed aggressor. When McLeod, Atkin, and Chaffee (1972) questioned high school students in Maryland and Wisconsin about their television viewing and social behavior, they found, as other investigators had, that exposure to television violence was positively associated with self-reported aggression. Most pertinent to the present issue, however, was that those students indicating a high degree of identification with violent television characters tended to be highly aggressive themselves. Huesmann, Eron, Klein, Brice, and Fischer (1983) also reported that children who watched violent television programs frequently and who identified with the aggressive characters tended to be highly aggressive in their dealings with peers. Aggressive fantasies generally might have a similar effect.

According to Rosenfeld et al. (1978), young boys who often fantasize about aggression tend to be highly aggressive. The data from these studies indicate that a highly aggressive imagination might keep the influence of the media exposure alive. Bandura (1971) maintained that the observers' imaginal and verbal representations of a witnessed incident can perpetuate the effects of that event. Huesmann (in National Institute of Mental [NIMH], 1982) maintained that children's hostile daydreams or aggressive make-believe play increase the chances that they will display overt aggression after seeing violence on the screen. In keeping with these concepts, continuing to think about the filmed violence and one's own aggression in the depicted situation might prolong the media-generated activation of aggressively related ideas and expressive-motor reactions. Some of the research results obtained by Singer and Singer (1981) are also consistent with this reasoning. They noted that children who engaged in imaginative play with a prosocial theme generally exhibited little aggression. In this case the children's prosocial thoughts could have activated ideas and feelings that were incompatible with aggression, thereby lessening their aggressive tendencies.

The meaning of the observed aggression.   Viewers can impart different kinds of meaning to the reported behavior in addition to defining it as aggressive or not. They might regard the depicted action as justified or unjustified, as warranted revenge for an earlier insult or an improper assault on an innocent victim as a profitable act yielding benefits for the aggressor, or as costly conduct leading to negative consequences. In many instances, perhaps because of a spreading activation of related concepts, these meanings apparently then generalize to affect the observers' interpretations of any aggression they themselves might display.

There is little doubt that the outcome of the model's aggression often influences the audience's willingness to engage in aggression themselves (Bandura, 1965, 1971). The viewers appear to draw a lesson from what they see: what happens on the screen (or is reported in the media) might also happen to them if they exhibited the same behavior (Bandura, 1971; Comstock, 1980; Comstock et al., 1978; Huesmann, in NIMH, 1982). As was suggested earlier, this phenomenon is readily interpreted in cognitive terms. Seeing the result of the model's action, the observers are reminded of other occasions in which there was a similar outcome. With this consequence prominently in mind, the frequency and probability of such a result are apt to be overestimated (as the availability heuristic suggests). Consequently, showing the actor punished for a given behavior tends to dampen their willingness to act in the same way, whereas a report that the behavior had favorable consequences often increases their inclination to follow suit.

The audience can be affected by the outcome of the aggression they watch even if the movie aggressor is not directly affected. Goranson (1969) found that his angry subjects attacked their tormentor only weakly after learning that the movie aggression victim died of the injuries received. In this case the thought of the possible unfortunate consequences of aggression apparently was uppermost in the observers' minds, and these ideas evidently led the subjects to restrain their assault on their insulter. It is important to note that Goranson's subjects had no ill feelings toward the movie aggression victim. Nor did they associate that movie person with another individual whom they might have wanted to hurt. In such a case, if the victim in the film had suffered rather than died, the angry observers conceivably might have regarded the victim's pain as gratifying for them. The observed aggression could then have been seen as successful aggression leading to a desired consequence—revenge—and the end result might have been a disinhibition (Berkowitz, 1974; Donnerstein & Berkowitz, 1981).

This matter of the observed aggression's outcome cannot be ignored if an adequate understanding of the effects of movie violence is to be gained. The old-fashioned Western movies might have had an adverse impact on their viewers because they never showed any tragic consequences of aggression. Characters fell down when they were shot but no one was seen suffering. There is an interesting and suggestive difference between U.S. and Japanese television programming in this regard. According to Iwao, de Sola Pool, and Hagiwara (1981), Japanese and American TV films have approximately the same amount of violence, but the Japanese movies are much more likely to show the victim suffering and are especially more apt to depict the protagonists as victims. This emphasis on the protagonists' pain could lessen the audience's willingness to act aggressively.

Other related phenomena are less obvious but may also affect the viewers' inhibitions against carrying out the reported behavior. A fairly substantial body of research has demonstrated that the audience members' attitude toward the observed aggressor and the victim influences their willingness to attack their own tormentors. In these investigations, initiated by Berkowitz and Rawlings (1963) and replicated by Berkowitz and his colleagues (Berkowitz, 1965; Berkowitz, Corwin, & Heironimus, 1963; Berkowitz & Geen, 1967; Berkowitz, Parke, Leyens, & West, 1974; Berkowitz & Powers, 1979) and others (e.g., Geen & Stonner, 1973; Hoyt, 1970; Meyer, 1972), the angry male subjects were given a brief introduction to the violent movie they were about to see that portrayed the victim of the observed aggression in a certain manner. In some instances this movie character was described as an immoral and unpleasant person, whereas in other cases the character was depicted favorably. At the conclusion of the scene, all of the men had an opportunity to punish the person who had insulted them earlier. The experiments all found that the subjects attacked their tormentor more severely after seeing the "bad guy" being assaulted than after watching the "good man" being hurt.

Berkowitz interpreted the results of his studies as being due to differences in the perceived justification of the witnessed aggression. That is, the subjects presumably regarded the villain's punishment as justified aggression, whereas the "good guy's" beating was viewed as morally unwarranted. The observers then interpreted their own possible attacks on their tormentor in the same way. In essence, the thought of the movie violence as good, justified aggression presumably activated other ideas of morally proper aggression. However, other researchers extended the original findings in a way that suggests a slightly different interpretation. Beginning with Hoyt (1970), investigators (Geen & Stonner, 1973, 1974; Meyer, 1972) showed that provoked observers were most punitive toward their insulter if they had been led to think of the witnessed violence as vengeance for an earlier injustice. Believing themselves to have been ill-treated, the subjects evidently applied the movie-activated thoughts of revenge to their own situation so that their inhibitions against aggression were lessened. Those who had not been angered, however, might have regarded these ideas as inappropriate or even wrong, which might have produced increased restraints (Geen & Stonner, 1973). Geen (1976) concluded that the viewers compared their own motivational states with those of the actors in the violent incident and used cues from this incident "as information concerning [what is] appropriate behavior" (p. 212). Whatever the exact meaning of the observed aggression, the context in which it occurs clearly can affect the viewers' inhibitions against aggression.

Nature of available target.   The probability of overt aggression after seeing violence depends on the nature of the potential target as well as the other factors which have been discussed. The viewers are unlikely to attack someone who might punish them, but there are also more subtle and interesting effects that should be noted. Most important, a series of experiments has demonstrated that after watching an aggressive scene, angry observers tend to direct the strongest aggression toward those around them who are associated with the victim of the witnessed violence (Berkowitz & Geen, 1967; Donnerstein & Berkowitz, 1981; Geen & Berkowitz, 1966, 1967). In most of these studies deliberately provoked subjects were shown a filmed fight and then were given an opportunity to punish their tormentor. The results indicated that the participants punished their antagonist more severely if the antagonist had the same name as the loser of the observed fight as opposed to having the winner's name or a name not used in the movie. A more recent experiment by Donnerstein and Berkowitz (1983) extends the generality of this phenomenon. The male subjects in this study were first provoked by a woman. Some of the subjects then saw a film clip in which a woman was assaulted by two men. In accord with the earlier findings, when these subjects were able to punish the insulting woman, their aggression was more intense if she had the same name as the female victim in the movie than if she had a different name. The portrayed assault might have activated thoughts in the angry viewers concerning the satisfaction of attacking a woman (probably because they had just been provoked by a woman). These thoughts could have been strengthened when the subjects faced the female antagonist having the same name as the film victim, perhaps because her name functioned as a retrieval cue. The result was the strong aggression toward her. In general, then, potential targets who remind viewers of the victim of violence they had recently seen might be especially likely to draw hostility toward themselves, particularly if the observed aggression was gratifying.

Reality of the observed incident. All of the factors just mentioned, such as the meaning of the witnessed event, will affect the viewers only to the extent that they attend to this occurrence. Moreover, they are especially inclined to be influenced if they are highly involved in the observed scene, thinking of themselves as carrying out the reported behaviors. The scene's reality can help determine how involved they will be in what they see.

A number of experiments suggest that viewers are more likely to be aggressively incited by a violent occurrence if this event is realistic rather than fictional. Noble (1973) reported that the constructiveness of children's play was more adversely affected by realistic rather than stylistic depictions of aggression. Feshbach (1972) has more direct evidence in a better controlled investigation. All of the children in his study saw a movie of a campus riot. Half of them were told this was a fictitious film; the others were informed they were watching a newsreel of an actual incident. When the children were able to punish a person soon afterward, those who had viewed the supposedly real violence were more aggressive. Berkowitz and Alioto (1973) extended this finding to young adults. The angry college men in their experiment were more punitive toward their provocateur after watching a war scene that was described as realistic rather than a staged depiction.

Research by Geen and his colleagues provides important additional information. An experiment by Geen and Rakosky (1973) suggests that the observers' definition of the witnessed aggression as only fictitious seemed to distance them from the event psychologically so that it had less of an impact on them. Subjects who were reminded that the fight they were about to see was fictional were less physiologically aroused by it than were those subjects who were not given this reminder. Consistent with this finding, in a later study Geen (1975) reported that angry men shown a real fight instead of a staged one were more likely to maintain their high level of physiological arousal during the movie and to give their tormentor strong punishment soon afterward. The subjects in these investigations were less likely to have aggression-activating thoughts as they watched the violent incident if they regarded the event as only fictional.

Another experiment indicates that the observer's focus on the artistic nature of the scene can have a similar result. Leyens, Cisneros, and Hossay (1976) asked some of their subjects to attend to the aesthetic qualities of the aggression-related pictures shown to them. These subjects were less aggressive toward the person who had insulted them earlier than were those subjects who were also exposed to aggressive pictures but who were not given this "decentration" instruction. In other words, the subjects seeing the aggressive pictures without the aesthetic focus were more aggressive than controls seeing aggressive pictures with the aesthetic focus. The researchers noted that the attention to the aesthetic qualities had not altered the aggressive meaning of the pictures, so it could only be that it led to a weaker activation of aggression-facilitating ideas.

Leyens and his associates pointed out an intriguing implication of their findings. It may be possible to lessen the aggression-inciting capacity of violent communications without imposing censorship by teaching viewers to focus on the aesthetic or physical aspects of the movies they watch. A research team led by Huesmann and Eron (Huesmann et al., 1983) followed a comparable line of reasoning, emphasizing the reality versus fictional dimension. As part of their research project, schoolchildren in the experimental condition were required to write essays on why televised violence was unreal and bad. This procedure, based on social-psychological studies of role playing, was intended to inculcate an unfavorable attitude toward violent programs as well as to strengthen the children's awareness of the fictional nature of these shows. The training procedure seemed to affect their subsequent behavior. Not only were the experimental subjects less aggressive than their controls (as rated by peers), but there was no relationship between television violence viewing and peer-rated aggression in the experimental group, although such a relationship did exist in the control condition. The children in the experimental group might have learned to think about televised violence in a way that dampened the aggression-activating capacity of these aggressive movies.

Conclusion

Criticisms of the heavy diet of violence in American movies and television programs typically are based on two principal fears: (1) the fear that children will learn to favor and use aggression as a way of solving their interpersonal problems, and (2) the fear that many persons will become indifferent to the suffering caused by violence. It certainly is not wrong to be concerned about these matters, but the present essay emphasizes another type of danger: people can get ideas from the communications reporting violent incidents and, for a short time afterward at least, these thoughts can help foster antisocial behavior.

The media can be a force for good as well as bad, and I have suggested that appropriate media-activated thoughts and memories can facilitate helpfulness and prosocial conduct generally. The outcome depends on the action that is communicated. Newspapers, radio, and television make news as well as report it. They can promote socially desirable behavior by publicizing instances of such conduct, or they can increase the likelihood of aggression by depicting violent incidents in either realistic or fictitious form. My guess is that realistic portrayals of violence are more inclined to have these adverse consequences (assuming that they are highly vivid and capture the audience's full attention).

Of course, it could be argued that the present analysis exaggerates the impact of the mass media. Even if the reasoning spelled out here is upheld by further research, some might say that the consequences are due to only one or a few exposures to media communications. Frequent viewing could conceivably lead to an even smaller effect so that the audiences become inured to the scenes or stories reported by the media. The trivialization of aggression or desensitization to aggression discussed earlier might be interpreted in such a manner: As the observers repeatedly encounter violent scenes, they might become habituated to events of this type so that there is a decreasing priming effect and a decline in the activation of aggression-related ideas and inclinations. The desensitization, then, presumably reflects this reduced activation.

This essay has implicitly rejected this habituation interpretation of desensitization. I have suggested that the signs of desensitization to aggression with repeated exposure to aggressive scenes are basically due to an increased acceptance of aggressive behavior. Aggressive ideas theoretically are more likely to be activated with this repeated exposure and, as a consequence, the observers are more apt to think (at least for a short time) that aggression is proper or worthwhile. Because of this increased acceptance of aggression, their concerns and anxiety about aggression presumably diminish. Thus, I have proposed that the lowered level of physiological arousal resulting from several viewings of aggressive movies might actually reflect a reduced internal conflict or a decreased aggression anxiety, but not a decline in the observer's inclination to aggression. The previously discussed experiment by Thomas (1982) has yielded findings consistent with this thesis.

Even if habituation is involved in the desensitization to aggression, this does not necessarily mean that there is a lower probability of open aggression with frequent exposure to aggressive scenes. The habituation could create a diminution of two different reaction tendencies: (1) ideas and inclinations facilitative of aggression, and (2) ideas and other responses that tend to inhibit overt aggression. Available evidence suggests, although only tentatively, that any habituation might result in a faster decrease in the inhibitory as compared with the facilitative tendencies. Again, overt aggression is then more likely.

This is not to say that antisocial and prosocial actions are inevitable when antisocial or prosocial incidents are reported. The mass communications only affect the probability of this behavior, and many other factors can intervene to affect the chances that the media-activated thoughts will be translated into overt acts. This report has examined a number of these moderating influences, but even when they are taken into account, there undoubtedly is only a relatively small likelihood that any one person will openly display the type of behavior that was portrayed. However, this low probability must be considered in the context of the audience size. For example, the chance that only one individual in one hundred thousand will exhibit overt aggression as a result of the depicted violence means that a hundred more violent acts will occur in an audience of 10 million. This particular example may have underestimated the probability of overt aggression and certainly minimized the size of American audiences. Whatever the exact numbers, our society has to decide whether the benefits of portrayed aggression outweigh the cost.

REFERENCES

Aderman, D., & Berkowitz, L. (1970). Observational set, empathy, and helping. *Journal of Personality and Social Psychology, 14,* 141–148.

Anderson, C. A.(1983). Imagination and expectation:The effect of imagining behavioral scripts on personal intentions. *Journal of Personality and Social Psychology, 45,* 293–305.

Anderson, J., & Bower, G. (1973). *Human associative memory.* Washington, DC: V. H. Winston.

Andison, F. (1977). TV violence and viewer aggression: A cumulation of study results 1956–1976. *Public Opinion Quarterly, 41,* 314–331.

Archer, D., & Gartner, R. (1976). Violent acts and violent times: A comparative approach to postwar homicide rates. *American Sociological Review, 41,* 937–963.

Bandura, A. (1965). Influence of models' reinforcement contingencies on the acquisition of imitative responses. *Journal of Personality and Social Psychology, 1,* 589–595.

Bandura, A. (1971). *Social learning theory.* New York: General Learning Press.

Bandura, A. (1973). *Aggression: A social learning analysis.* Englewood Cliffs, NJ: Prentice-Hall.

Bandura, A., Ross, D., & Ross, S. (1963). Imitation of film-mediated aggressive models. *Journal of Abnormal and Social Psychology, 66,* 3–11.

Bargh, J., & Pietromonaco, P. (1982). Automatic information processing and social perception: The influence of trait information presented outside of conscious awareness on impression formation. *Journal of Personality and Social Psychology, 43,* 437–449. Berkowitz, L. (1965). Some aspects of observed aggression. *Journal of Personality and Social Psychology, 2,* 359–369.

Berkowitz, L. (1970). Aggressive humor as a stimulus to aggressive responses. *Journal of Personality and Social Psychology, 16,* 710–717.

Berkowitz, L. (1973). Words and symbols as stimuli to aggressive responses. In J. Knutson (Ed.), *Control of aggression: Implications from basic research* (pp. 113–143). Chicago: Aldine.

Berkowitz, L. (1974). Some determinants of impulsive aggression: Role of mediated associations with reinforcements for aggression. *Psychological Review, 81,* 165–176.

Berkowitz, L., & Alioto, J. (1973). The meaning of an observed event as a determinant of its aggressive consequences. *Journal of Personality and Social Psychology, 28,* 206–217.

Berkowitz, L., Corwin, R., & Heironimus, M. (1963). Film violence and subsequent aggressive tendencies. *Public Opinion Quarterly, 27,* 217–229.

Berkowitz, L., & Geen, R. (1967). Stimulus qualities of the target of aggression: A further study. *Journal of Personality and Social Psychology, 5,* 364–368.

Berkowitz, L., & Macaulay, J. (1971). The contagion of criminal violence. *Sociometry, 34,* 238–260.

Berkowitz, L., Parke, R., Leyens, J., & West, S. (1974). The effects of justified and unjustified movie violence on aggression in juvenile delinquents. *Journal of Research in Crime and Delinquency, 11,* 16–24.

Berkowitz, L., & Powers, P. (1979). Effects of timing and justification of witnessed aggression on the observers' punitiveness. *Journal of Research in Personality, 13*, 71–80.

Berkowitz, L., & Rawlings, E. (1963). Effects of film violence on inhibitions against subsequent aggression. *Journal of Abnormal and Social Psychology, 66*, 405–412.

Blackman, J., & Hornstein, H. (1977). Newscasts and the social actuary. *Public Opinion Quarterly, 41*, 295–313.

Bollen, K., & Phillips, D. (1982). Imitative suicides: A national study of the effects of television news stories. *American Sociological Review, 47*, 802–809.

Bower, G. (1981). Mood and memory. *American Psychologist, 36*, 129–148.

Buvinic, M., & Berkowitz, L. (1976). Delayed effects of practiced versus unpracticed responses after observation of movie violence. *Journal of Experimental Social Psychology, 12*, 283–293.

Carver, C., Ganellen, R., Froming, W., & Chambers, W. (1983). Modeling: An analysis in terms of category accessibility. *Journal of Experimental Social Psychology, 19*, 403–421.

Clark, M., & Isen, A. (1982). Toward understanding the relationship between feeling states and social behavior. In A. Hastorf & A. Isen (Eds.), *Cognitive social psychology* (pp. 73–108). New York: Elsevier.

Collins, A., & Loftus, E. (1975). A spreading-activation theory of semantic memory. *Psychological Review, 82*, 407–428.

Collins, W., & Getz, S. (1976). Children's social responses following modeled reactions to provocation: Prosocial effects of a TV drama. *Journal of Personality, 44*, 488–500.

Comstock, G. (1975). *Television and human behavior: The key studies.* Santa Monica, CA: Rand.

Comstock, G. (1980). New emphases in research on the effects of television and film violence. In E. Palmer & A. Dorr (Eds.), *Children and the faces of television* (pp. 129–148). New York: Academic Press.

Comstock, G., Chaffee, S., Katzman, N., McCombs, M., & Roberts, D. (1978). *Television and human behavior.* New York: Columbia University Press.

Cook, T. D., Kendzierski, D. A., & Thomas, S. V. (1983). The implicit assumptions of television research: An analysis of the 1982 NIMH report on television and behavior. *Public Opinion Quarterly, 47*, 161–201.

Donnerstein, E., & Berkowitz, L. (1981). Victim reactions in aggressive erotic films as a factor in violence against women. *Journal of Personality and Social Psychology, 41*, 710–724.

Donnerstein, E., & Berkowitz, L. (1983). *Effects of film content and victim association on aggressive behavior and attitudes.* Unpublished manuscript, University of Wisconsin–Madison.

Doob, A., & Climie, R. (1972). Delay of measurement and the effects of film violence. *Journal of Experimental Social Psychology, 8*, 136–142.

Doob, A., & MacDonald, G. (1979). Television viewing and fear of victimization: Is the relationship causal? *Journal of Personality and Social Psychology, 37*, 170–179.

Dorr, A. (1981). Television and affective development and functioning: Maybe this decade. *Journal of Broadcasting, 25*, 335–345.

Drabman, R., & Thomas, M. (1974). Does media violence increase children's toleration of real-life aggression? *Developmental Psychology, 10*, 418–421.

Eron, L. (1982). Parent-child interaction, television violence, and aggression of children. *American Psychologist, 37*, 197–211.

Eron, L., Huesmann, L., Lefkowitz, M., & Walder, L. (1972). Does television violence cause aggression? *American Psychologist, 27*, 253–263.

Feshbach, S. (1972). Reality and fantasy in filmed violence. In J. Murray, E. Rubinstein, & G. Comstock (Eds.), *Television and social behavior* (vol. 2, pp. 318–345). Washington, DC: Department of Health, Education, and Welfare.

Some Effects of Thoughts on Anti- and Prosocial Influences of Media Events

Friedrich, L., & Stein, A. (1973). Aggressive and prosocial television programs and the natural behavior of preschool children. *Monographs of the Society for Research in Child Development, 38* (4, Serial No. 151).

Geen, R. (1975). The meaning of observed violence: Real versus fictional violence and effects of aggression and emotional arousal. *Journal of Research in Personality, 9,* 270–281.

Geen, R. (1976). Observing violence in the mass media: Implications of basic research. In R. Geen & E. O'Neal (Eds.), *Perspectives on aggression* (pp. 193–234). New York: Academic Press.

Geen, R. (1981). Behavioral and physiological reactions to observed violence: Effects of prior exposure to aggressive stimuli. *Journal of Personality and Social Psychology, 40,* 868–875.

Geen, R., & Berkowitz, L. (1966). Name-mediated aggressive cue properties. *Journal of Personality, 34,* 456–465.

Geen, R., & Berkowitz, L. (1967). Some conditions facilitating the occurrence of aggression after the observation of violence. *Journal of Personality, 35,* 666–676.

Geen, R., & Rakosky, J. (1973). Interpretations of observed violence and their effects of GSR. *Journal of Experimental Research in Personality, 6,* 289–292.

Geen, R., & Stonner, D. (1973). Context effects in observed violence. *Journal of Personality and Social Psychology, 25,* 145–150.

Geen, R., & Stonner, D. (1974). The meaning of observed violence: Effects on arousal and aggressive behavior. *Journal of Research in Personality, 8,* 55–63.

Gerbner, G., Gross, L., Morgan, M., & Signorielli, N. (1980). The "mainstreaming" of America: Violence profile No. 11. *Journal of Communication, 30,* 10–29.

Gerbner, G., Gross, L., Signorielli, N., Morgan, M., & Jackson-Beeck, M. (1979). The demonstration of power. Violence profile No. 10. *Journal of Communication, 29,* 177–195.

Goranson, R. (1969). *Observed violence and aggressive behavior: The effects of negative outcomes to the observed violence.* Unpublished doctoral dissertation. University of Wisconsin.

Goranson, R. (1970). Media violence and aggressive behavior: A review of experimental research. In L. Berkowitz (Ed.), *Advances in experimental social psychology* (vol. 5, pp. 1–31). New York: Academic Press.

Greenwald, A. G. (1970). Sensory feedback mechanisms in performance control: With special reference to the ideo-motor mechanism. *Psychological Review, 77,* 73–99.

Hawkins, R., & Pingree, S. (1980). Some processes in the cultivation effect. *Communication Research, 7,* 193–226.

Hearold, S. (1979). *Meta-analysis of the effects of television on social behavior.* Unpublished doctoral dissertation, University of Colorado.

Holloway, S., Tucker, L., & Hornstein, H. (1977). The effects of social and nonsocial information on interpersonal behavior of males: The news makes news. *Journal of Personality and Social Psychology, 35,* 514–522.

Hornstein, H. A., LaKind, E., Frankel, G., & Manne, S. (1975). The effects of knowledge about remote social events on prosocial behavior, social conception, and mood. *Journal of Personality and Social Psychology, 32,* 1038–1046.

Hoyt, J. (1970). Effect of media violence "justification" on aggression. *Journal of Broadcasting, 16,* 455–464.

Huesmann, L., Eron, L., Klein, L., Brice, P., & Fischer, P. (1983). Mitigating the imitation of aggressive behaviors by changing children's attitudes about media violence. *Journal of Personality and Social Psychology, 44,* 899–910.

Iwao, S., de Sola Pool, I., & Hagiwara, S. (1981). Japanese and U.S. media: Some cross-cultural insights in TV violence. *Journal of Communication, 31,* 28–36.

James, W. (1890). *Principles of psychology.* New York: Holt.

Josephson, W. (1982). *The effects of violent television upon children's aggression: Elici-

tation, disinhibition, or catharsis? Unpublished doctoral dissertation. University of Manitoba.

Klatzky, R. (1980). *Human memory* (2nd ed.). San Francisco: Freeman.

Landman, J., & Manis, M. (1983). Social cognition: Some historical and theoretical perspectives. In L. Berkowitz (Ed.), *Advances in experimental social psychology* (vol. 16, pp. 49–123). San Francisco: Academic Press.

Lang, P. J. (1979). A bio-informational theory of emotional imagery. *Psychophysiology, 16,* 495–512.

Leifer, A., & Roberts, D. (1972). Children's response to television violence. In J. Murray, E. Rubinstein, & G. Comstock (Eds.), *Television and social behavior* (vol. 2). Washington, DC: U.S. Government Printing Office.

Leventhal, H. (1980). Toward a comprehensive theory of emotion. In L. Berkowitz (Ed.), *Advances in experimental social psychology* (vol. 13, pp. 140–207). New York: Academic Press.

Leyens, J., Cisneros, T., & Hossay, J. (1976). Decentration as a means for reducing aggression after exposure to violent stimuli. *European Journal of Social Psychology, 6,* 459–473.

Leyens, J., & Parke, R. (1975). Aggressive slides can induce a weapons effect. *European Journal of Social Psychology, 5,* 229–236.

Leyens, J., & Picus, S. (1973). Identification with the winner of a fight and name mediation: Their differential effects upon subsequent aggressive behavior. *British Journal of Social and Clinical Psychology, 12,* 374–377.

Liebert, R., Sprafkin, J., & Davidson, E. (1982). *The early window: Effects of television on children and youth* (2nd ed.). New York: Pergamon Press.

Malamuth, N., & Check, J. (1981). The effects of mass media exposure on acceptance of violence against women: A field experiment. *Journal of Research in Personality, 15,* 436–446.

Mann, J., Berkowitz, L., Sidman, J., Starr, S., & West, S. (1974). Satiation of the transient stimulating effects of erotic films. *Journal of Personality and Social Psychology, 30,* 729–735.

McLeod, J., Atkin, C., & Chaffee, S. (1972). Adolescents, parents and television use: Adolescent self-report measures from Maryland and Wisconsin samples. In G. Comstock & E. Rubinstein (Eds.), *Television and social behavior* (vol. 3, pp. 173–238). Washington, DC: U.S. Government Printing Office.

Myer, T (1972). Effects of viewing justified and unjustified real film violence on aggressive behavior. *Journal of Personality and Social Psychology, 23,* 21–29.

Milavsky, J., Kessler, R., Stipp, H., & Rubens, W. (1982). *Television and aggression: The results of a panel study.* New York: Academic Press.

Murray, J. (1980). *Television and youth: 25 years of research and controversy.* Boys Town, NE: Boys Town Center for Study of Youth Development.

Murray, J., & Kippax, S. (1979). From the early window to the late night show: International trends in the study of television's impact on children and adults. In L. Berkowitz (Ed.), *Advances in experimental social psychology* (vol. 12, pp. 254–320). New York: Academic Press.

National Institute of Mental Health. (1982). *Television and behavior: Ten years of scientific progress.* Vol 1. *Summary report.* Washington, DC: U.S. Government Printing Office.

Noble, G. (1973). Effects of different forms of filmed aggression on children's constructive and destructive play. *Journal of Personality and Social Psychology, 26,* 54–59.

Palmer, E., & Dorr, A. (Eds.). (1980). *Children and the faces of television: Teaching, violence, selling.* New York: Academic Press.

Parke, R., Berkowitz, L., Leyens, J., West, S., & Sebastian, R. (1977). Some effects of violent and nonviolent movies on the behavior of juvenile delinquents. In L. Berkowitz

(Ed.), *Advances in experimental social psychology* (vol. 10, pp. 136–172). New York: Academic Press.

Phillips, D. (1974). The influence of suggestion on suicide: Substantive and theoretical implications of the Werther effect. *American Sociological Review, 39,* 340–354.

Phillips, D. (1979). Suicide, motor vehicle fatalities, and the mass media: Evidence toward a theory of suggestion. *American Journal of Sociology, 84,* 1150–1174.

Phillips, D. (1980). Airplane accidents, murder, and the mass media: Towards a theory of imitation and suggestion. *Social Forces, 58,* 1001–1024.

Phillips, D. (1982). The impact of fictional television stories on U.S. adult fatalities: New evidence on the effect of mass media on violence. *American Journal of Sociology, 87,* 1340–1359.

Phillips, D. (1983). The impact of mass media violence on U.S. homicides. *American Sociological Review, 48,* 560–568.

Rosenfeld, E., Maloney, S., Huesmann, R., Eron, L., Fischer, P., Musonis, V., & Washington, A. (1978). *The effect of fantasy behaviors and fantasy-reality discriminations upon the observational learning of aggression.* Paper presented at the annual meeting of the International Society for Research on Aggression, Washington, DC.

Rushton, J. (1979). Effects of prosocial television and film material on the behavior of viewers. In L. Berkowitz (Ed.), *Advances in experimental social psychology* (vol. 12, pp. 322–351). New York: Academic Press.

Shiffrin, R., & Schneider, W. (1977). Controlled and automatic human information processing: II. Perceptual learning, automatic attending, and a general theory. *Psychological Review, 84,* 127–190.

Silverman, L., & Sprafkin, J. (1980). The effects of Sesame Street's prosocial spots on cooperative-play between young children. *Journal of Broadcasting, 24,* 135–147.

Singer, J., & Singer, D. (1981*). Television, imagination and aggression.* Hillsdale, NJ: Erlbaum.

Sprafkin, J., Liebert, R., & Poulos, R. (1975). Effects of a prosocial televised example on children's helping. *Journal of Experimental Child, 20,* 119–126.

Tannenbaum, P., & Gaer, E. P. (1965). Mood changes as a function of stress of protagonist and degree of identification in a film-viewing situation. *Journal of Personality and Social Psychology, 2,* 612–616.

Tarde, G. (1912). *Penal philosophy.* Boston: Little, Brown.

Thomas, M. (1982). Physiological arousal, exposure to a relatively lengthy aggressive film, and aggressive behavior. *Journal of Research in Personality, 16,* 72–81.

Thomas, M., & Drabman, R. (1977). *Effects of television violence on expectations of others' aggression.* Paper presented at the annual meeting of the American Psychological Association, San Francisco, CA.

Thomas, M., Horton, R., Lippincott, E., & Drabman, R. (1977). Desensitization to portrayals of real-life aggression as a function of exposure to television violence. *Journal of Personality and Social Psychology, 35,* 450–458.

Turner, C., & Berkowitz, L. (1972). Identification with film aggressor (covert role taking) and reactions to film violence. *Journal of Personality and Social Psychology, 21,* 256–264.

Turner, C., & Layton, J. (1976). Verbal imagery and connotation as memory induced mediators of aggressive behavior. *Journal of Personality and Social Psychology, 33,* 755–763.

Tyler, I. R. (1980). Impact of directly and indirectly experienced events: The origin of crime-related judgments and behaviors. *Journal of Personality and Social Psychology, 39,* 13–28.

Vaughan, K., & Lanzetta, J. (1981). The effect of modification of expressive displays on vicarious emotional arousal. *Journal of Experimental Social Psychology, 17,* 16–30.

Velten, E. (1968). A laboratory task for the induction of mood states. *Behavior Research and Therapy, 6,* 473–482.

Wheeler, L. (1966). Toward a theory of behavioral contagion. *Psychological Review, 73,* 179–182.

Wober, J. (1978). Televised violence and paranoid perception: The view from Great Britain. *Public Opinion Quarterly, 42,* 315–321.

Worchel, S. (1972). The effect of films on the importance of behavioral freedom. *Journal of Personality, 40,* 417–435.

Wyer, R., Jr., & Hartwick, J. (1980). The role of information retrieval and conditional inference processes in belief formation and change. In L. Berkowitz (Ed.), *Advances in experimental social psychology* (vol. 13, pp. 243–284). New York: Academic Press.

Wyer, R., Jr., & Srull, T. (1981). Category accessibility: Some theoretical and empirical issues concerning the processing of information. In E. Higgins, C. Herman, & M. Zanna (Eds.), *Social cognition* (vol. 1, pp. 161–197). Hillsdale, NJ: Erlbaum.

Zillmann, D., & Bryant, J. (1982). Pornography, sexual callousness, and the trivialization of rape. *Journal of Communication, 32,* 10–21.

Zillmann, D., Bryant, J., Comisky, P., & Medoff, N. (1981). Excitation and hedonic valence in the effect of erotica on motivated intermale aggression. *European Journal of Social Psychology, 11,* 233–252.

Richard B. Felson

Mass Media Effects on Violent Behavior

Watching violence is a popular form of entertainment. A crowd of onlookers enjoys a street fight just as the Romans enjoyed the gladiators. Wrestling is a popular spectator sport not only in the United States, but in many countries in the Middle East. People enjoy combat between animals—cock fights in Indonesia, bull fights in Spain, and dog fights in rural areas of this country. Violence is frequently depicted in folklore, fairy tales, and other literature. Local news shows provide extensive coverage of violent crimes in order to increase their ratings.

Technological advances have dramatically increased the availability of violent entertainment. The introduction of television was critical, particularly in making violent entertainment more available to children. More recently, cable systems, videocassette recorders, and video games have increased exposure. Hand-held cameras and video monitors now permit filming of actual crimes in progress. Economic competition for viewers, particularly young viewers, has placed a premium on media depictions of violence.

Not long after the introduction of television in American households, there occurred a dramatic increase in violent crime (Centerwall, 1989). Some scholars and commentators see a causal connection. The most common argument is that children imitate the violence they see on television. The process of imitation is emphasized by social learning theory—a well-established approach in social psychology (Bandura, 1983). For both practical and theoretical reasons, then, an interest developed in examining whether exposure to violence in the media affects the incidence of violence.

Violence usually refers to physical aggression. Aggression is

With permission from the *Annual Review of Sociology*, vol. 22, 1996, pp. 103–128, © 1996, by Annual Reviews.

Figure 36. Harvey Keitel takes aim in Quentin Tarantino's Reservoir Dogs, *a film awash in blood and mayhem.*

usually defined as any behavior involving an intent to harm another person. Some studies of media effects, however, examine behaviors that do not involve an intent to harm. For example, a common procedure is to see whether children will hit a "Bobo" doll after observing an adult model do so or after being exposed to media violence. It seems unlikely that hitting a Bobo doll involves an intent to do harm (Tedeschi et al., 1974). Other studies include measures of nonviolent criminal behavior, most of which do not involve an intent to do harm. Of course, it depends on what is meant by intent, a term most researchers do not define. Tedeschi and Felson (1994) define an intent to do harm as a behavior in which the actor expects the target will be harmed and values that harm.[1] Offenders who commit larceny and other nonviolent crimes know that the victim will be harmed, but in most cases they do not value that harm; harm is not their goal.

In the first section of this essay, I discuss the empirical evidence regarding whether media violence has a causal effect on the aggressive behavior of viewers. I review the classic studies, the meta-analyses, and some more recent research. In the second section I examine the theoretical processes that might explain short-term effects, should they exist, and discuss relevant evidence. I do the same for long-term effects in the third section.[2]

Empirical Evidence Regarding Media Effects on Aggression

The relationship between exposure to media violence and aggression has been examined using laboratory experiments, field experiments, natural experiments, and longitudinal analyses based on correlational data. I review some of the key research in each of these domains.

Laboratory Experiments

Laboratory experiments examine short-term effects of media violence. Most studies show that subjects in laboratory experiments who observe media violence tend to behave more aggressively than do subjects in control groups. A meta-analysis of these studies reveals consistent and substantial media effects (Andison, 1977). However, research is inconsistent in showing whether it is necessary to provoke subjects before showing violence to get an effect (Freedman, 1984). Thus, it is not clear whether media exposure acts as an instigator of aggression in the laboratory or merely as a facilitator.

Researchers have raised questions about the external validity of laboratory experiments in this area (Freedman, 1984; Cook et al., 1983). They point out that the laboratory situation is very different from situations leading to violence outside the laboratory (e.g., Tedeschi & Felson, 1994). For subjects to engage in aggressive behavior in the laboratory, the behavior must be legitimated. Subjects are told, for example, that the delivery of shocks is a teaching method or part of a game. Subjects are then subjected to an attack by a confederate and given a chance to retaliate. Unlike aggressive behavior outside the laboratory, there is no possibility that this will be punished by third parties or that this will subject them to retaliation from the target. It is unknown to what extent these differences limit the generalizability of experimental studies. Evidence suggests that aggression measures in many laboratory studies do involve an intent to harm (Berkowitz & Donnerstein, 1982). Experimental subjects may not be so different from those who engage in violence outside the laboratory, who see their behavior as legitimate, and who do not consider its costs.[3]

The demand cues in these studies are probably a more significant problem. Demand cues are instructions or other stimuli that indicate to subjects how the experimenter expects them to behave.[4] Experimenters who show violent films are likely to communicate a message about their attitudes toward aggression. A violent film may imply to subjects that the experimenter is a permissive adult or someone not particularly offended by violence. Just a few subjects aware of the demand and compliant could account for the mean differences in aggression found between experimental conditions.

The laboratory is a setting that exaggerates the effects of conformity and social influence (see Gottfredson & Hirschi, 1993). The extent of compliance in laboratory settings is dramatically demonstrated in Milgram's (1974) well-known research on obedient aggression. Subjects' behavior is easily influenced for at least three reasons: (1) The standards for behavior are unclear and the situation is novel (Nemeth, 1970); (2) subjects are influenced by the prestige of the experimenter and the scientific enterprise; (3) subjects want to avoid being perceived as psychologically maladjusted by the psychologist-experimenter (Rosenberg, 1969).

Field Experiments

Concerns about external validity have stimulated researchers to employ field experiments. Field experiments retain the advantages of experimental design but avoid the problem of demand cues since subjects do not usually know they are being studied. A number of such studies have been carried out in institutionalized settings (Feshbach & Singer, 1971; Leyens et al., 1975; Parke et al., 1977). In these studies, boys are exposed to either violent or nonviolent programming, and their aggressive behavior is observed in the following days or weeks. Each of the studies has some important methodological limitations (see Freedman, 1984). For example, although the boys in each treatment lived together, the studies used statistical procedures that assumed that each boy's behavior was independent. Even if one overlooks the limitations, the results from these studies are inconsistent. In fact, one of the studies found that the boys who watched violent television programs were less aggressive than the boys who viewed nonviolent shows (Feshbach & Singer, 1971).

The results of field experiments have been examined in at least three meta-analyses. Hearold's (1986) meta-analysis of a broad range of experimental studies revealed an effect for laboratory experiments but no effect for field experiments. A meta-analysis that included more recent studies, however, did find an effect for field experiments (Paik & Comstock, 1994). Finally, Wood et al.'s meta-analysis (1991) was restricted to field studies of media violence on unconstrained social interaction.[5] In all of these studies children or adolescents were observed unobtrusively after being exposed to an aggressive or nonaggressive film. In sixteen studies subjects engaged in more aggression following exposure to violent films, while in seven studies subjects in the control group engaged in more aggression. In five of the studies there was no difference between control and experimental groups.

Natural Experiments: The Introduction of Television

These studies take advantage of the fact that television was introduced at different times in different locations. They assume that people who are exposed to television will also be exposed to a high dose of television violence. This is probably a reasonable assumption given the extremely high correlation between television viewing and exposure to television violence (Milavsky et al., 1982).

Hennigan et al. (1982) compared crime rates in American cities that already had television with those that did not. No effect of the presence or absence of television was found on violent crime rates in a comparison of the two kinds of cities. Furthermore, when cities without television obtained it, there was no increase in violent crime. There was an increase in the incidence of larceny, which the authors attributed to relative deprivation suffered by viewers observing affluent people on television.[6]

Joy et al. (1986) examined changes in the aggressive behavior of children after television was introduced into an isolated Canadian town in the 1970s. The town was compared to two supposedly comparable towns that already had television. Forty-five children in the three towns were observed on the school playground in first and second grade and then again two years later. The frequency of both verbal and physical aggression increased in all three communities, but the increase was significantly greater in the community in which television was introduced during the study. Some of the results were not consistent with a television effect, however. In the first phase of the study, the children in the community without television were just as aggressive as the children in the communities that already had television. Without television they should have been less aggressive. The children in the community where television was introduced then became more aggressive than the children in the other communities in the second phase, when all three communities had television. At this point, the level of aggressive behavior in the three communities should have been similar. To accept the findings, one must assume that the community without television at the beginning of the study had more aggressive children than the other communities for other reasons, but that this effect was counteracted in the first phase by the fact that they were not exposed to television. That assumption implies that there are other differences between the communities and thus casts doubt on the findings of the study.

Centerwall (1989) examined the relationship between homicide rates and the introduction of television in three countries: South Africa, Canada, and the United States. Television was introduced in South Africa in 1975, about twenty-five years after Canada and the United States. The white homicide rate increased dramatically in the United States and Canada about fifteen years after the introduction of television, when the first generation of children who had access to television were entering adulthood. The white homicide rate declined slightly in South Africa during this time period. While Centerwall ruled out some confounding factors (e.g., differences in economic development), causal inference is difficult, given the many differences between the countries involved. In addition, Centerwall could not determine at the time he wrote whether the level of violence had increased fifteen years after the introduction of television in South Africa; thus an important piece of evidence was missing.

Centerwall also examined the effect of the introduction of television in the United States. He found that urban areas acquired television before rural areas, and their homicide rates increased earlier. However, social changes in general are likely to occur in urban areas before they occur in rural areas. He also found that households of whites acquired television sets before households of blacks, and their homicide rates increased earlier as well. It is difficult to imagine an alternative explanation of this effect.

Still, the methodological limitations of these studies make it difficult to have confidence in a causal inference about media effects. The substantial differences between the comparison groups increase the risk that the relationship between the introduction of television and increases in aggression is spurious.

Natural Experiments: Publicized Violence

The effects of highly publicized violent events on fluctuations in homicide and suicide rates over time have been examined in a series of studies (see Phillips, 1986 for a review). Phillips (1983) found an increase in the number of homicides after highly publicized heavyweight championship fights. Modeling effects were only observed when the losing fighter and the crime victims were similar in race and sex. The loss of prize fights by white fighters was followed by increases in deaths through homicide of white males on days 2 and 8. The loss of prize fights by blacks was followed by an increase in homicide deaths for black males on days 4 and 5. The rise in the homicide rate was not canceled out by a subsequent drop, suggesting that the prize fights affected the incidence and not just the timing of homicides.

Baron and Reiss (1985) attribute these effects to the fact that prize fights tend to occur during the week and homicides are more likely to occur on weekends. They were able to replicate Phillips's findings by selecting weeks without prizefights and pretending that they had occurred. In response to this critique, Phillips and Bollen (1985) selected different weeks and showed that the weekend effect could not account for all of the findings. Miller et al. (1991) replicated some of Phillips's results, but found that the effect only occurred on Saturdays following highly publicized fights.

Freedman (1984) has criticized Phillips's research on other methodological grounds, and Phillips (1986) has addressed these criticisms. There are still unresolved questions, such as why effects tended to occur on different days for different races. In addition, experimental results suggest that watching boxing films does not affect the viewer's aggressive behavior. Geen (1978) found that, when provoked, college students were more aggressive after viewing vengeful aggression but not after viewing a boxing match (see also Hoyt, 1970).

Longitudinal Surveys

Survey research demonstrates that the correlation between the amount of exposure to television violence and frequency of aggressive behavior generally varies between 0.10 and 0.20 (Freedman, 1984; see Paik & Comstock, 1994 for slightly higher estimates). There are good reasons to think the relationship is at least partly spurious. For example, children with favorable attitudes toward violence may be more likely to engage in violence and also more likely to find violence entertaining to watch. Also, children who are more closely supervised may be less likely to engage in violence and less likely to watch television. Intelligence, need for excitement, level of fear, and commitment to school are other possible confounding variables. Wiegman et al. (1992) found that intelligence was negatively associated with both exposure to violence and aggressive behavior.

Longitudinal data has been used to examine whether viewing television violence produces changes in aggressive behavior. These studies statistically control for aggression at *T*1 in order to isolate causal effects on aggression at *T*2. Spuriousness is still possible if some third variable is associated with exposure to media violence and changes in aggressive behavior over time.

The main longitudinal evidence for a causal link between viewing violence and aggressive behavior has been provided by Eron, Huesmann, and their associates (Eron et al., 1972; Huesmann & Eron, 1986). In the first study, they examined the effect of children's exposure to television violence at age 8 on aggressive behavior at age 18. A measure of viewing television violence at Time 1 was obtained by asking parents the names of their children's favorite television shows. These shows were coded for the level of violence depicted. Aggressive behavior at Time 2 was measured by ratings of aggressiveness by peers, self-reports, and the aggression subscale on the MMPI.[7] Effects of television violence were found only for boys and only on the peer nomination measure.

In addition to the inconsistent results, there are some measurement problems in this study (see Surgeon General's Report on Television Violence, 1972; Freedman, 1984). First, the aggression measure included items referring to antisocial behavior that do not involve aggression. Second, the measure of television exposure is based on parents' beliefs about the favorite programs of their children. Later research found that parental reports of their children's favorite programs are not strongly correlated to children's self-reports of total exposure (Milavsky et al., 1982).

Three-year longitudinal studies of primary schoolchildren were later carried out in five countries: Australia, Israel, Poland, Finland, and the United States (Huesmann & Eron, 1986). Aggression was measured by the same peer nomination measure as the one used in the earlier research. The children were asked to name one or two of their favorite programs and to indicate how often they watched them. Complex and inconsistent results were obtained. In the United States, television violence had a significant effect on the later aggressiveness of females but not males, a reversal of the effect found in their first study (Huesmann & Eron, 1986). An effect of the violence of favorite programs on later aggression was found only for boys who rated themselves as similar to violent and nonviolent television characters. A similar conditional effect was found for males in Finland, but there was no effect of viewing television violence on later aggressiveness of females (Lagerspetz &

Viemero, 1986). In Poland a direct effect of violence in favorite programs was found on later aggressiveness for both males and females (Fraczek, 1986). No effect of early viewing of television violence was found on subsequent aggressiveness for either males or females in Australia (Sheehan, 1986), or among children living in a kibbutz in Israel (Bachrach, 1986). A television effect was found for city children in Israel when the measure of aggression was a single item asking "who never fights." But the effect did not occur on the same peer nomination measure that had been used in the other cross-national studies.

Negative evidence was obtained in a large-scale, methodologically sophisticated, longitudinal study carried out by Milavsky et al. (1982). Their study was based on data collected from 3,200 students in elementary and junior high schools in Fort Worth and Minneapolis. Students identified the programs they had watched in the past four weeks and indicated how many times they had watched them; these were coded for violent content.[8] The authors refined the peer nomination measure of aggression used by Eron et al. to include intentional acts of harm-doing, but not general misbehavior.

There was no evidence that any of the measures of exposure to television violence produced changes in aggressive behavior over time. The authors corrected for measurement error and used a variety of time lags, subsamples, and measures of exposure to television violence and aggressive behavior. In spite of a thorough exploration of the data, they found no evidence that exposure to violence on television affected the aggressive behavior of children. While the coefficients in most of the analyses were positive, they were all close to zero and statistically insignificant. The abundance of positive correlations led some critics to reject Milavsky et al.'s conclusion of no effect (e.g., Friedrich-Cofer & Huston, 1986).

A more recent longitudinal study in the Netherlands also failed to find a media effect (Wiegman et al., 1992). The children were surveyed in either the second or fourth grade and then again two years later. Peer nominations were used as a measure of aggressive behavior. The lagged effect of exposure on aggressive behavior was small and statistically insignificant.

It is difficult to reach a conclusion on the long-term effects of viewing television violence from these longitudinal studies. The studies that used better measurement failed to find an effect. In the studies where an effect was found, the relationship was between favorite show violence and subsequent aggression, rather than the amount of exposure to television violence, and Milavsky et al. did not replicate that effect. The findings reported in the cross-national studies were inconsistent and had as many negative findings as positive ones. Therefore one must conclude that longitudinal studies have not demonstrated a relationship between the amount of violence viewed on television and subsequent aggressive behavior.[9]

Theoretical Explanations of Situational Effects

The experimental results described above show that exposure to media violence can have at least a short-term effect on aggressive behavior. In this section, I consider theoretical reasons for expecting situational effects. I also review some of the evidence regarding these theoretical mechanisms.

Cognitive Priming

According to a cognitive priming approach, the aggressive ideas in violent films can activate other aggressive thoughts in viewers through their association in memory pathways (Berkowitz, 1984). When one thought is activated, other thoughts that are strongly connected are also activated. Immediately after a violent film, the viewer is primed to respond aggressively because a network of memories involving aggression is retrieved. Evidence indicates that media violence does elicit thoughts and emotional responses related to aggression (Bushman & Geen, 1990).

Huesmann (1982) makes a similar argument. He suggests that children learn problem-solving scripts in part from their observations of others' behavior. These scripts are cognitive expectations about a sequence of behaviors that may be performed in particular situations. Frequent exposure to scenes of violence may lead children to store scripts for aggressive behavior in their memories, and these may be recalled in a later situation if any aspect of the original situation—even a superficial one—is present.

The classic studies of these effects involve the exposure of subjects to the fight scene from a film, *The Champion*, starring Kirk Douglas. In one of these studies subjects were either shocked frequently or infrequently by a confederate, witnessed the fight scene, or viewed a neutral film, and then had an opportunity to shock the confederate, whose name was either Bob or Kirk (Berkowitz & Geen, 1966). Subjects gave the confederate the most shocks in the condition when they had been provoked, had viewed the violent film, and the confederate had the same name as the film's star.

Tedeschi and Norman (1985) attribute the results from these studies to demand cues (see also Tedeschi & Felson, 1994). They point out that experimenters mention the fact that the confederate's first name is the same as Kirk Douglas's in their instructions, and that they justify to subjects the beating that Kirk Douglas received. A series of studies have shown that it is necessary to provide this justification to get a violent film effect (Geen & Berkowitz, 1967; Berkowitz, 1965; Berkowitz et al., 1962; Berkowitz & Rawlings, 1963; Meyer, 1972b).

Josephson (1987) examined the combined effects of exposure to a violent film and retrieval cues in a field experiment with second- and third-grade boys. The boys were exposed to either a violent film (in which a walkie-talkie was used) or a nonviolent film. The boys were also frustrated either before or after the film. Later they were interviewed by someone holding either a walkie-talkie or a microphone. After the interview, the boys played a game of field hockey and their aggressive behavior was recorded. It was predicted that boys who were exposed to both violent television and a walkie-talkie would be most aggressive in the game, since the walkie-talkie would lead them to retrieve scripts associated with the violent film. The hypothesis was confirmed for boys who were, according to teacher ratings, aggressive. Boys who were identified as nonaggressive inhibited their aggression when exposed to the walkie-talkie and the film. Josephson suggested that for these nonaggressive boys, aggression may be strongly associated with negative emotions such as guilt and fear which, when primed, may inhibit aggression. If we accept this post hoc interpretation, it suggests that media violence may increase or inhibit the violent behavior of viewers, depending on their initial predisposition. Such effects are likely to be short-term, and they may have no effect on the overall rate of violence.

Arousal from Pornography

According to Bandura (1973), emotional arousal facilitates and intensifies aggressive behavior. The facilitating effect of emotional arousal occurs only when the individual is already prone to act aggressively. If the individual is predisposed to behave in some other way, then emotional arousal will facilitate that behavior. Arousal energizes any behavior that is dominant in the situation.

Zillmann (1983) explains the facilitative effects of arousal in terms of excitation transfer. He has proposed that arousal from two different sources may combine with one another and be attributable to the same source. When the combined arousal is attributed to anger, the individual is likely to be more aggressive than would have been the case if only the anger-producing cue has been present.

Some research has examined whether the arousal produced by pornography facilitates aggressive behavior. A series of experiments have been carried out in which subjects are exposed to sexual stimuli and then allowed to aggress against another person, who may or may not have provoked them. The prediction is that arousal produced by pornography should increase aggression when a subject has been provoked. The message communicated by pornography and the gender of actor and target should not matter unless they affect the level of arousal.

Experiments that have examined the effects of arousal from pornography have produced mixed results. Some studies have found that erotic films increased the aggressiveness of subjects who had been provoked by the victim, while others have shown that pornography has an inhibitory effect (Zillman, 1971; Meyer, 1972a; Zillmann et al., 1974; Baron & Bell, 1973, 1977; Donnerstein et al., 1975).

Researchers have developed hypotheses to provide explanations for the conditions under which opposite effects are obtained (Baron, 1974; White, 1979). Zillmann et al. (1981) explained the contradictory findings using an arousal–affect hypothesis. They proposed that arousal has both an excitation component and an affective component. If arousal is accompanied by negative affect, it should add to the arousal produced by anger and increase the level of aggression. If arousal is accompanied by positive affect, it should subtract from the arousal produced by anger and decrease the level of aggression. The findings from research on the arousal-affect hypothesis are inconclusive (see Sapolski, 1984; Tedeschi & Felson, 1994 for reviews).

Even if these results are real, their significance for pornography effects outside the experimental lab seems trivial. They suggest, for example, that a man enjoying a pornographic film is less dangerous when provoked, while a man who dislikes the film, but is still aroused by it, is more likely to retaliate for a provocation. Perhaps the findings have more implications for the effects of arousal from other sources. For example, it is possible that arousal from the car chase in the Rodney King incident contributed to the violent behavior of the police.

It is difficult to manipulate arousal in the laboratory without also affecting the meanings subjects give to those manipulations (Neiss, 1988). Experimenters who show pornographic films communicate information about their values and expectations and thus create demand cues. I discuss this issue in the next section.

Sponsor Effects

Demand cues provide a general explanation of short-term media effects in the experimental laboratory. Wood et al. (1991) suggest that demand cues may be a type of "sponsor effect" that occurs outside the experimental laboratory as well:

> Viewers are likely to believe that the violent presentation is condoned by the media sponsor, whether it be an experimenter, one's family, the television networks or movie studios, or society in general. . . . Sponsor effects are not artifacts of laboratory procedures; they also occur in field settings (Wood et al., 1991, 373).

Wood et al.'s (1991) concept of sponsor effects appears to include both social learning and situational conformity. Social learning involves socialization and enduring effects on the viewer. Viewers may be more likely to internalize a media message if they think it is sponsored by someone they respect. A sponsor effect would enhance whatever message is being conveyed.

Field and laboratory experiments seem more likely to produce sponsor effects involving situational conformity. By showing a violent film, sponsors may communicate that they are not very strict or that they have a permissive attitude toward aggressive behavior. Young people, who are normally inhibited in front of adults, may engage in aggressive behavior if they think that they can get away with it. For example, students often misbehave when they encounter less experienced substitute teachers. According to this line of thinking, young people who are exposed to media violence should feel disinhibited and should be more likely to misbehave in a variety of ways, at least while adults are present. When the sponsors of the film are no longer present, the effects should disappear.

Meta-analyses show that exposure to violence is related to nonaggressive forms of antisocial behavior. Hearold (1986) performed a meta-analysis of experiments that included studies of effects of exposure to media violence on antisocial behavior generally. The effects of media violence on antisocial behavior were just as strong as the effects of media violence on violent behavior. A more recent meta-analysis that focused on all types of studies yielded similar results (Paik & Comstock, 1994).

A study performed by Friedrich and Stein (1973) provides an example of an experiment showing general effects of exposure to media violence on antisocial behaviors. They found that nursery school children exposed to violent cartoons displayed more aggression during free play than children exposed to neutral films. However, they also found that children exposed to violence had lower tolerance for minor delays and lower task persistence, and displayed less spontaneous obedience in regard to school rules. These behaviors clearly do not involve an intent to harm.

Additional evidence for a sponsor effect comes from a study by Leyens et al. (1975). They found that subjects delivered more shock to another person when they anticipated that the experimenter would show them violent films; it was not necessary for them to actually see the films. The investigators attributed this effect to priming, based on the assumption that the mere mention of violent films primes aggressive thoughts. It seems just as likely that sponsor effects were involved: an experimenter who is willing to show a violent film is perceived as more permissive or more tolerant of aggression.

The effects of exposure to television violence on antisocial behavior generally cast doubt on many of the theoretical explanations usually used to explain media effects on violence. Explanations involving cognitive priming or arousal cannot explain why those who view violence should engage in deviant behavior generally. Explanations that stress modeling (to be discussed) cannot explain this pattern of effects either. It is possible, however, that viewers imitate the low self-control behaviors of the characters they observe in television and films, rather than violence specifically. Children model the self-control behavior of adults in experimental situations (Bandura & Walters, 1963), but it is not clear whether socialization or short-term situational effects are involved.

Sponsor effects may also explain the results of experimental studies involving exposure to pornography. Paik and Comstock's (1994) meta-analysis shows effects of both pornography and violent pornography on antisocial behavior in general. Experimenters who show pornography, especially violent pornography, may imply that they condone or at least are tolerant of taboo behavior (Reiss, 1986). Subjects may be disinhibited in this permissive atmosphere and engage in more antisocial behavior.

In sum, these studies suggest that subjects may assume a more permissive atmosphere when they are shown a violent film, and that their inhibitions about misbehavior generally are reduced. It is not yet clear whether their behavior reflects short-term conformity or longer-term socialization. Research is needed to determine whether subjects who view violent films in experiments engage in more aggression and other misbehavior in the absence of sponsors.

Television Viewing as a Routine Activity

According to the routine activity approach, crime should be less frequent when the routine activities of potential offenders and victims reduce their opportunities for contact (e.g., M. Felson, 1986). Any activity that separates those who are prone to violence from each other, or from potential victims, is likely to decrease the incidence of violence.

Messner uses this approach to argue that watching television can decrease the incidence of violence in society (Messner, 1986; Messner & Blau, 1987). Since people watch television at home, the opportunities for violence, at least with people outside the family, are probably reduced. When people watch television, they may also interact less often with other family members, so the opportunities for domestic violence may also be reduced. Messner found that cities with high levels of television viewing have lower rates of both violent and nonviolent crime (Messner, 1986; Messner & Blau, 1987). However, in an aggregate analysis of this type, one cannot determine the specific viewing habits of offenders or victims of criminal violence.[10]

The routine activities of young adult males are particularly important since they are most prone to use violence. Young adult males do not spend as much time as other groups watching television (Dimmick et al., 1979). According to the routine activity approach, their level of violence would be lower if they did.

Theoretical Explanations Involving Socialization

It is widely believed that people are more violent because they learn to be violent from their parents, their peers, and the mass media. These socialization effects tend to endure since they involve changes in the individual. The evidence on the versatility of criminal offenders casts doubt on the importance of this socialization process. Considerable evidence suggests that those who commit violent crime tend to commit nonviolent crime and other deviant acts as well. Studies of arrest histories based on both official records and self-reports show a low level of specialization in violent crime. For example, West and Farrington (1977) found that 80 percent of adults convicted of violence also had convictions for crimes involving dishonesty. Violent acts were also related to noncriminal forms of deviant behavior, such as sexual promiscuity, smoking, heavy drinking, gambling, and having an unstable job history.

The evidence that most offenders are versatile challenges the notion that violent offenders are more violent because of a special proclivity to engage in violence, due to exposure to media violence or any other factor. Individual differences in the propensity to engage in criminal violence reflect for the most part individual differences in antisocial behavior generally. Variations in the socialization of self-control and other inhibitory factors are probably important causal factors (Gottfredson & Hirschi, 1990). Theories that emphasize specific socialization to violence are likely to be limited in their utility, since most violent offenders are generalists.

The versatility argument should not be overstated. Some people do specialize in violence, and exposure to media violence may play a role in their socialization. There are a variety of reasons one might expect viewers to learn aggressive behavior from the media. First, media depictions of violence may suggest novel behaviors to viewers that they otherwise might not have considered. Second, vicarious reinforcements and legitimation of violent actions may increase the tendency to model media violence. Third, viewers become desensitized about violence after a heavy diet of it on television. Finally, people may get a false idea of reality from observing a great deal of violence on television and develop unrealistic fears. I now examine each of the processes more closely.

Learning Novel Forms of Behavior

Bandura (1983) has argued that television can shape the forms that aggressive behavior takes. Television can teach skills that may be useful for committing acts of violence, and it can direct viewers' attention to behaviors that they may not have considered. For example, young people may mimic karate and judo moves, or they may learn effective tactics for committing violent crime. This information may give direction to those who are already motivated to engage in aggression. Such a modeling process could lead to more severe forms of aggression. It could increase the frequency of violence if people who are motivated to harm someone choose a violent method they have observed on television.

There is anecdotal evidence that bizarre violent events have followed soon after their depiction on television, suggesting a form of copycat behavior. In one widely reported case in Boston, six young men set fire to a woman after forcing her to douse herself with fuel. The scene had been depicted on television two nights before. In another instance, four teenagers raped a 9-year-old girl with a beer bottle, enacting a scene similar to one in the made-for-TV movie *Born Innocent*. Such incidents may be coincidental, but they suggest the possibility that unusual and dramatic behaviors on television are imitated by viewers who might never otherwise have imagined engaging in such behaviors.

Modeling can also be used to explain contagion effects observed for highly publicized violence, such as airline hijackings, civil disorders, bombings, and political kidnapping. The tendency for such events to occur in waves suggests that at least some viewers imitate real events that are reported on television. However, the central argument about the relationship of viewing violence on television and viewers' aggressive behavior focuses on fictional events.

Vicarious Reinforcement and Legitimations

Bandura (1983) also suggested that television may inform viewers of the positive and negative consequences of violent behavior. Audiences can be expected to imitate violent behavior that is successful in gaining the model's objectives in fictional or nonfictional programs. When violence is justified or left unpunished on television, the viewer's guilt or concern about consequences is reduced. Thus Paik and Comstock's (1994) meta-analysis found that the magnitude of media effects on antisocial behavior was greater when the violent actor was rewarded or the behavior was legitimated.

It is not at all clear what message is learned from viewing violence on television. In most plots, the protagonist uses violence for legitimate ends while the villain engages in illegitimate violence. The protagonist usually uses violence in self-defense or to mete out an appropriate level of punishment to a dangerous or threatening criminal. Television conveys the message that while some forms of violence are necessary and legitimate, criminal violence is evil.

The consequences of the illegitimate violence portrayed in fictional television and film are more negative than the consequences of illegitimate violence in real life. In real life violent people often evade punishment, while in television, the villain is almost always punished. Thus, one could argue that television violence might reduce the incidence of criminal violence, since crime doesn't pay for TV criminals. Another difference is in the appeal of those who engage in illegitimate violence. In fictional television, those who engage in illegitimate violence tend to lack any attractive qualities that would lead to sympathy or identification. In real life, illegitimate violence may be committed by loved ones or others who are perceived to have desirable qualities.

Other factors may limit the effects of any message about the legitimacy, or the rewards and costs of violence. First, the lessons learned from the media about violence may be similar or redundant to the lessons learned about the use of violence conveyed by other sources. In fact, most viewers probably approve of the violent behavior of the protagonists. The influence of television on viewers who already agree with its message would be weak at best. Second, the audience may not take the message from fictional plots seriously. Modeling is more likely to occur after viewing nonfiction than after viewing fiction (Feshbach, 1972; Berkowitz & Alioto, 1973).[11] Third, the violent contexts and provocations observed on television are likely to be very different from the contexts and provocations people experience in their own lives. Evidence suggests that viewers take context and intentions into account before they model aggressive behavior (Geen, 1978; Hoyt, 1970). Straus (Baron & Straus, 1987), on the other hand, suggests that people are likely to be influenced by the violence they observe regardless of its context, message, or legitimacy. According to cultural spillover theory, violence in one sphere of life leads to violence in other spheres.

Finally, some young children may miss the more subtle aspects of television messages, focusing on overt acts rather than on the intentions or contexts in which such acts occur. Collins et al. (1984) found that kindergarten and second-grade children were relatively unaffected by an aggressor's motives in their understanding of a violent program. They focused more on the aggressiveness of the behavior and its ultimate consequences. However, even if young children imitate the violence of models, it is not at all clear that they will continue to exhibit violence as they get older. When they are older, and they pay attention to the intentions and context in violent television, their behavior is more likely to reflect the messages they learn. It is also at these later ages that violent behavior, if it should occur, is likely to be dangerous.

Creating Unrealistic Fear

Bandura (1983) claims that television distorts knowledge about the dangers and threats present in the real world. The notion that television viewing fosters a distrust of others and a misconception of the world as dangerous has been referred to as the "cultivation effect" (Gerbner & Gross, 1976). Research shows that heavy television viewers are more distrustful of others and overestimate their chances of being criminally victimized (see Ogles, 1987 and Gunter, 1994 for reviews).[12] The assumption is that these fears will lead viewers to perceive threats that do not exist and to respond aggressively. It is just as plausible that such fears would lead viewers to avoid aggressive behavior against others, if they feel it is dangerous and might lead to victimization. Persons who fear crime may also be less likely to go out at night or go to places where they may be victimized. If viewing television violence increases fear, it might decrease the level of violence.

Desensitization

Frequent viewing of television violence may cause viewers to be less anxious and sensitive about violence. Someone who becomes desensitized to violence may be more likely to engage in violence. This argument assumes that anxiety about violence inhibits its use.

Desensitization has been examined indirectly using measures of arousal. Research shows that subjects who view violent films are less aroused by violence later on (Thomas et al., 1977; see Rule & Ferguson, 1986 for a review). In addition, heavy viewers of television violence tend to respond less emotionally to violence than do light viewers.

There is no evidence that desensitization produces lower levels of violent behavior.[13] Nor is it clear what effect should occur. Studies of desensitization measure arousal not anxiety, and arousal can facilitate violent behavior, according to the literature cited earlier (e.g., Zillmann, 1983). If viewers are exposed to a heavy diet of television violence, one might argue that they will be less aroused by violence and therefore less likely to engage in violence. In addition, if viewers become desensitized to violent behavior on television, they may become indifferent to its message. Desensitization could thereby weaken the effect of a heavy diet of television violence.

Messages from Pornography

The discussion of situational effects of pornography on aggression focused on arousal as a mediating variable. Feminists have argued that pornography has special effects on violence against women because of the message it communicates (Dworkin, 1981; MacKinnon, 1984). Exposure to pornography supposedly leads to negative attitudes toward women which, in turn, affects the likelihood of rape and other forms of violence against women. It is argued, for example, that pornography leads male viewers to think of women as sex objects or as promiscuous (Linz & Malamuth, 1993). Furthermore, some erotica portrays scenes of rape and sadomasochism. In such fictional forms the female victim may express pleasure during and after being raped, suggesting that women enjoy such treatment. Males who view such films may be induced to believe that forceful sexual acts are desired by women. In addition, unlike illegitimate violence not associated with sex, violence in pornographic films rarely has negative consequences for the actor (Palys, 1986; Smith, 1976).

Evidence does not support the hypothesis that exposure to non-violent pornography leads to violence toward women. Most experimental studies show no difference in aggression toward women between subjects exposed to pornographic films and control groups (for reviews, see Donnerstein, 1984; Linz & Malamuth, 1993). Research outside the laboratory has not demonstrated that exposure to pornography and violence toward women are even correlated, much less causally related. There is evidence that rapists report less exposure to pornography than controls, not more (see Linz & Malamuth, 1993 for a review). Studies of the relationship between exposure to pornography and use of sexual coercion among college students yield mixed results (Demare et al., 1993; Boeringer, 1994).

Research using aggregate data has also failed to demonstrate a relationship between exposure to pornography and violence against women. Studies of the effect of changes in restrictions on pornography on rape rates show inconsistent results. States in which sex-oriented magazines are popular tend to have high rape rates (Baron & Straus 1987). However, it is questionable whether the state is a meaningful unit of analysis, given the heterogeneity within states. Gentry (1991) found no relationship between rape rates and circulation of sexually oriented magazines across metropolitan areas.

Effects of violent pornography have been reported in laboratory experiments, at least under certain conditions (see Linz & Malamuth, 1993 for a review). Some studies show that an effect is obtained only if the sexual assault has positive consequences. In this case, subjects are told that the woman became a willing participant in the coercive sexual activities, and she is shown smiling and on friendly terms with the man afterward (Donnerstein, 1980). However, in a more recent study, exposure to a rape scene with positive consequences did not increase subjects' aggression toward women (Fisher & Grenier, 1994).

The effects of exposure to violence with positive consequences have been examined in a field experiment. College students were exposed either to two films that showed women responding positively to men who had attacked them or to two neutral films (Malamuth & Check, 1981). Subjects completed a survey that they thought was unrelated to the films several days later. Males who had viewed the violent films showed greater acceptance of violence against women. Note that these films did not involve pornography. Pornographic films in which the victim of sexual aggression is perceived as experiencing a positive outcome are quite rare (Garcia & Milano, 1990).

The experimental evidence is mixed concerning whether pornography or violent pornography affects male attitudes toward women, according to Linz's (1989) review of the literature. Evidence that men who have negative attitudes toward women are more likely to engage in violence against women is also inconsistent. Some studies find that men who engage in sexual coercion have different attitudes toward women and rape than do other men, while other studies do not (Kanin, 1969; Malamuth, 1986; Ageton, 1983; Rapapport & Burkhart, 1984). It may be that sexually aggressive men are more likely to have antisocial attitudes generally. Thus, convicted rapists are similar to males convicted of other offenses in their attitudes toward women and women's rights (e.g., Howells & Wright, 1978) and in their belief in rape myths (Hall et al., 1986).

The literature on violence and attitudes toward women is plagued by conceptual and measurement problems. Measures of belief in rape myths are problematic (Tedeschi & Felson, 1994). In addition, traditional attitudes about gender roles do not necessarily involve negative attitudes toward women and may be negatively associated with violence toward women and exposure to pornography. Thus, rape rates are twice as high at private colleges and major universities than at religiously affiliated institutions (Koss et al., 1987). Males who report greater exposure to pornography have more (not less) liberal attitudes toward gender roles (Reiss, 1986). Finally, even if a correlation between certain attitudes regarding women and violence could be established, the causal interpretation would be unclear. For example, it may be that men express certain beliefs to justify coercive behavior already performed (Koss et al., 1985).

One limitation on the impact of pornography or any media

effect is selective exposure (McGuire, 1986). Media effects are likely to be limited to the extent that viewers choose programming that already reflects their values and interests. The argument in regard to media violence is that violence is so pervasive on television that all viewers, including impressionable children, are exposed. In the case of pornography, particularly violent pornography, there is much more selective exposure, since those interested in viewing this material must make a special effort to do so. In addition, the viewers of pornography are usually adults, not children.

Pornography provides fantasies for masturbation. Viewers may select material depicting activities that they already fantasize about. When they substitute commercially produced fantasies for their own fantasies, the content is not necessarily more violent. Palys (1986) found that less than 10 percent of scenes in pornography videos involved some form of aggression. A study of college students revealed that approximately 39 percent of men and women reported that they had fantasized about forced sex (Loren & Weeks, 1986).

The versatility evidence is also relevant to the literature on pornography and rape. Most rapists do not specialize in rape or in violent crime (Alder, 1984; Kruttschnitt, 1989). Therefore, theories that emphasize socialization of rape-supportive attitudes, whether learned from the media or elsewhere, are going to have limited utility for understanding individual differences in the proclivity to rape.

In summary, some experimental research suggests that violent pornography that depicts women enjoying the event can lead male subjects to engage in violence against women in the laboratory. The effect of these films appears to be similar to the effects of violent films without a sexual theme. Demand cues provide an alternative explanation of these results as well (see Reiss, 1986). The external validity of these studies is questionable given the rarity of these themes in pornography, and given selective exposure.

Summary and Conclusions

The inconsistencies of the findings make it difficult to draw firm conclusions about the effects of exposure to media violence on aggressive behavior. Most scholars who have reviewed research in the area believe that there is an effect (Friedrich-Cofer & Huston, 1986; Centerwall,

1989). Other scholars have concluded that the causal effects of exposure to television have not been demonstrated (Freedman, 1984; McGuire, 1989).

Given the pervasiveness of media violence, it would be surprising if it had no effect on viewers. I agree with those scholars who think that exposure to television violence probably does have a small effect on violent behavior (Cook et al., 1983). The reason that media effects are not consistently observed is probably because they are weak and affect only a small percentage of viewers. These weak effects may still have practical importance since, in a large population, they would produce some death and injuries. However, it seems unlikely that media violence is a significant factor in high crime rates in this country. Changes in violent crimes mirror changes in crime rates generally. In addition, the people who engage in criminal violence also commit other types of crime. An explanation that attributes violent behavior to socialization that encourages violence cannot easily explain the versatility of most violent criminals.

It seems likely that some people would be more susceptible to media influence than others. Therefore it is puzzling that research has not shown any consistent statistical interactions involving individual difference factors and media exposure. The failure to find individual difference factors that condition the effects of media exposure on aggressive behavior contributes to skepticism about media effects.

It seems reasonable to believe that the media directs viewers' attention to novel forms of violent behavior they might not otherwise consider. The anecdotal evidence is convincing in this area. There appear to be documented cases in which bizarre events on television are followed by similar events in the real world; the similarities seem too great to be coincidental. In addition, hijackings and political violence tend to occur in waves. Many parents have observed their children mimicking behaviors they've observed in films. Whether this process leads to a greater frequency of violence is unclear.

There is some evidence that the effects observed in laboratory experiments, and less consistently in field experiments, are due to sponsor effects. The fact that children who are exposed to violence tend to misbehave generally casts doubt on most of the other theoretical explanations of media effects. The issue has particular significance for laboratory research, where subjects know they are being studied and may be responding to demand cues. Research is needed in which sponsor effects are isolated and controlled. A field experiment in which subjects imitate violent behavior they have observed in the absence of the sponsor, but do not misbehave otherwise, would be convincing. Alternatively, there may need to be further development of the theoretical argument that self-control behavior is modeled.

It is not clear what lesson the media teaches about the legitimacy of violence, or the likelihood of punishment. To some extent that message is redundant with lessons learned from other sources of influence. The message is probably ambiguous and is likely to have different effects on different viewers. Young children may imitate illegitimate violence if they do not understand the message, but their imitative behavior may have trivial consequences. Out of millions of viewers, there must be some with highly idiosyncratic interpretations of television content who intertwine the fantasy with their own lives, and as a result have an increased probability of engaging in violent behavior.

NOTES

1. An alternative definition is that intentional harm involves deliberate harm or expected harm. However, teachers sometimes give low grades with the expectation that it will make their students unhappy, but their behavior should not be defined as aggressive, unless they also value that harm. Tedeschi and Felson (1994) substitute the term *coercion* for *aggression* and include coercive actions in which the actor values compliance as well as harm.

2. This chapter borrows from Tedeschi and Felson (1994).

3. According to Freedman (1984), effects outside the laboratory are likely to be weaker than laboratory effects because violent programs are mixed with other types of programs. Friedrich-Cofer and Huston (1986) dispute this point, arguing that experimental research underestimates media effects. They claim that the stimuli used in experimental research are brief and often less violent than typical television programs and that the presence of experimenters inhibits subjects from engaging in aggressive behavior in laboratory settings.

4. Any cue that indicates which direction the experimenter prefers would be a demand cue. In their strongest form demand cues give away the experimenter's hypothesis to subjects, who then compliantly act to confirm the hypothesis. In their weaker form, demand cues simply guide behavior without creating awareness of the hypothesis.

5. Some of the studies were in laboratory settings, but subjects did not know that their aggressive behavior was being observed as part of the study.

6. The hypothesis that consumerism, promoted by advertising and the depiction of wealth on television, leads to more financially motivated crime has never been tested, to my knowledge.

7. An important requirement of such studies is that they control for the aggressiveness of the viewer at the earlier time period, when looking at the effect of earlier exposure on later aggression. Eron and Huesmann do so in later reanalyses of their data.

8. Also included were parental reports of a child's favorite programs, and self-reports of children of their favorite programs. These measures of exposure to television violence were poor indicators of overall exposure.

9. Valkenburg et al. (1992) found that violent programming increased the level of

aggressive-heroic fantasies found in a longitudinal analyses among Dutch children. However, nonviolent dramatic programming had the same effect.

10. Viewing violent television and viewing television are so highly correlated across cites that it does not matter which measure is used in analysis. The notion of catharsis provides an alternative explanation, but it cannot explain the negative relationship between exposure to television violence and the incidence of nonviolent crime.

11. In Paik and Comstock's (1994) meta-analyses the strongest effects were observed for cartoon programs. However, the subjects in these studies were children, and children may be more easily influenced.

12. There is some evidence that the relationship is spurious; see Gunter's (1994) review.

13. Emergency room personnel may become desensitized to the consequences of violent behavior, but there is no evidence that they are more violent than other groups of people.

REFERENCES

Ageton, S. (1983). *Sexual assault among adolescents.* Lexington, MA: Lexington.

Alder, C. (1984). The convicted rapist: A sexual or a violent offender? *Criminal Justice Behavior 11,* 157–177.

Andison, F. S. (1977). TV violence and viewer aggression: A cumulation of study results: 1956–1976. *Public Opinion Quarterly 41,* 314–31.

Bachrach, R. S. (1986). The differential effect of observation of violence on kibbutz and city children in Israel. In L. R. Huesmann & L. D. Eron (Eds.), *Television and the aggressive child: A cross-national comparison,* (pp. 201–238. Hillsdale, NJ: Erlbaum.

Bandura, A. (1973). *Aggression: A social learning analysis.* Englewood Cliffs, NJ: Prentice-Hall.

Bandura, A. (1983). Psychological mechanisms of aggression. In R. Geen & E. I. Donnerstein (Eds.), *Aggression: Theoretical and empirical reviews* (vol. 1, pp. 1–40). New York: Academic.

Bandura, A., & Walters, R. H. (1963). *Social learning and personality development.* New York: Holt, Rinehart & Winston.

Baron, J. N., & Reiss, P. C. (1985). Same time next year: Aggregate analyses of the mass media and violent behavior. *American Sociological Review, 50,* 347–363.

Baron, L., & Straus, M. A. (1987). Four theories of rape: A macrosocial analysis. *Social Problems, 34,* 467–489.

Baron, R. A. (1974). The aggression-inhibiting influence of heightened sexual arousal. *Journal of Personality and Social Psychology, 30,* 318–322.

Baron, R. A., & Bell, P. A. (1973). Effects of heightened sexual arousal on physical aggression. *Proceedings of the 81st Annual Convention of the American Psychological Association, 8,* 171–172.

Baron, R. A., & Bell, P. A. (1977). Sexual arousal and aggression by males: Effects of type of erotic stimuli and prior provocation. *Journal of Personality and Social Psychology, 35,* 79–87.

Berkowitz, L. (1965). Some aspects of observed aggression. *Journal of Personality and Social Psychology, 2,* 359–369.

Berkowitz, L. (1984). Some effects of thought on anti- and pro-social influences of media effects. *Psychological Bulletin, 95,* 410–427.

Berkowitz, L., & Alioto, J. T. (1973). The meaning of an observed event as a determinant of its aggressive consequences. *Journal of Personality and Social Psychology, 28,* 206–217.

Berkowitz, L., Corwin, R., & Heironimus, M. (1962). Film violence and subsequent aggressive tendencies. *Public Opinion Quarterly, 27,* 217–229.

Berkowitz, L., & Donnerstein, E. (1982). External validity is more than skin deep: Some answers to criticism of laboratory experiments. *American Psychologist, 37,* 245–257.

Berkowitz, L., & Geen, R. G. (1966). Film violence and the cue properties of available targets. *Journal of Personality and Social Psychology, 3,* 525–530.

Berkowitz, L., & Rawlings, E. (1963). Effects of film violence: An inhibition against subsequent aggression. *Journal of Abnormal Social Psychology, 66,* 405–412.

Boeringer, S. (1994). Pornography and sexual aggression: Associations of violent and nonviolent depictions with rape and rape proclivity. *Deviant Behavior, 15,* 289–304.

Bushman, B. J., & Geen, R. G. (1990). Role of cognitive-emotional mediators and individual differences in the effects of media violence on aggression. *Journal of Personality and Social Psycholology, 58,* 156–163.

Centerwall, B. S. (1989). Exposure to television as a cause of violence. In G. Comstock (Ed.), *Public communication and behavior* (vol. 2, pp. 1–58. Orlando: Academic.

Collins, W. A., Berndt, T. J., & Hess, V. L. (1984). Observational learning of motives and consequences for television aggression: A developmental study. *Child Development, 45,* 799–802.

Cook, T. D., Kendzierski, D. A., & Thomas, S. V. (1983). The implicit assumptions of television: An analysis of the 1982 NIMH Report on Television and Behavior. *Public Opinion Quarterly, 47,* 161–201.

Demare, D., Lips, H. M., & Briere, J. (1993). Sexually violent pornography, anti-women attitudes, and sexual aggression: A structural equation model. *Journal of Research in Personality, 27,* 285–300.

Dimmick, J. W., McCain, T. A., & Bolton, W. T. (1979). Media use and the life span. *American Behavioral Scientist, 23,* 7–31.

Donnerstein, E. (1980). Aggressive erotica and violence against women. *Journal of Personality and Social Psychology, 39,* 269–277.

Donnerstein, E. (1984). Pornography: Its effect on violence against women. In N. M. Malamuth & E. Donnerstein (Eds.), *Pornography and sexual aggression* (pp. 53–81). New York: Academic.

Donnerstein, E., Donnerstein, M., & Evans, R. (1975). Erotic stimuli and aggression: Facilitation or inhibition. *Journal of Personality and Social Psychology, 32,* 237–244.

Dworkin, A. (1981). Pornography: Men possessing women. New York: G. P. Putnam's Sons.

Eron. L. D., Huesmann, L. R., Lefkowitz, M. M., & Walder, L. O. (1972). Does television violence cause aggression? *American Psychologist, 27,* 253–263.

Felson, M. (1986). Routine activities, social controls, rational decisions and criminal outcomes. In D. Cornish & R. Clarke (Eds.), *The reasoning criminal: Rational choice perspectives on offending.* New York: Springer-Verlag.

Feshbach, S. (1972). Reality and fantasy in filmed violence. In J. P. Murray, E. Rubinstein, & G. A. Comstock (Eds.), *Television and social behavior* (vol. 2, pp. 318–345). Washington DC: U.S. Government Printing Office.

Feshbach, S., & Singer, R. (1971). *Television and aggression.* San Francisco: Jossey Bass.

Fisher, W. A., & Grenier, G. (1994). Violent pornography, antiwoman thoughts, and antiwoman acts: In search of reliable effects. *Journal of Sex Research, 31.* 23–38.

Fraczek, A. (1986). Socio-cultural environment, television viewing, and the development of aggression among children in Poland. In L. R. Huesmann & L. D. Eron (Eds.), *Television and the aggressive child: A cross-national comparison* (pp. 119–160. Hillsdale, NJ: Erlbaum.

Freedman, J. L. (1984). Effects of television violence on aggressiveness. *Psychological Bulletin, 96,* 227–246.

Friedrich, L. K., & Stein, A. H. (1973). Aggressive and prosocial television programs and the natural behavior of preschool children. *Monograph of the Society for Research in Child Development, 38* (4, Serial No. 151).

Friedrich-Cofer, L., & Huston, A. C. (1986). Television violence and aggression: The debate continues. *Psychological Bulletin, 100,* 364–371.

Garcia, L. T., & Milano, L. (1990). A content analysis of erotic videos. *Journal of Law Psychiatry, 14,* 47–64.

Geen, R. G. (1978). Some effects of observing violence upon the behavior of the observer. In B. Maher (Ed.), *Progress in experimental personality research* (vol. 8). New York: Academic.

Geen, R. G. (1983). Aggression and television violence. In R. G. Geen & E. I. Donnerstein (Eds.), *Aggression: Theoretical and empirical reviews* (vol. 2, pp. 103–125). New York: Academic.

Geen, R. G, & Berkowitz, L. (1967). Some conditions facilitating the occurrence of aggression after the observation of violence. *Journal of Personality, 35,* 666–676.

Gentry, C. S. (1991). Pornography and rape: An empirical analysis. *Deviant Behavior, 12,* 277–288.

Gerbner, G., & Gross, L. (1976). Living with television: The violence profile. *Journal of Communication, 26,* 173–199.

Gottfredson, M., & Hirschi, T. (1990). *A general theory of crime.* Stanford: Stanford University Press.

Gottfredson, M., & Hirschi, T. (1993). A control theory interpretation of psychological research on aggression. In R. B. Felson & J. T. Tedeschi (Eds.), *Aggression and violence: Social interactionist perspectives* (pp. 47–68). Washington, DC: American Psychological Association.

Gunter, B. (1994). The question of media violence. In J. Bryant & D. Zillman (Eds.), *Media effects: Advances in theory and research* (pp. 163–212). Hillsdale, NJ: Erlbaum.

Hall, E. R., Howard, J. A., & Boezio, S. L. (1986). Tolerance of rape: A sexist or antisocial attitude. *Psychology of Women Quarterly, 10,* 101–118.

Hearold, S. (1986). A synthesis of 1043 effects of television on social behavior. In G. Comstock (Ed.), *Public communication and behavior* (vol. 1, pp. 65–133). San Diego, CA: Academic.

Hennigan, K. M., Del Rosario, M. L., Heath, L., Cook, T. D., Wharton, J. D., & Calder, B. J. (1982). The impact of the introduction of television on crime in the United States. *Journal of Personality and Social Psychology, 42,* 461–477.

Howells, K., & Wright, E. (1978). The sexual attitudes of aggressive sexual offenders. *British Journal of Crimnology, 18,* 170–173.

Hoyt, J. L. (1970). Effect of media violence 'justification' on aggression. *Journal of Broadcasting, 14,* 455–464.

Huesmann, L. R. (1982). Television violence and aggressive behavior. In D. Pearl, L. Bouthilet, & J. Lazar (Eds.), *Television and behavior: Ten years of scientific progress and implications for the eighties* (vol. 2, pp. 220–256). Washington, DC: National Institute of Mental Health.

Huesmann, L. R., & Eron, L. D. (1986). The development of aggression in American children as a consequence of television violence viewing. In L. R. Huesmann & L. D. Eron (Eds.), *Television and the aggressive child: A cross-national comparison* (pp. 45–80). Hillsdale, NJ: Erlbaum.

Josephson, W. L. (1987). Television violence and children's aggression: Testing the priming, social script, and disinhibition predictions. *Journal of Personality and Social Psychology, 53,* 882890.

Joy, L. A., Kimball, M. M., & Zaback, M. L. (1986). Television and children's aggressive behavior. In T. M. Williams (Ed.), *The impact of television: A natural experiment in three communities* (pp. 303–360). New York: Academic.

Kanin, E. J. (1969). Selected dyadic aspect of male sex aggression. *Journal of Sex Research,* 5, 12–28.

Koss, M. P., Gidycz, C. A., & Wisniewski, N. (1987). The scope of rape: Incidence and prevalence of sexual aggression and victimization in a national sample of students in higher education. *Journal of Consultation in Clinical Psychology,* 55, 162–170.

Koss, M. P., Leonard, K. E., Beezley, D. A., & Oros, C. J. (1985). Non-stranger sexual aggression: a discriminate analysis classification. *Sex Roles,* 12, 981–992.

Kruttschnitt. C. (1989). A sociological, offender-based, study of rape. *Sociological Quarterly,* 30, 305–329.

Lagerspetz, K., & Viemero, V. (1986). Television and aggressive behavior among Finnish children. In L. R. Huesmann & L. D. Eron (Eds.), *Television and the aggressive child: A cross-national comparison* (pp. 81–118). Hillsdale, NJ: Erlbaum.

Leyens, J. P., Camino, L., Parke, R. D., & Berkowitz, L. (1975). Effects of movie violence on aggression in a field setting as a function of group dominance and cohesion. *Journal of Personality and Social Psychology,* 32, 346–360.

Linz, D. (1989). Exposure to sexually explicit materials and attitudes toward rape: A comparison of study results. *Journal of Sex Research,* 26, 50–84.

Linz, D., & Malamuth, N. (1993). *Pornography.* Newbury Park: Sage.

Loren, R. E. A., & Weeks, G. (1986). Sexual fantasies of undergraduates and their perceptions of the sexual fantasies of the opposite sex. *Journal of Sex Education Therapy,* 12, 31–36.

MacKinnon, C. (1984). Not a moral issue. *Yale Law Policy Review,* 2, 321–345.

Malamuth, N. M. (1986). Predictors of naturalistic sexual aggression. *Journal of Personality and Social Psychology,* 50, 953–962.

Malamuth, N. M., & Check, J. V. P. (1981). The effects of mass media exposure on acceptance of violence against women: A field experiment. *Journal of Research in Personality,* 15, 436–446.

McGuire, W. J. (1986). The myth of massive media impact: Savagings and salvagings. In G. Comstock (Ed.), *Public communication and behavior* (vol. 1, pp. 175–257). Orlando: Academic.

Messner, S. F. (1986). Television violence and violent crime: An aggregate analysis. *Social Problems,* 33, 218–235.

Messner, S. F., & Blau, J. R. (1987). Routine leisure activities and rates of crime: A macro-level analysis. *Social Forces,* 65, 1035–1052.

Meyer, T. P. (1972a). The effects of sexually arousing and violent films on aggressive behavior. *Journal of Sex Research,* 8, 324–331.

Meyer, T. P. (1972b). Effects of viewing justified and unjustified real film violence on aggressive behavior. *Journal of Personality and Social Psychology,* 23, 21–29.

Milavsky, J. R., Stipp, H. H., Kessler, R. C., & Rubens, W. S. (1982). *Television and aggression: A panel study.* New York: Academic.

Milgram, S. (1974). *Obedience to authority: An experimental view.* New York: Harper & Row.

Miller, T. Q., Heath, L., Molcan, J. R., & Dugoni, B. L. (1991). Imitative violence in the real world: A reanalysis of homicide rates following championship prize fights. *Aggressive Behavior,* 17, 121–134.

Neiss, R. (1988). Reconceptualizing arousal: Psychobiological states in motor performance. *Psychological Bulletin,* 103, 345–366.

Nemeth, C. (1970). Bargaining and reciprocity. *Psychological Bulletin,* 74, 297–308.

Ogles, R. M. (1987). Cultivation analysis: Theory, methodology and current research on television-influenced constructions of social reality. *Mass Communication Review,* 14, 43–53.

Padget, V. R., Brislin-Slutz, J., & Neal, J. A. (1989). Pornography, erotica, and attitudes toward women: The effects of repeated exposure. *Journal of Sex Research, 26,* 479–491.

Paik, H., & Comstock, G. (1994). The effects of television violence on antisocial behavior: A meta-analysis. *Communication Research, 21,* 516–545.

Palys, T. S. (1986). Testing the common wisdom: The social content of video pornography. *Canadian Psychology, 27,* 22–35.

Parke, R. D., Berkowitz, L., Leyens, J. P., West, S., & Sebastian, R. J. (1977). Some effects of violent and nonviolent movies on the behavior of juvenile delinquents. In L. Berkowitz (Ed.), *Advances in experimental social psychology* (vol. 10, pp. 135–172). New York: Academic.

Phillips, D. P. (1983). The impact of mass media violence on U.S. homicides. *American Sociological Review, 48,* 560–568.

Phillips, D. P. (1986). The found experiment: A new technique for assessing the impact of mass media violence on real-world aggressive behavior. In G. Comstock (Ed.), *Public communication and behavior* (vol. 1, pp. 259–307). San Diego, CA: Academic.

Phillips, D. P., & Bollen, K. A. (1985). Same time last year: Selective data dredging for unreliable findings. *American Sociological Review, 50,* 364–371.

Rapaport, K., & Burkhart, B. R. (1984). Personality and attitudinal characteristics of sexually coercive college males. *Journal of Abnormal Psychology, 93,* 216–221.

Reiss, I. L. (1986). *Journey into sexuality: An exploratory voyage.* Englewood Cliffs, NJ: Prentice-Hall.

Rosenberg, M. J. (1969). The conditions and consequences of evaluation apprehension. In R. Rosenthal & R. Rosnow (Eds.), *Artifacts in behavioral research.* New York: Academic.

Rule, B. G., & Ferguson, T. J. (1986). The effects of media violence on attitudes, emotions, and cognitions. *Journal of Social Issues, 42,* 29–50.

Sapolsky, B. S. (1984). Arousal, affect, and the aggression-moderating effect of erotica. In N. M. Malamuth & E. Donnerstein (Eds.), *Pornography and sexual aggression* (pp. 83–115). New York: Academic.

Sheehan, P. W. (1986). Television viewing and its relation to aggression among children in Australia. In L. R. Huesmann & L. D. Eron (Eds.), *Television and the aggressive child: A cross-national comparison* (pp. 161–200). Hillsdale, NJ: Erlbaum.

Smith, D. D. (1976). The social content of pornography. *Journal of Communication, 29,* 16–24.

Straus, N. (1991). Discipline and divorce: Physical punishment of children and violence and other crime in adulthood. *Social Problems, 38,* 133–154.

Surgeon General's Scientific Advisory Committee on Television and Social Behavior. (1972). *Television and growing up: The impact of televised violence.* Report to the Surgeon General, U.S. Public Health Service. HEP Publ. No. HSM 72-9090. Rockville, MD: National Institute of Mental Health, U.S. Government Printing Office.

Sykes, G., & Matza, D. (1961). Juvenile delinquency and subterranean values. *American Sociological Review, 26,* 712–719.

Tedeschi. J. T., & Felson, R. B. (1994). *Violence, aggression, and coercive actions.* Washington, DC: American Psychological Association.

Tedeschi, J. T., & Norman, N. (1985). Social mechanisms of displaced aggression. In E. J. Lawler (Ed.), *Advances in group processes: Theory and research* (vol. 2). Greenwich, CT: JAI.

Tedeschi, J. T., Smith, R. B. III, & Brown, R. C. Jr. (1974). A reinterpretation of research on aggression. *Psychological Bulletin, 89,* 540–563.

Thomas, M. H., Horton, R. W., Lippincott, E. C., & Drabman, R. S. (1977). Desensitization to portrayals of real-life aggression as a function of exposure to television violence. *Journal of Personality and Social Psychology, 35,* 450–458.

Valkenburg, P. M., Vooijs, M. W., & Van der Voort, T. H. (1992). The influence of television on children's fantasy styles: A secondary analysis. *Imagination, Cognition, Personality, 12*, 55–67.

West, D. J., & Farrington, D. P. (1977). *The delinquent way of life.* London: Heinemann.

White, L. A. (1979). Erotica and aggression: The influence of sexual arousal, positive affect, and negative affect on aggressive behavior. *Journal of Personality and Social Psychology, 37*, 591–601.

Wiegman, O., Kuttschreuter, M., & Baarda, B. (1992). A longitudinal study of the effects of television viewing on aggressive and antisocial behaviors. *British Journal of Social Psychology, 31*, 147–164.

Wood, W., Wong. F. Y., & Chachere, J. G. (1991). Effects of media violence on viewers' aggression in unconstrained social interaction. *Psychological Bulletin, 109*, 371–383.

Zillman, D. (1971). Excitation transfer in communication-mediated aggressive behavior. *Journal of Experimental and Social Psychology, 7, 419–434.*

Zillman, D. (1983). Arousal and aggression. In R. G. Geen & E. I. Donnerstein (Eds.), Aggression: *Theoretical and empirical reviews* (vol. 1, pp. 75–101). New York: Academic.

Zillmann, D., Bryant, J., Comisky, P. W., & Medoff, N. J. (1981). Excitation and hedonic valence in the effect of erotica on motivated intermale aggression. *European Journal of Social Psychology, 11*, 233–252.

Zillmann, D., Hoyt, J. L., & Day, K. D. (1974). Strength and duration of the effect of aggressive, violent, and erotic communications on subsequent aggressive behavior. *Communication Research, 1*, 286–306.

Contributors

JOHN BAILEY is a Hollywood cinematographer whose work includes *The Out-of-Towners*, *As Good As It Gets*, and *In the Line of Fire*, and, as director, *China Moon*.

LEONARD BERKOWITZ is Professor Emeritus of Psychology at the University of Wisconsin–Madison and has published extensively on mass media effects.

CAROL J. CLOVER is Professor of Rhetoric and Scandinavian at the University of California–Berkeley. She is author of *Men, Women and Chainsaws*.

BOSLEY CROWTHER was the film critic for *The New York Times*.

RICHARD B. FELSON is Professor of Sociology at University of Albany (SUNY), where his research has focused on the social psychology of violence.

RONALD GOLD covered the Hollywood industry for *Variety*, the trade paper for the motion picture business.

DEVIN MCKINNEY is an independent writer-researcher whose work on film has appeared in *Film Quarterly*.

JOSEPH MORGENSTERN was the film critic for *Newsweek*.

STEPHEN PRINCE is Associate Professor of Communication Studies at Virginia Tech. His books include *A New Pot of Gold: Hollywood Under the Electronic Rainbow, 1980–1989*, *Savage Cinema: Sam Peckinpah and the Rise of Ultraviolent Movies*, and *The Warrior's Camera: The Cinema of Akira Kurosawa*.

Vivian C. Sobchack is Professor and Associate Dean of Film and Television at the University of California–Los Angeles. Her books include *Meta-Morphing: Visual Transformation and the Culture of Quick-Change, The Persistence of History: Cinema, Television and the Modern Effect,* and *Address of the Eye: A Phenomenology of Film Experience.*

David Thomson is the author of *Beneath Mulholland: Thoughts on Hollywood and Its Ghosts, Rosebud: The Story of Orson Welles,* and *A Biographical Dictionary of Film.*

Jack Valenti is President of the Motion Picture Association of America.

Index